# ARCHAIC
# GREECE

# ARCHAIC GREECE

*The Age of Experiment*

ANTHONY SNODGRASS

University of California Press

Berkeley and Los Angeles

University of California Press
Berkeley and Los Angeles, California

First California Paperback Printing 1981
ISBN 0-520-04373-1

Printed in the United States of America
1 2 3 4 5 6 7 8 9

# Contents

For Anne-Marie

# Preface

I began to write this book sitting at a table over which were scattered half a dozen books dealing wholly or partly with the same period, the majority of them written by personal friends. Now, more than a year later, they are still there, joined by one or two others which have been published since then. I can think of no better way of acknowledging my most obvious debts than to express here my gratitude to their authors. In two cases, those of Aristotle and of Victor Ehrenberg, it is too late to do this personally; but I now convey my thanks to the others – Michel Austin, Nicolas Coldstream, Moses Finley, George Forrest, Sally Humphreys, Ann Jeffery, Chester Starr and Pierre Vidal-Naquet – whose works will be found listed, with many others, in the bibliography. They cannot be saddled with any responsibility for my own book, not least because none of them has seen any part of it in draft. If this preface nevertheless arouses in the reader a suspicion that there are already more than enough books about archaic Greece, and that most of them have been written by the members of a tightly-knit circle of conspirators, then I can only hope that what follows will weaken the second of these beliefs, if not the first.

Cambridge, 1979

# List of Figures

# List of Plates

# Introduction

'The archaic period is perhaps the most important period in Greek history'

*M. M. Austin and P. Vidal-Naquet,*
*Economic and Social History of Ancient Greece* (1977), p. 49.

Until quite recently, it is doubtful whether anyone would have ventured an opinion like this, at least in public. On the accepted view, the Archaic period was by definition merely a prelude to the decisive achievements of Classical Greece. It did not make any difference which criterion one chose to appeal to – literary, intellectual, artistic, political – there appeared to be an unanswerable case for the supremacy of the Classical period as a whole and, in Greece, of the fifth century BC in particular. Professional historians, so far from dissenting from this view, tended to endorse it with special warmth. The Classical period was the age in which their most highly esteemed ancient authorities had lived, and about which they had mainly written. It was natural, therefore, to conclude that the Classical period was of the greatest historical importance; and school and university curricula have continued to reflect this belief.

Why, then, is there room for a dissenting view today? The answer is that ancient historians have undertaken a major reappraisal of their subject. In so doing, they have acknowledged several lessons from historians of other periods. To begin with, there has been some change in attitudes towards the ancient written sources, whose dominance had once been almost total. It was, after all, strange that ancient historians were prepared to describe as 'sources' these accounts, many of which (in addition to their fragmentary or contradictory character) were written centuries after the events in question. Once a wider range of evidence came to be admitted, and a wider range of problems tackled, it was natural to apply these methods to a wider span of time as well. There were, for example, categories of evidence in which the Archaic period was richer than the Classical. Much has also been learned from other disciplines besides history, whether in method, or by analogy, or more directly by drawing on independent sources of evidence for the ancient world itself.

Archaeology is one of these independent sources and, since this book is written by an archaeologist, it is right to say something about its potential contribution and about its recent development. For Classical archaeology, as traditionally understood, was bound by limitations at least as clear as those which have operated in ancient history. The artistic achievements of the Greeks were so awe-inspiring that to discover, classify and interpret them seemed for long a sufficient goal. Inscriptions were left to the historians, field-surveys to the prehistorians, while excavations were directed primarily towards the recovery of works of art. Classical archaeologists who pursued such aims were likely to look at the products of the Classical period, and then to fall in with the majority view that this period had been the focal point of Greek cultural history. But here, too, lessons are now being learned from elsewhere: above all, from non-Classical archaeology. If it is accepted elsewhere that the field of archaeology is the *entire* material culture – so far as it is recoverable – of an ancient society, then why should this not be true of Classical archaeology as well? It is probably true that Classical archaeologists are slower to accept such arguments than ancient historians have been in the corresponding case, but there are still signs of change to be seen.

Two consequences of these new attitudes in ancient studies seem to me of vital importance, and they have formed the main inspiration for the writing of this book. First, by enlarging their horizons in this way, ancient history and Classical archaeology have also come much closer together. Once historians extend their interests from political and military events to social and economic processes, it is obvious that archaeological evidence can offer them far more; once Classical archaeologists turn from the outstanding works of art to the totality of material products, then history (thus widely interpreted) will provide them with a more serviceable framework, not least because Greek art is notoriously deficient in historical reference. As a result of this *rapprochement*, it will be difficult for a future researcher to embark on an historical subject in the field of Archaic Greece without becoming involved in archaeological questions, or vice versa.

The second, more interesting, consequence is that the Archaic period of Greek history appears in an entirely new light. No longer is it of interest solely because of what it led to; suddenly it becomes possible to see it as, in some respects, a complete episode in its own right. It would be pointless to deny the magnitude of the intellectual revolution which divided the Archaic period from the Classical, transforming something remarkable into something unique. But opposite that intellectual revolution, we have to set up another, earlier revolution of a more material or structural kind, although it also had its purely intellectual component. This 'structural revolution' took place not merely within the Archaic period but at its beginning. It established the economic basis of Greek society, as well as the main outlines of its social framework; it drew the political map of the Greek world in a form that was to endure for four centuries; it set up, with even greater permanence, the forms of state that were to determine Greek political history; it provided the interests and goals, not merely for Greek but for Western art as a whole, which were to be pursued over the next two and a half millennia; it gave Greece in the Homeric epics, an ideal of behaviour and a memento of past glory to sustain it; it provided much of the physical basis, and perhaps also of the spiritual basis, of Greek religion; and it furnished many lesser things, among them the means for Greek society to defend its independence militarily. Not all of these features were without parallel in other, older cultures; but it is doubtful whether, before or since, they have ever come about in one country with such concertedness and above all with such speed.

The Archaic period of Greek history is thus bounded, at either end, by these two revolutions. It is a field of study of which, despite generations of past work, we know neither as much as we need, nor as much as we might know in the present state of our evidence. This book is only a preliminary step in approaching the problems afresh, not a definitive statement; it is undeniably attempting to make a case as well as, indeed in preference to, presenting a subject; omissions, even quite major ones, are inevitable. There will be mistakes, too. But both will have served a purpose of a kind if they help to provoke wider discussion.

# Structural Revolution:
# the Human Factor

About the tall white gods who landed from their open boat,
Skilled in the working of copper, appointing our feast-days,
Before the islands were submerged, when the weather was calm,
    The maned lion common,
An open wishing-well in every garden;
    When love came easy.

Perfectly certain, all of us, but not from the records, . . . .

W. H. Auden, *The Orators*

By the ninth century BC, all significant trace of the former Mycenaean civilization had disappeared from the Greek world, apart from its physical vestiges. That complex and highly-stratified society, with its kings ruling from citadels and palaces, its elaborate system of land-ownership, its laboriously detailed monitoring of production and taxation, its specialization of crafts, its armed forces and its road network, was gone for ever. Not that the Greeks had forgotten the Mycenaean episode; if translated backwards in time, they would have been able to recognize most of its outstanding features. But the fact was that their own activities now bore so small a resemblance to those of their ancestors that there was little that they could have usefully learned from them. It is, for example, doubtful whether there was a single Greek alive who could have understood the symbols of the various writing-systems of the Bronze Age Aegean, much less convinced society of their utility. Like the other out-

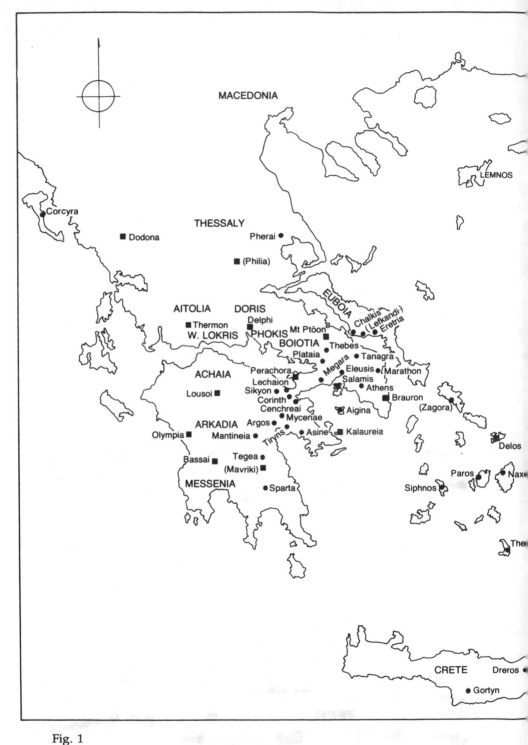

Fig. 1
Greece – sites mentioned in the text. (Solid squares indicate sanctuary sites)

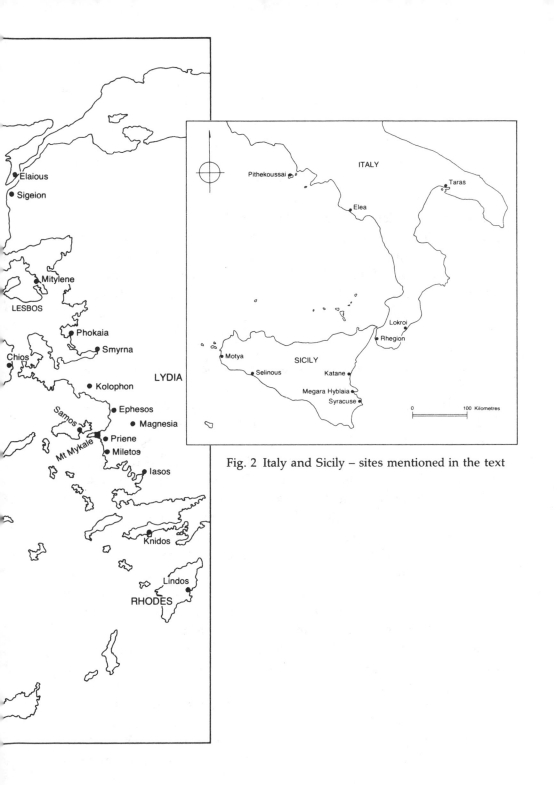

Fig. 2 Italy and Sicily – sites mentioned in the text

wardly impressive attributes of the Mycenaean world, they had
been ultimately dependent on a social system for which Greece
had no further use; the same was apparently true of the fortified
citadels, the elaborately-built tombs, the frescoes, the ornate but
impractical weaponry, the personal seals and signets engraved
with such skill and labour. These things were an object of awe
and perhaps wistful nostalgia, hardly of serious emulation; just
as today even fervent imperialists would be taken aback if presented with a detailed plan of re-conquest. One of the greatest
attractions of a Heroic Age is the impracticability of any return to
it. In the case of Iron Age Greece, the change of outlook is
merely a local manifestation of a greater change which passed
over the Old World at the end of the Bronze Age, and which can
be recognized in different forms from the Celtic West to China.
It was as if the adoption of a new basic material, iron, had
brought with it a new ethos, as severely practical as the metal
itself.

But if the old world had been entirely obliterated, then neither
had the new, in the form of the historical Hellenic world, yet
arrived. By the eighth century BC, and especially its latter part,
we can see the outlines of that world clearly delineated, but in
the ninth there are still too many unfamiliar features. For a start,
although there were nucleated settlements, there can have been
no city life, mainly because the settlements were so small and
few. We have at least one instance, Lefkandi in Euboia, where
we can believe that a substantial proportion of the community's
graves have been discovered. There are some 63 burials in an
earlier cemetery whose period of use is estimated at about 125
years; then a further total of 82 in two later cemeteries, covering
about 100 years which bring us into the ninth century. If we
make the assumption of an average life-expectancy of 30 years,
we may be being generous (for comparison in the late eighteenth
century of our era it was 28.8 in France, while about 1850 it was
40.2 in England as a whole, but only 24.2 for men in Manches-
ter); even so, the extant graves will then represent a community
rising from about 15 persons in the earlier phase to about 25 in
the later. If there is a way of making a fair comparison with

earlier, Mycenaean settlements, it is perhaps by considering analogous evidence from the cemetery of Perati in eastern Attica, which centres on the twelfth century BC – the very end of the Mycenaean era – and which is fairly self-contained. Its extant burials number about 600, covering a period estimated at 110–115 years; on the same assumption as before, this will mean a community of about 160 people in the associated settlement. Fortuitous or not, these figures of the shrinkage in settlement-size echo the message of the general evidence of depopulation over the whole country, as we shall see presently.

If ninth-century Greece lacked sizeable towns, this is only one of a series of characteristic features of historical Greek culture which are missing. There is no writing. There is no community of artistic and technological development across the Aegean world. There is no colonization outside the Aegean, and even within it there are famous sites – Sparta, Tegea, Mantineia, Eretria, Ephesos, Chios town – where, if anyone was yet living, we have not found material trace of them. There is but a handful of sanctuaries where we can see any physical trace of cult, and that on a minimal scale. Among the sites that *are* prominent, there are at least three – Lefkandi, Zagora on Andros and the partially Greek trading settlement established by the end of the century at Al Mina in Syria – whose role in later developments was so slight that we do not even know their Classical names for sure. There is hardly a single temple which can be shown archaeologically to have been constructed within the ninth century. Of the personalities and deeds which later Greek tradition would have assigned to this century, almost all can be shown to belong later; what is left is a handful of empty names.

To bring this state of affairs to an end required a revolution indeed. Of the many elements of this revolution which we can detect today, almost all look forward, in that they are intelligible and even familiar to us from later history. Yet the first in importance, and one of the first chronologically, was a development for which nature must take perhaps greater credit than man: the population explosion of eighth-century Greece. The presence of this phenomenon has been vaguely perceived by modern scho-

larship for some years past, but it is, at such an ill-documented
period, extremely difficult to measure. Nor is it quite self-
evident that such a development was either desirable in itself or
necessary for the growth of Greek culture. It is therefore worth
pausing to consider both the size and the implications of this
change in the Aegean scene.

To begin with, we can see today that Greece in the preceding
dark age must have been woefully under-populated. A crude
calculation, based on the numbers of known sites in occupation,
will show the genesis of this predicament. For the Aegean area
as a whole in the thirteenth, twelfth and eleventh centuries BC, it
was calculated a few years ago that the number of known sites
was something in the order of 320, 130 and 40 respectively for
the three centuries. Fieldwork since then has added a few to
these totals, but completeness is not relevant to this kind of
computation: it is the *relationship* of the figures which counts,
and this is not likely to be materially altered – erratic as the earlier fieldwork had been, there is no cogent reason why it should
have produced such differential results, unless widespread
abandonment of settlements had in fact taken place. If the
*number* of settlements were really reduced to something like
one-eighth of its former level between the thirteenth and the
eleventh centuries BC, then we may add to this our earlier finding that the evidence of two of our most thoroughly-explored
cemeteries hints at an equally drastic fall in the *size* of settlements over a slightly different time-span, between the twelfth
and the tenth centuries approximately. It all adds up to a picture
of depopulation on an almost unimaginable scale, and there may
indeed be an element of fortuitous exaggeration in these figures.

Yet there is one thing which provides independent and rather
startling confirmation of the reality of this decline in population:
it is that the statistical evidence of the subsequent *rise* in population after 800 BC shows this to have been equally dramatic in its
steepness, as we shall soon see. This evidence is derived from
data of a slightly different kind, namely the numbers of burials
per generation in certain communities and areas; and the potential flaws in these data are of a different order from those of the

earlier period of depopulation. It is quite possible that exaggeration has once again crept in, but it is a somewhat suspicious coincidence for it always to operate in the same direction. A high proportion of the evidence, in all the relevant periods, comes from burials rather than settlements, so that it will hardly do to explain the shortfall in the years between about 1100 and 800 BC by claiming that people were using some unrecognized and therefore undatable pottery at that time: this might cover the case of settlements, but not that of cemeteries unless there were a large number of undated graves, which is not the case. The most respectable route of escape from the conclusion of depopulation might be that there is some hidden selectivity in the burial-practices of Greece which operates only between 1100 and 800, and leads us to underestimate the numbers of burials and indeed to overlook whole sites for the disposal of the dead. Some such practice as exposure of the dead, to the total exclusion of burial, would meet the case. But there is no shred of positive evidence for such a custom; and furthermore we can point to the fact that the cemeteries which we do have represent a fairly complete range of ages and sexes, while their general poverty is such as to make it an almost laughable claim that they should represent any kind of élite or privileged group.

For all these reasons, I believe that it is now the most sensible course to accept that there was indeed a most drastic depopulation of Greece at the end of the Bronze Age. Of course, it may be that the level of population in the thirteenth century BC, the last era of the Mycenaean heyday, was dangerously high and that this contributed to the economic disaster which may well have brought about the downfall of that culture. But if so, then the pendulum subsequently swung much further than was good for Greece. It does not require too much imagination to picture some of the effects of living in small settlements, some of them shrunken survivals of the greater Mycenaean ones among whose ruins they were set, with long distances between them and with large areas of usable land unoccupied. The memory of ancestral achievements must have been clear enough to emphasize the falling-off to the latter-day Greeks (if also to console them for it);

nowhere more so than in the field of population where the
power of the former armies was not easily forgotten, while the
size of the towns, together with the manpower and specialization of labour required for their associated feats of engineering,
were features inherent in the still-visible remains. (Compare the
evidence of the relative sizes of Perati and Lefkandi, neither of
them probably a centre of major importance, pp. 18–19.)

The low level of population in the eleventh-century Aegean as
a whole shows no sign of having risen any more markedly in the
tenth and ninth centuries than does that of the settlement of
Lefkandi. These are not questions on which one can speak with
any certainty; one can only say that nothing, least of all the
quantities of surviving pottery, does anything to suggest a major
recovery. This is especially clear on the Greek mainland: across
the Aegean in Ionia, where comparatively recent settlements
had been established on largely unexploited territory, and on the
Aegean islands, many of which were probably entirely deserted
and offered scope for new settlers to make a fresh start, the picture may have been more positive; some at least of the factors

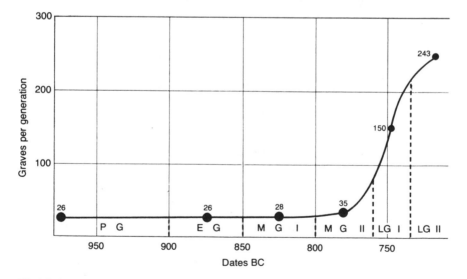

Fig. 3 Estimated population-growth in Athens and Attica, *c.* 950–700 BC (the
points are located at the mid-point of each pottery-phase; chronology after
J. N. Coldstream, *Greek Geometric Pottery* (1968))

which govern changes in population – in morale, in health and above all in availability of resources – may have already begun to operate favourably.

If so, this was nothing compared with what was to happen in the eighth century. I have tried elsewhere to calculate the rate of population-growth in one area, Attica, at this time, using the evidence of the datable burials from this region (Fig. 3). My conclusion was that in the space of two thirty-year generations, between about 780 and 720 BC, the population may have multiplied itself by a factor of approximately seven, and I tried to show grounds for finding this credible. In the accompanying diagram (Fig. 4), I have elaborated on this conclusion by further subdividing the burials into those from within the area of Athens itself, and those from the Attic countryside around it. The result suggests a slight net emigration from the town to the country, in that the curve rises more steeply towards the end for the latter area than for the former; we have no grounds for inferring any significant immigration from outside at this period. I have also shown (Fig. 4 dashed line) the apparent growth, based

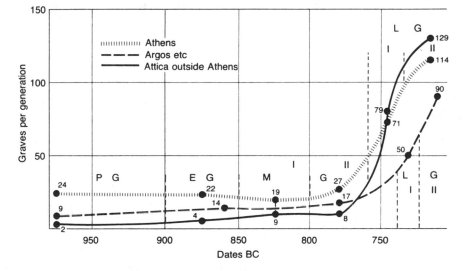

Fig. 4 Estimated population-growth of (i) Athens, (ii) the Argolid and (iii) the Attic countryside, *c.* 950–700 BC (points located as in Fig. 3 but the dates and durations of the periods are different at Argos; Argive chronology after P. Courbin *La Céramique géometrique de l'Argolide* (1966))

on a parallel calculation, for one of the few other regions which offer something approaching an adequate sample on which to base one's conclusions: the Argolid with the town of Argos and a group of lesser towns in or near the Argive plain (Asine, Lerna, Mycenae, Nauplia and Tiryns, with a few outlying graves). Being from essentially town-centred cemeteries, this evidence is to be compared with that from the town of Athens (Fig. 4, barred line); the relationship within the Argive group is *not* like that between Athens and its territory, since the other centres were at this time largely independent of Argos, as the Attic countryside was not. The Argive graph shows an increase from approximately the same period as the Athenian one. Despite the exodus that we have inferred, from Athens to the country, the Argive increase looks slighter, but this is very prob- ably the result of a much smaller sample (182 closely datable graves, as against 424 from Athens and 673 from Attica as a whole). The *rate* of increase in the Argolid and in Athens town is similar; and in the long term the salient feature is the marked rise in population everywhere during the eighth century. Its appearance in the Argolid makes the alternative explanations for Attica (p. 21 above) seem even less likely, for the burial-customs both traditional and contemporary were quite different in the Argolid.

Once again, it is possible to imagine some of the consequences for Greek society of a dynamic change like this. As settlements increase in number, communication between them becomes easier and more frequent; new ideas spread more widely; the pace of change accelerates. As the same settlements increase in size, greater division of labour becomes possible and, more important, political change becomes almost mandatory. A loose organization under a dominant family, with *ad hoc* decisions taken by a local ruler and only occasional assemblies of any larger group, becomes unworkable when the community more than doubles in size within a single generation. Greater resources of land are needed; new houses and whole settlements have to be built. Problems arise of a kind never experienced in the collective memory; and long-term decisions, some of them hard ones, have to be made. The survival of the group is now replaced, as the top priority, by more unfathomable considerations. A tighter and more complex social organization is needed.

If the population factor, on its own, could thus create a potentially revolutionary situation, it still requires some specific political steps to fulfil the potential. The eighth-century Greeks produced one great notion which was in many respects new, although it drew on some natural sources of inspiration in the earlier history of their land, and perhaps on others from outside. The dominant geographical unit in their past, especially the recent past had been a region of territory, whose area could reach a thousand square miles or more; we can be more certain about this geographical element than about the corresponding political one. One thinks naturally of a tribal system, but in recent years this hypothesis has been very strongly contested. On the face of it, tribal survivals in later Greek political systems are strong enough to suggest a considerable previous importance. Greek historical records abound in tribal names, and many states also show evidence for the survival of a hierarchy of lesser subdivisions of the tribe: the *phratry* or 'brotherhood' which at least purported to be a kinship-grouping, and the smaller *genos*, a group of related families (although not every tribesman necessarily belonged either to phratry or genos). What is more, the same tribal names recur, again and again, among different states speaking the same dialect of Greek: among the Ionic-speakers, a recurrent group of four tribe-names, among those speaking Doric a different group of three. This would make best sense if the system derived from a stage when all the Ionic Greeks were still united in mainland Greece, and the Doric-speakers similarly but separately concentrated.

But at this point difficulties begin to arise, and they have been recently developed by French scholars who have argued, with great thoroughness and ingenuity, that this whole picture of a 'tribal order' in early Greece is a mirage. It is indeed a surprising fact that, of the two main forms of state in the historical Greek world, it is only in the more advanced one, the *polis* (below p. 28), that the apparatus of tribal survivals occurs, and not in the simpler *ethnos* (p. 42), which so much more closely resembled the supposed ancestral model of organization. The next obstacle is that the subdivisions of the system are suspiciously hard to trace, and the genos in its technical sense of an established social organization is entirely absent, in the texts of Homer and Hesiod. If we argue that the system was already, by their time, in an advanced state of decay, then it is reasonable to ask why it later reappears, in robust health albeit in a 'technical' form, in the states of the historical period, with the genos particularly widely attested. Furthermore there is disagreement as to precisely what form the genos took in historical times, with some arguing that it had changed its nature from being a kind of clan-organization to which everyone of a certain minimal status belonged into an exclusive aristocratic group, while others hold that, on the contrary, it had allowed its original prowess to be diluted by the admission of non-aristocratic outsiders. These and other difficulties largely disappear if we merely make the assumption that the system had no ancient pedigree; that the tribe, phratry and genos were the late and artificial creations of the developed Greek state, in whose workings they played an indispensable part, enabling such matters as military enlistment and minor religious festivals to be handled by small and manageable groups.

This is a clever theory and, like others of its kind, it is destructive as well as constructive in its effects. For if there was no tribal order in the era before the formation of the Greek states, then what system was there? To what group larger than the family did men owe allegiance? Archaeology may help here, for it suggests that, throughout the dark age and even to some extent in the last years of the Mycenaean epoch, some organized entity had existed which – whatever its name – could function over fairly large geographical areas. When common features of material culture appear in each such area, and change as the boundaries of the territory are reached, it is fair to infer some human grouping which is coterminous with the area; and it is difficult to think of a better model than a tribal system to explain these phenomena. We have our first glimpse of these divisions in the full Bronze Age, in one or two features (but not many) of the culture of the Mycenaeans, and this is not surprising: every civilization can be expected to show *some* degree of regional differentiation, and the remarkable thing is that the divisions at this period are not stronger. But later we see them, more strongly marked, in such things as the burial-practices of the Protogeometric period, when central control had broken down, the trappings of civilization had disappeared, and loose-knit groups were scattered thinly over the landscape. The regional schools of Geometric pottery in the ninth and eighth centuries BC reveal them in an even more clearly developed form. Nor are they detectable only in material objects. The spread of the alphabet to Greece leads to the growth of a mass of 'epichoric' alphabets, each distinguishable in minor ways from its neighbours in the same dialect-group, and more obviously from those in other groups; their divisions more or less coincide with those of the material phenomena. This regional pattern calls out for an explanation: what ties can have bound together the practices of men living in such small numbers and at times more than fifty miles apart? Certainly they were such ties as could survive the growth of the historical city-state, offer a rival to it as a focus for loyalty, and on occasions supplant it; while in areas where the city-state did not arise, they continued to define the political unit of the ethnos. Geographical and environmental factors are hardly enough on their own; furthermore, the pattern must have had to grow up in reaction against the very different tendencies of the Mycenaean world, which had been characterized by entrenched and affluent monarchies, living on a pattern superficially similar to each other but markedly different from that of their subjects. The ensuing dark age is the best time for such a system to have grown up; it is comforting, too, that *some* form of tribal state seems to be detectable in the Homeric poems, although at certain points it is overlaid with reminiscences of the Mycenaean kingdoms (as for example in the *Catalogue of Ships* in book ii of the *Iliad*) and at others contaminated by the poet's awareness of the growth of the city-state in his own time; and although as a result the incidence of substantial towns is

unrealistically high. The standard way for Homer to refer to a
king's subjects, to a state, or to a component in the armies at
Troy, is by the plural ethnic – 'the Myrmidons', 'the Boiotians',
'the Cilicians' and so forth. This bears the stamp of tribalism, if
of a simple kind, without the elaborate substructure of phratry
and genos.

There may be ways in which a tribal system could accommodate a soaring rise in population without disintegrating. But in
the event the more advanced communities in Greece adopted a
different solution, one which led to urbanization, but only by an
indirect route. The distribution of these more developed states
coincides fairly well with that of the more advanced areas of
Mycenaean culture, where towns had once existed. Memory of
the names of the former towns, though not always their location, certainly survived. But the new system was to be no mere
re-establishment of the old. The towns were to be quite different
physically and, above all, they were to form part of a quite different political system. We know that in the Mycenaean world a
kingdom normally included a number of towns all subject to the
king's rule, and we suspect a very marked discrimination between town and country. These were features that were not to be
revived in the new states.

As so often happens, the name adopted for the new institution was a well-worn term with many meanings besides the one
now intended. 'Polis', since the time when it outgrew its earlier
meaning of 'citadel' or 'stronghold', had probably meant merely
a conurbation of a certain minimum size. Now, in its strictest
usage, it came to mean a settlement with two essential and new
qualities: first, political independence (not always unqualified)
from its neighbours; second, political unity with a tract of country surrounding it, this time entirely unqualified, in that no formal distinction was normally made between the inhabitants of
the countryside and the inhabitants of the main settlement.
Although in one or two cases the institution of monarchy survived into the lifetime of the new system, and although it later
proved possible to reconcile the two in the rather different
régime of the Archaic tyrannies, the growth of the polis coin-

cided with the general disappearance of hereditary monarchies. The idea of a king ruling over a single town and its territory had perhaps not been quite unknown in Mycenaean times; but we do not find it in the *Catalogue of Ships*, the place in Homer where above all we should expect it to occur if it were a regular Mycenaean feature and its appearances elsewhere in the poems are few and controversial. Appropriately enough in the cases where hereditary monarchy still lingered on in the eighth century and later, the word now used for 'king', *basileus*, had in Mycenaean Greek apparently signified a mere nobleman or petty chieftain.

Nor was the typical early polis simply a Mycenaean town resurrected: hardly surprisingly, since the process which had begun in the Neolithic period and reached its final stage in the

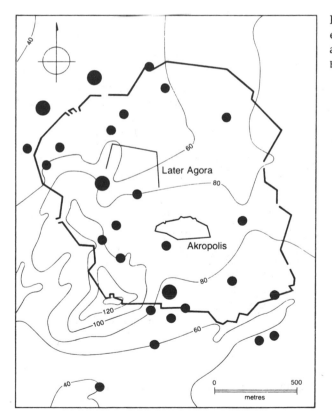

Fig. 5 Distribution of early burials (ninth and eighth centuries BC) in Athens

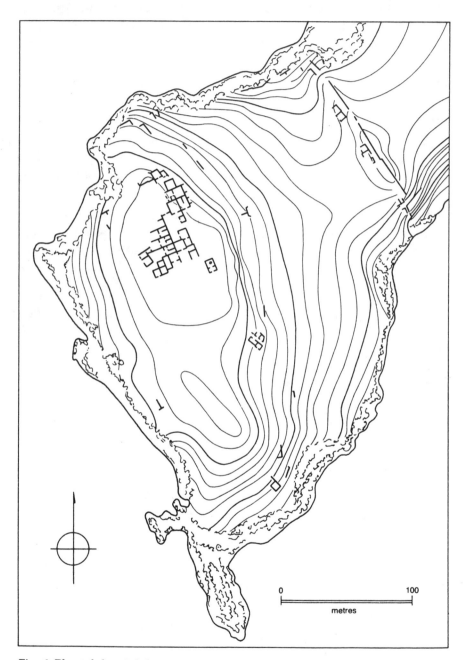

Fig. 6 Plan of the eighth-century settlement at Zagora on Andros

Mycenaean town had suffered a total interruption. The most obvious difference was in the degree of concentration. Mycenaean towns tended to be centred on a fortified citadel, which housed either the royal palace or, in subordinate towns, a chieftain's or governor's stronghold. The town-houses could often not be accommodated inside, although in the cause of security they tended to crowd against the outer walls or slopes of the citadel as closely as they could. By contrast the early polis, except in special geographical circumstances, was hardly a town at all, but rather a fairly close cluster of villages – close enough, certainly, to make use of a communal citadel which would in many cases be none other than the former Mycenaean royal citadel (cf. Fig. 5). The villages would also, in some cases, be sufficiently close together for a really sharp rise in population to have the automatic effect of unifying them physically. When particular factors of remoteness or vulnerability applied, a fortification-wall around the whole site was often a very early feature. But even then, the area thus enclosed was not always entirely built up: sometimes it was dotted with clusters of housing, as if the 'village' habit was so engrained as to survive in rather inappropriate circumstances (Fig. 6).

The Greeks launched this new model of settlement with such success that it rapidly grew to become, in reality, what we usually call it when translating 'polis': a city-state. But where had the idea come from in the first place? Some of the difficulties of deriving it from the Mycenaean era have already been seen. In default of such an origin, the natural place to look next is outside Greece. The city-state is such a characteristic feature of Greek civilization that the tendency has been to assume that – along with other such features, from the Hellenic temple to the ideal of individual freedom – it was the spontaneous creation of the Greek people. But the truth may be more complex. At a time when the Greeks were in fresh contact with the older civilizations of the Near East, it would have been surprising if many of their ideas had not been coloured by that relationship; a society recovering from such a profound economic, social and demographic recession as that which had enveloped Greece will be

eager to learn from those who have progressed further. So with
the city-state, there was at least one potential model within the
ken of eighth-century Greeks: that of the Phoenician coastland.
The cities of Phoenicia had some important qualities in common
with the Greek polis as it eventually emerged: they were mutu-
ally independent; each was ruled by its own monarchy with the
aid of a political assembly, and had a small territory of its own; a
further point whose significance will become apparent later is
that the population of each city was united by devotion to the
same religious cults. What we do not know is whether, like the
Greek polis, they extended their citizenship to the free indigenous population of their own territories; but if they did, this
makes the parallel closer.

    If there was some influence here, we should look for it at the
time when the Greek polis took on its distinctive form. There is
some disagreement as to when this was, particularly in the last
thirty years, since the excavation of the Ionian site of Old
Smyrna revealed urbanization beginning to take place in the
ninth century, and a fortification-wall surrounding the settlement from about 850 BC onwards – an unexpectedly early
appearance for both phenomena. More recently, other sites have
shown fortifications no later than 800 BC: Iasos in Caria (further
south on the coast of Asia Minor) and Zagora on the island of
Andros. Are all these to be taken as signs of the rise of the polis
idea in the ninth century? If so, we should at once concede that
the Greek mainland had as yet no part in the process, for neither
fortification nor anything approaching urban concentration is
visible so early there; excavations in Athens and Corinth suggest
strongly that, until well after this time, they still conformed to
the pattern of scattered and unfortified villages that we noted
just now (p. 31). But in fact the early fortifications outside the
mainland can perhaps be explained otherwise. Security was
clearly a prime motive behind them: there was a tradition that
dark age settlements like Smyrna and Iasos had been planted in
the face of native resistance, and the potential threat of surrounding alien population certainly existed. It is significant that
the most important Mycenaean settlement on this coast, Miletos,

had not had the usual fortified stronghold within the settlement but instead a defensive circuit which apparently ran round the whole of it. If this was an abiding local consideration here, then for Zagora and other sites in the Cycladic islands piracy is likely to have been an equally persistent threat. If it was simply that no settlement of any size or prosperity could afford to do without a fortification, then this need carry no implication of citizenship or other recognition for those inside it, much less for any who lived in the adjacent countryside. A tribal community could own towns and strongholds without conferring a special status on them, and the Ionian and Cycladic towns may have been closer to this model in their very early stages.

So fortification and urbanization, being neither necessary nor sufficient conditions for the advent of the polis, are poor criteria for its formation. Will any other serve better? A possible answer lies in the field of religion. Every Greek polis was, among other things, a religious association; its citizens accepted a community of cult, with a patron deity presiding over each state. To impose this regularity of worship was probably a difficult feat after the diversity of local practices which must have existed in the conditions of the dark age. The presiding deity was very often female (as for example Athena at Athens, Sparta and elsewhere; Hera in Argos, Tiryns and Samos; probably Artemis at Smyrna), but Apollo was also strong in this role (as at Corinth, Eretria in Euboia, Thermon in Aitolia or Dreros in Crete). A necessary element in such an official cult was a central city sanctuary – not necessarily a temple at first, but a sanctified place at which all could detect the deity's presence. An approximate indication of the establishment of such a cult will be given, first at the date of the earliest dedications on a site which can be identified as that of the patron god, and later by the construction of an actual temple. Both criteria prove to indicate that the same period, the eighth century BC, was the critical one. In each of the examples mentioned above, the dedications begin within that century or occasionally just before; the first temple-construction is usually towards its end or just afterwards. An eighth-century date for the decisive phase in the rise of the Greek polis is, among other things, compatible with the idea that the Phoenician model could have had some influence on it: this is a time at which Graeco-Phoenician relations were on a familiar level without becoming indiscriminately close – just as they are portrayed in the *Odyssey*, in fact.

Of the actual processes of formation, written records present us with one classic model, that of synoecism. Here too, as with the 'polis', the term is an irritatingly ambiguous one in Greek usage. It covers everything from the notional acceptance of a single political centre by a group of townships and villages whose inhabitants stay firmly put, to the physical migration of a population into a new political centre, which could be either an existing or a purpose-built city. The crucial element in all cases is the political unification. The earliest case of synoecism of which we hear, that of Attica, took place long before the advent of historical records, probably in the ninth and eighth centuries BC, and is described for us in the often anachronistic phrases of much later writers: Thucydides portrays it as a unification of magistracies, council-chambers and town-halls (ii 15, 2); Livy, despite the distancing effect of writing in Latin, perhaps catches more of the spirit of seeing it as a *contributio* (strictly, a form of federation) of people who had been hitherto villagers (*pagatim habitantes*) (xxxi 30, 6). But it is clear enough that the Attic synoecism conformed to the abstract and not the physical model. The people of Attica, whether settled in Athens, in country villages, or actually on their holdings, agreed to accept Athens as their political centre. Athens itself, as we have seen, was no more than an unusually substantial and close constellation of villages in the eighth century, and that is the latest period at which this synoecism can have taken place. But other synoecisms followed, some rapidly and others many centuries later, in which populations were moved bodily into the city. There is a faint hint that something of the kind could have happened with another early case, that of Corinth. Here the population of the surrounding Corinthia seems to have dwindled after the eighth century, but the case is also linked with the other great migratory phenomenon of the age, colonization abroad. And colonization in turn is closely bound up with the twin issues of population, which we have been considering, and of agricultural land, to which we must now turn.

In an era as dynamic as that of the eighth century in Greece, it is almost to be expected that we should find some kind of economic revolution underlying the more obvious developments, and this I think we do. The evidence is very scanty, but it all points in the same direction. Throughout history, the loose structure of tribalism has constantly been associated with stock-raising. It is the natural medium of subsistence both for a nomadic people and for a widely-scattered sedentary one; it is also a common form of wealth in insecure environments. Some or all of these considerations applied to the preceding dark age in Greece and there are signs, if we look for them, that stock-rearing had flourished then. Homer speaks with more than one voice on this question as on others, but there is no denying that herds form the predominant medium of wealth, and meat the regular diet, of his heroes. Yet it is a fact, not just of Greek but of all Mediterranean civilization in later centuries, that arable farming and a grain-based diet predominate. This facet of Homer's picture is therefore likely to derive from an early epoch; and here too, as with the tribal system itself, the likeliest context is that of the dark age. A severely diminished population, unable to cultivate all the available land, can effectively occupy and use it by pastoral methods. Even such a paradox as the survival of place-names for deserted sites can be easily explained by the hypothesis of grazing herds. Archaeological evidence has as yet made only a limited contribution to this question, but there are two areas in particular where further material should prove enlightening: the study of animal-bones from settlement-sites, and even from graves where they are often left as refuse from funerary feasts; and the study of dated pollen-deposits. As far as they go, both classes of evidence give some support to the hypothesis of dark age pastoralism: the bones from the grave-side feasts attest to widespread consumption of the meat of domestic animals, especially sheep and goats, in the eleventh, tenth and ninth centuries BC; while the pollen-analyses hint at sharp local reductions in arable farming at the same period, with an apparent growth in olive-cultivation. By contrast, there is evidence from the eighth century and even from the later ninth that arable farming has begun to gain ground. We find, espe-

*Plate 1*  cially in Attica, model granaries being included in the grave-goods that accompany the dead, a practice which should point to the economic preoccupations of the deceased in their lifetime. Again, in several passages of Homer the 'stock-rearing' stratum is overlaid by a thinner, and probably later, stratum of arable farming: the clearest instances are given by the formulaic phrases found in the *Odyssey*, 'barley-meal, the marrow of mankind' and the generic phrase 'bread-eating' to denote civilized humanity as distinct from gods and savages. Most explicit of all is the message conveyed by Hesiod's *Works and Days*, composed probably at a date close to 700 BC. It is a poetic manual of arable farming which shows awareness of its wider economic context and social implications, yet reverts to a fairly rudimentary level of instruction in husbandry – a combination which suggests an uneven spread of experience, and thus a moment when the decisive concentration on arable farming was in the very process of diffusion across Greece.

There is a parallel, of far wider significance, in later history for the kind of agricultural revolution which I have postulated here. In northern Europe in the earlier Middle Ages, the adoption of the open field system was also accompanied by a big rise in population in some localities, to a level far above even that of Roman times. Furthermore, some authorities argue that the severe depopulation of the intervening centuries, so far from impeding the onset of the new system, actually facilitated its progress, since it left large areas of land unburdened with ownership-rights, and thus available for a new method of distribution. The similarities between these conditions and those at the end of the dark age of Greece are clear. If there was also a real similarity in the effects, then the impact of the later revolution for Europe, and ultimately for the world, would suggest a proportionate significance for the earlier one within the narrow confines of the Greek world.

In particular, there was surely a close connection between the political phenomenon of the advent of the polis and the economic one of the switch to arable farming – for in the Classical era of Greek history there is no closer link than that between citizenship of the polis and ownership of land. Three centuries after this period, in 403 BC, it seems that between three-quarters and four-fifths of the citizens of Athens were still landowners (that is, all but 5,000 of a total citizen population of between 20,000 and 25,000). Such a regime of smallholders was in total contrast to the pastoralism which I believe had prevailed in earlier centuries. This made the original apportionment of plots of land, and the subsequent legislation as to their transferability, especially significant matters. Although we may doubt the literal truth of later claims that the land-lots were totally inalienable, it is clear that legislation was often introduced early on to keep their number and size as constant as possible. When there is a continuing rise in population within a state, such provisions will obviously lead to tension; emigration is the most familiar and

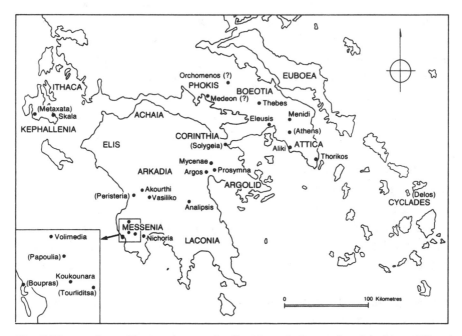

Fig. 7 Hero-cults at Bronze Age tombs (bracketed sites: cult only after *c.* 650 BC)

perhaps in the long run the least painful remedy that suggests
itself.

But before we consider the logical consequence, in the form of
the colonization process, there is a category of evidence which
may bear on the problem of land-ownership at home.
Repeatedly, when Greeks of the historical period engaged in
land-disputes, we hear of their having recourse to the legendary
past as a source of justification: if a party could claim to be
linked by descent or other close association, plausibly or even
implausibly, with a legendary personage who had once inhabited
a place, then their claim to ownership of that place was greatly
enhanced. Where no really eligible personage existed, it was
necessary to invent him, if only by forming a personal name out
of the name of the locality in question; but the trump-card was
the physical discovery of the legendary hero, in the form of a
skeleton in a tomb. Herodotus tells two excellent stories about
such practices in sixth-century Greece: first, how the tide was
turned in the hitherto unsuccessful warfare of Sparta against
Tegea when the resourceful Spartan Lichas, with some help
from the Delphic oracle and a garrulous Tegean blacksmith,
located the bones of Orestes and brought them to Sparta; and
again how Kleisthenes, tyrant of Sikyon, in order to pursue his
anti-Argive policy, actually persuaded the Thebans to exhume
the remains of the legendary hero Melanippos, deadly enemy of
the Argive Adrastos, so that he could re-inter him on the site
where Adrastos was worshipped and thus 'drive out' the cult of
Adrastos (i 68; v 67, 2–4). Even more pragmatic was the use to
which the hero Theseus was put by the fifth-century Athenian
Kimon. The legend that the great hero of Athens had been killed
and buried on the island of Skyros gave Kimon, first, a pretext
for conquering the island and then, when he had 'found'
Theseus' bones, a sensational political success when he brought
them back to Athens (Plutarch, *Life of Theseus* xxxvi 1–2; *Life of
Kimon* viii 3–6). I believe that we can trace the beginnings of this
practice, albeit at a lowly and unofficial level, in the later eighth
century. From shortly after 750 BC, in the regions of Attica,
Boiotia, Phokis, the Argolid and Messenia, with a few outlying

occurrences in the islands, we begin to find the almost entirely new practice of making dedications in, or otherwise showing reverence to, tombs of the Bronze Age. In nearly every case, *Plate 7* these are of the Mycenaean age – that is to say, of a period about 500 years earlier than the institution of cult. Separated as they were by centuries of change, migration and sheer oblivion from the world in which the burials had been made, the worshippers must have known that they were working in the dark. The people of Eleusis who, at this date, surrounded with an enclosure-wall a group of graves identified with those of the Seven Against Thebes, heroes of the generation before the Trojan War, in fact chose not Mycenaean but even earlier Middle Helladic burials: an archaeological error of about 300 years. But they and their contemporaries went ahead with their veneration and dedications; and what is more, they convinced a more sophisticated posterity: the Eleusis graves were pointed out, more than 800 years later, to the traveller Pausanias; while the dedications at many graves, once instituted, go on well into the Classical period. What thinking or imagining lay behind this odd practice? The likeliest explanation is that it originated in local attempts to consolidate the ownership of land. As such, it would be unconnected with the contemporary rise of the city sanctuaries (p. 33) except in the very indirect sense that both are linked with the rise of the polis, and thus with settled land-holding. But by instituting a cult of a local hero, a community could acquire a sense of security in an age of apparently fluid and unpredictable settlement. Some at least of these cults became important enough to be taken over officially, at any rate in Athens, and transplanted to the city; but of the cults at graves of which we know archaeologically, most continue to be practised *in situ*. Only in rare cases can we guess at the pretended identification of the dead. It is also noteworthy that the cults do not appear in all regions of Greece: they are conspicuously absent, for example, from three regions – Lakonia, Crete and Thessaly – where we know that land-ownership was not distributed among a free peasantry, but was worked by a population of serfs who were bound to the lands on behalf of its owners, their masters. One can imagine only too well that there would be no attraction for such people in this crude proprietary propaganda, while the owners of the land would often live some way off. But elsewhere, the practice makes best sense as that of a social class which was humble and potentially insecure, but had aspirations; the offerings are never intrinsically precious, but they are not rubbish either – indeed, their quality is often above that of offerings in contemporary burials.

All this emphasis on land becomes intelligible when we reflect that it was the only significant medium of wealth; that it was itself on occasion the personified object of worship and offerings; that a new political system was being widely introduced in which it was the only qualification for citizenship; and that (if I am right) its full fruitfulness was only now in the process of being rediscovered after centuries of neglect. Competition for land was at its most intense in the newly-arising polis. There is little doubt that, as Thucydides held, of the manifold causes and facets of colonization this one is the most fundamental. In many areas, land-shortage would in any case have resulted from the rise in population, and the measures taken over ownership may have accentuated it. At all events, from around 735 BC groups of aristocrats and their followings began to set out, with a rather abrupt intensity, for the West. These were not however the very earliest Greek settlements overseas, even if we set aside the rather different case of the Ionian migration in the early dark ages. We now know in some detail about the early development of Pithekoussai on Ischia, the earliest Greek settlement commonly called a 'colony'. It was planted by the cities of Chalkis and Eretria no later than the second quarter of the eighth century; since the site of one of its mother-cities, Eretria, has been shown (also by very recent excavation) to have been settled no earlier than 800 BC itself, this seems surprising. We have little sign that, in these early years of the century, the pressure of population had anywhere begun to be significant. It is therefore encouraging to find that the evidence from early Pithekoussai points strongly to a commercial motive behind this pioneer western enterprise, and not the usual agricultural one of land-shortage. The desire for access to the great mineral wealth of Etruria may have been the foremost consideration. It looks, therefore, as though the success of this isolated venture, conceived for a special and non-recurrent purpose, later suggested a ready-made solution for a new and different problem which afflicted a much wider area of Greece. Thus people from Chalkis and Eretria themselves, together with others from Corinth, Sparta, Naxos, Paros, Lindos and other towns in Rhodes and in Crete – all of them city-states – and men from Achaia and Lokris, which were not, all alike within little more than a generation then turned to colonization as one solution to their troubles.

The foundation of these colonies and the fact that the majority of them were swiftly successful will have encouraged political developments in the homeland. In a true colony, the survival of the settler depended on his being allocated a portion of land in the territory surrounding the town, exactly the principle on which citizenship was determined in the polis at home. But Pithekoussai, although showing some of the expected physical characteristics of a polis – it is centred on a natural akropolis, on the coast of an island of 46 square miles, for whose population it was presumably the only urban centre – may yet not conform to the true polis pattern. For one thing, the soil of this steep and rocky island was not well suited to agriculture; for another, there are the chronological difficulties posed by its early date. Signs of a pre-existing polis system in the Greek homeland are hard to detect as early as *c.* 770 BC, even if the particular problem about Eretria (p. 40) can be resolved by the explanation that the mother-city had itself recently moved from an older site, and that this very move was part of the process of *synoikismos*, the physical and political unification of a city-state; something similar could have happened, roughly simultaneously, at Chalkis.

A town in the Greek homeland, founded as it necessarily was by countrymen, posed new problems for the status of the free population living around it. Without their assistance in the cultivation of the land, the town could not survive. In many civilizations, the countrymen would have become in some way subordinated to the dictates of the town-dwellers, or even have gravitated *en masse* to the town; in others, their own smaller villages might have aspired to become autonomous communities. The Greek solution was different, and, once it had been applied with success in the colonies of the third quarter of the eighth century, all Greeks must have become aware of its possibilities: why should those who stayed at home be treated worse than those who had emigrated? That some kind of lateral influence operated is suggested by the fact that the form of the colonizing state did not always determine that of the colony. An early foundation like Lokroi in Italy could become a polis, despite the fact that its settlers came from a region, Lokris, where the city-state was not prevalent and where urbanization of any kind was laggardly.

This last point brings us face to face, however incidentally, with a substantial and often ignored fact. Just as the polis as a state-form was not the peculiar property of Greek lands, so too it was not universal in them. Alongside it there continued to flourish a very different conception of the state, the ethnos. In many studies of ancient Greece the ethnos is almost ignored, either as being an embarrassing legacy of a more primitive era, or more respectably because its contribution to the great intellectual revolution of the fifth century seems so marginal when compared to that of the polis. There are some problems of definition here. In its purest form, the ethnos was no more than a survival of the tribal system into historical times: a population scattered thinly over a territory without urban centres, united politically and in customs and religion, normally governed by means of some periodical assembly at a single centre, and worshipping a tribal deity at a common religious centre. But between this extreme and that of the polis, there were many intermediate stages possible: if a number of urban centres grew up within the territory of the ethnos, they might attain intermittent autonomy as separate states, and pay only occasional homage to the concept of a unified 'nationality'; if on the other hand a single city grew to power, it might forcibly establish itself as the political centre of at least a part of the ethnos, and make this part effectively into a polis: if both these processes happened succes-

sively, in that order, a very large polis might be the final product. The importance of the ethnos lies, chronologically as geographically, near the boundaries of classical Greek culture: firstly
it recalls the antecedent culture of the dark age, and secondly,
by remaining in inconspicuous existence throughout the rise and
fall of the polis, it provided the basis for a fresh venture in
state-formation in the autumn of Greek civilization. What it
offered above all was size: a disadvantage in the eyes of a true
child of the polis like Aristotle ('a polis with excessive population
becomes like an ethnos', he wrote (*Politics* 1326 b 4)), but an
advantage when the issue was power – particularly when, after

Fig. 8 Greece: the extent of city life (drawn after E. Kirsten *Die griechische Polis*
*als historisch-geographisches Problem des Mittelmeerraumes* (1956), figure 13)

Aristotle's death, Greece was embroiled in the 'Great Power' politics of the Hellenistic age. The form of this revitalization of the ethnos was that of a federation of autonomous entities, each of which could individually have been either polis or ethnos previously, but which was prepared to accept a central political and military authority; often, the whole federation was still called by the name of ethnos. The success of the notion is shown by the fact that the Achaean League of the third century BC attracted no less than 60 cities into its orbit, including such distinguished former exponents of the polis idea as Argos, Corinth, Sikyon and Megara.

But we should not read these impressive attributes into the ethnos of the early days. The most common forms at this date were those of the primarily rural 'canton-state' like Lokris or Doris; and the fairly loose union of towns and their territories like Arkadia, Achaia or Boiotia – towns which, to tell the truth, were individually given the label 'polis' by contemporary Greeks without discrimination, a usage which has blurred the distinctions for modern minds. They cannot nevertheless be designated as city-states. The point at issue is that of political autonomy versus mere urbanization; the difference in effect is shown if we compare a map showing the extent of city-life, the polis in its loosest Greek sense, with one showing the much smaller extent of the true city-state (cf. Figs. 8&9). The former was drawn by E. Kirsten, to illustrate the fact that urbanism is more or less co-extensive with the earlier spread of Mycenaean culture. What this suggests is that *urbanization* in Greece was in some way indebted to the Mycenaean precedent; it gives no ground for attributing any such origins to the political idea of the city-state, and we have already seen (pp. 28–31) how unlikely this would be.

The maps show that not even urbanization, let alone the city-state system, won unanimous acceptance among the Greeks, particularly in the western half of the Greek mainland. Yet the superiority of both seemed, to their own products, beyond all argument; they explained the rejection of city-life on the part of a substantial number of Greeks by more or less condescending

Fig. 9 Greece: the extent of the city-state (shaded) and of the ethnos (unshaded) in the Archaic period

references to the backwardness of the latter. Modern analysts have offered different explanations of their own, like that of Kirsten who attributed the divergence of practices between eastern and western Greece to geological and ecological factors, operative in Mycenaean as in Classical times. But the ancients would probably have claimed as adherents of the polis-system many Greeks whose cities fell under the authority of an ethnos of the more developed type: the people of Tegea and Mantineia in Arkadia, for example, or of Thebes and Plataia in Boiotia. It took a purist like Aristotle to make the point that 'a polis differs even from an ethnos where the people live, not in scattered villages,

but like the Arkadians' (*Politics* 1261 a 27). Certainly there is no
reason to think that such Greeks were any less fervent believers
in city life. One of the most cogent expositions of its merits is a
speech put into the mouth of Alexander the Great, who quelled
the discontent of his troops in Mesopotamia by appealing to the
services his father had done them: 'Philip . . . gave you cloaks to
wear instead of sheepskins, brought you down from the moun-
tains to the plains, made you a match in war for your barbarian
neighbours, so that you no longer relied on natural fastnesses
for your defence, as much as on your own courage; *and* he made
you into city-dwellers, endowing you with excellent laws and
customs' (Arrian, *Anabasis* vii 9, 2). This rehearsal of the benefits
of civilization was addressed to Macedonians who had never
experienced the system of the city-state. When we evaluate the
contribution to Greek civilization of those who did not live in
city-states we can, if we take a long-term view, see that their
systems had a greater durability built into them, and that this
resilience had not a little to do with the apparently technical
discrepancies to which Aristotle was referring in the quotation
about the Arkadians. In the Archaic period, too, a city like Tegea
or Thebes owned a higher allegiance than did Athens, and could
in adversity fall back on a broader base of supprt. It is only if we
concentrate exclusively on the achievements, intellectual, artistic, political and military, of the fifth and earlier fourth centuries
BC that we shall judge the contribution of these Greeks to be
slight or marginal.

Throughout Greek history, a rough but detectable correlation
can also be seen between the polis-system and the growth of
democracy on the one hand, and the ethnos and oligarchy on
the other. Such significant political phenomena of the Archaic
period as tyranny, too, prove to have been largely confined to
the polis. In this field it seems that progress was especially difficult in the environment of the ethnos; and there is an amusing
illustration of this on one of the rare occasions when historical
processes were reversed. The city of Mantineia was razed and its
inhabitants dispersed into villages by the Spartans after a war in
385 BC. Initially, says Xenophon, there was resentment; 'but

since the landowners were living nearer to the estates which they owned in the vicinity of the villages, and had an aristocratic government and were rid of the troublesome demagogues, they became pleased at what had been done' (*Hellenica* v 2, 7). The Mantineians, like Alexander's audience, had not belonged to a fully autonomous city-state; it was urbanism in general that they were passing judgment on, and in some respects they and other city-dwellers outside the polis system had contributed quite substantially to Greek culture in the past. If we look back to the material revolution of the later eighth century in Greece, we find that it did not wholly run its course in the context of the embryo city-state, even though the subsequent birth of the latter was to be its most conspicuous achievement; the developed ethnos, too, was after all essentially a creation of this era, by the refinement of the primitive tribal order into a settled cultural unit, less distinctively Greek than the polis, but also more adaptable.

All this and much else was achieved in Greece within the short space of about a hundred years, between the early eighth and the early seventh centuries BC. Before this episode, the Greek world was an enclave whose boundaries hardly extended beyond Rhodes or Ithaka to the east and west, Macedonia and Crete to the north and south; the tentative contacts with southern Italy and the Levant had, as yet, no significant effect for anyone. After it, colonization and commerce had between them taken Greeks, repeatedly or even permanently, to the south of Spain, to Italy and Sicily, to North Africa, to the coast and even the hinterland of the Levant; the Greeks of Cyprus, isolated for so long, had been brought back into the cultural commonwealth. Before it, the low population and cultural level of the Greeks had made them certainly an obscure and perhaps even a backward people by the standards of the Mediterranean world; by its end, they were conspicuous everywhere as leaders and innovators. Before, they had been just another tribal society with fond memories of a better past; after, they were the expansive prophets of a new political system whose future must have seemed very bright. Before, they had orally-transmitted poetry of uncertain content and variable antiquity, which they were unable to record permanently; after, they had the songs of Homer and the means to write them down. The evidence of this extraordinary transformation is most clearly presented by their material culture: its growth, its range, its diffusion and its development. This evidence will form the subject of the next chapter.

# Structural Revolution:
# the Material Evidence

Clio loves those who bred them better horses,
Found answers to their questions, made their things,
Even those fulsome
Bards they boarded:

W. H. Auden 'Makers of History'

The remarkable developments of the eighth century in Greece, it is true, seem almost all to be centred round an abstract idea: the new conception of the state. But the material and technical advances associated with this idea soon developed a momentum of their own. It is difficult to decide whether any one of them should be treated as the independent and necessary advance without which the others would have been ineffective. The importance of an agricultural revolution (pp. 35–7), although potentially decisive, is too obscure and controversial to be invoked without further proof. Some would dispute the reality of any such revolution, others would claim that it was much more gradual and imperceptible than I have argued. But there is another area in which a change at least as dramatic is visible at this period, and that is metallurgy. The interpretation of this change is still far from obvious, but at least we can agree that it is there. We can first consider the historical background against which this change happened; then try, however crudely, to quantify it; and finally attempt to explain it.

In eighth-century Greece, 'metalwork' means large quantities of bronze and iron, a modicum of silver and gold, and a little

lead. Such a description could not be applied to any earlier era
of Greek metallurgy. As one moves backwards in time through
the ninth and tenth centuries BC, one finds an impoverishment,
steadily more acute, which reaches a climax in the years around
1000 BC when it seems that there was no real bronze industry at
all, and when gold, silver and even lead are almost absent; iron
reigns supreme, but only in a kingdom of the utmost poverty. If
one looks back further still, the pattern changes again because
iron virtually drops out of consideration; but the Mycenaean picture is otherwise extremely rich. The scope of the bronze industry is really impressive, with vessels, tools, weapons, defensive
armour and dress-accessories in a wide range of variant types.
Bronze fibulae and dress-pins were two common and important
classes of object added in the closing phases of Mycenaean civilization. Why the production of all these artefacts apparently
ceased is a problem which only marginally concerns us here;
there is, however, one factor which operates in the reverse direction in the question that we *are* faced with, the later revival of
the Greek metal industries. This is that of the tin trade and, to a
less marked degree, of the copper trade. A viable bronze industry requires considerable quantities of copper, and a supply of
tin that needs to be only about a tenth as large. In both cases,
requirements are modified by the fact that bronze is reusable,
through the melting down of existing objects. As long as the
Aegean remained in contact with Cyprus, the supplies of copper
were likely to be adequate: but tin is a different story. Opinions
differ as to which was the main source of tin for the Aegean,
whether in the Mycenaean or in the Classical period; but *no* convincing source has been found much nearer than a thousand
miles from Mycenae, and most of those that there were lay at
the ends of arduous and insecure overland routes. Without the
small but vital supply of tin, no effective bronze industry could
maintain itself for long, let alone develop. A people who, like
the Greeks, have ample supplies of iron ore and have mastered
even the rudiments of iron-working, will at least have an alternative metal technology when tin supplies are threatened or cut
off. When that eventuality arose in the eleventh and tenth cen-

turies BC, the rise of Greek iron-working followed swiftly. There may be a partial parallel with precious metals – for Greece also possessed silver deposits; and whereas gold, along with costly non-metallic materials like ivory and glass, became exceedingly rare at this same period, there is solid evidence for the progress of silver-extraction in Attica and the Argolid.

But when at last the metal trade revived, when copper and tin became freely available and gold and ivory could again be obtained, then Greece found herself with a much better economic basis than even at the height of the Mycenaean era. Iron was now available as an alternative to bronze, and there were many purposes for which aptitude or mere economy made it preferable; yet the unprecedented extent and frequency of Greek voyages overseas also meant that the tin and copper supplies were on a more secure basis than before. Choice was to a large extent free, as indeed it again was between native silver and imported gold. Doubtless it needed to be, with the huge increase in population which had now to be supported. Of the pressures which a population-boom would bring to bear on an ancient society, none are more immediate than those on farming-land and on metals. Both could be dynamic in their effects, but that on metals much the more so. In the case of Greece, the overall extension of agricultural land and the intensification of its use will have increased the sum of wealth; so, less directly, will the resultant diffusion of Greek settlers overseas. But there, it seems, the process halted for a time in its tracks, and lost itself in internal agrarian disputes and external territorial wars; there is no evidence that Greek agriculture achieved further technical advances for a while. Metals, unlike land, are portable, almost endlessly adaptable, and dynamic: they lead not to mere emigration, but to exchanges between the homeland and foreign parts; they encourage specialization of labour as well as just employment. Increased metal supplies stimulate not only internal developments in metallurgy: they invade other activities and transform them. A rise in metal-production, especially if the rate of increase exceeded that in the level of population, could change the whole economy. Is there a

point at which we can intercept this process, and verify empiri-
cally what is still no more than a hypothesis?

There is one class of evidence, until recently a most neglected
one, which is sufficiently bound up with this process to throw
some light on it. This is the metallic dedications from the Greek
sanctuaries. It is true that they represent metalwork in an
unproductive context, economically speaking: an object once
dedicated becomes static in every sense. But the mere existence
of this unproductive sector is a strong hint, if not a proof, of the
existence of a much larger productive counterpart: a weapon of
war, for example, will be dedicated only by a man who can
spare it, or has captured it from enemies who will then need to
*Plate 2*  supply its replacement; and although the great bronze tripods
may have been constructed exclusively for ceremonial uses,
these latter extended far beyond the field of dedications (as
prizes, for example, and in gift-exchange). Even objects
designed purely for dedication, like bronze figurines, were using
up valuable metal. So that an increase in dedication is, *prima
facie*, a sign of increased total resources; and in the event the rate
of increase that we find is of a startling order, as the following
figures show. (Different time-divisions have been used, according to the manner in which the objects have been published, and
one class of non-metallic finds is included for comparison; the
date of the relevant publication is shown on the right-hand
side.)

One does not need a computer to see that the rise in dedications in the eighth century is of an extraordinarily abrupt kind,
far more so than any conceivable rise in population. There may,
indeed there must, be at least one further hidden factor at work
behind these figures: an increasing *proportion* of the available
wealth is being dedicated to the gods. Some of the sanctuaries
probably did not even exist before the eighth century; even the
earliest dedications, while of eleventh or tenth century *type*, may
yet have enjoyed long use before their final dedication. But
when allowance is made for the distorting factors – increasing
population and increasing emphasis on dedications, which
operate in one direction, long retention of objects which oper-

ates in the other – figures of this order must convey a major rise of wealth in metals, both *in toto* and *per capita*. It is often, and rightly, pointed out that the rise in dedications roughly coincided with a falling-off in metallic and other grave-goods in Greek burials. This is certainly a significant fact, but first we must note that there is a chronological overlap: the sharp rise in sanctuary-dedications comes, as we have seen, during the eighth century, while the discontinuation of grave-goods falls at its very end; and secondly, to set things in proportion, let us note that the total yields of metalwork from graves are small by comparison with some of the figures we have just considered. In Attic and Argive graves of the tenth to eighth centuries BC, for example, it is only a proportion of the graves which contain

| | *Eleventh and tenth centuries BC* | *Ninth century* | *Eighth century* | |
|---|---|---|---|---|
| Bronze figurines at Delphi | 0 | 1 | 152 | (1969) |
| Bronze tripods at Mount Ptoön (Boiotia) | 0 | 0 | 7 | (1971) |
| Bronze dedications on Delos | 0 | 1 | 19 | (1973) |
| Terracotta figurines at Olympia | 10 | 21 | 837 | (1972) |
| | *Eleventh and tenth centuries BC* | *Ninth and early eighth* | *Later eighth and seventh* | |
| Bronze fibulae at Philia (Thessaly) | 0 | 2 | 1783+ | (1975) |
| Bronze pins at Philia | 1 | 4 | 37 | (1975) |
| Bronze fibulae at Perachora | 7 | 1 | 50+ | (1940) |
| Bronze pins at Perachora | 0 | 15 | 81 | (1940) |
| Bronze fibulae at the Argive Heraion | 16 | 10 | 88 | (1905) |
| Bronze pins at the Argive Heraion | 3 | c. 250 | c. 3070 | (1905) |
| Bronze fibulae at Lindos (Rhodes) | 0 | 52 | 1540 | (1931) |
| Bronze pins at Lindos | 0 | 0 | 42 | (1931) |

bronzes – between one third and a half at the height of the practice, less than one quarter after about 800 BC. The total numbers of fibulae and pins known from eighth-century graves in central and southern Greece are to be numbered in hundreds rather than thousands; tripods and pieces of armour are rarities, bronze figurines unknown.

We are dealing, therefore, with more than one simultaneous phenomenon here. There is a big social change with the re-direction of attention towards the communal sanctuary and away from the individual grave: more will be said of this development later. But independent of this, there is a change in the level of metal-use. People were beginning to use metal implements for tasks which either had been undertaken hitherto without the benefit of metal, or else had not been achieved at all before; this must have been of enormous benefit to technology. The material evidence does not offer us many glimpses of this transformation, but two fields where we can detect its impact are carpentry, with the appearance of lathe-turned furniture, especially the legs of funerary biers in contemporary vase-painting, and stone-working, with the increased incidence of dressed masonry (below, pp. 60–1), A third and yet more significant area where technological advance would be reflected would be communication by sea; and we do indeed hear from Thucydides of a major development in shipbuilding towards the end of the eighth century (i 13, 3). But this last was an activity which must, in turn, have contributed greatly to the increase in metal wealth, through the expansion into remoter areas rich in metallic ores, not to speak of its warlike potential, including the capture of booty from nearer neighbours. A circle is thus completed. What we are seeing is a phenomenon familiar in systems theory, the 'multiplier effect' whose operation in the same lands two thousand years earlier has been described by Professor Renfrew in his book *The Emergence of Civilization*. Advances, however impressive, in one area of human activity will not necessarily change the society which introduces them: an increase in food-production, for instance, will not in itself suffice to bring about a change in institutions. But the moment that two or more such independent areas witness major advances, and the results interact, the rate of progress – both material and social – may accelerate violently. We have evidence of a major re-settlement of agricultural land in Greece in the eighth century, and we may further suspect an intensification in land-usage; at the same period we have quite independent evidence of a sudden increase in metal supplies, and of a consequent diversification of metal products, some of them making possible a greater specialization of crafts, others already its product. We have also evidence, again quite independent, that overseas communications were increasing at this time both in extent and in frequency. The obvious indicator to use here is pottery: in the tenth century BC we know of just two Greek pots which definitely found their way beyond the Aegean sea-coasts and their hinterlands; in the ninth, there is still no more than a handful of sherds from a very few sites; by the end of the eighth, the exported pieces are almost literally too numerous to count and the known sites number over eighty. We cannot assume that the carriers were always Greek, nor may we know in every case what motives inspired their long and dangerous journeys. But although these various developments may not even be the most important material advances of the age, the point is that any two of them together would be capable of producing a change in society; while their concerted effect could well carry it across the borderline into full civilization.

The rise of the sanctuary-sites, as we shall see presently, is also one of these interacting processes. We have used the quantity of dedications to demonstrate the general and sudden rise in activity in the eighth century BC. But it should not be imagined that all Greek sanctuaries were of a similar nature and function. There is first a small group of sites which combined exceptional religious importance with relative remoteness from any great centre of political power. This enabled them to achieve a pan-Hellenic status, usually insulated from the inter-state dissension which dominated almost every aspect of Greek relations, and in some ways even an international one. Three names dominate this group: Olympia and Delphi, whose athletic festival and oracle, respectively, had already acquired much more than local esteem before the end of the eighth century; and the isle of Delos, famed as the birthplace of two of the twelve Olympian deities, Artemis and Apollo. With them we may place another oracular seat, Dodona in Epirus: this, too, achieved fame early enough to be known to Homer, although the material record of early dedications is a little disappointing in the light of this. Here also belongs a special class of inter-state sanctuary, best represented by the Panionion on Mount Mykale in Asia Minor, founded as a communal shrine by the league of the twelve original cities of Ionia. Other early league sanctuaries existed, such as that on the island of Kalaureia (Poros), but none is thoroughly explored. Olympia, Delphi and Delos, as we should expect, have all produced a wealth of dedications both from this early period and from later times; with the subsequent rise of Greek monumental sculpture and architecture, for example, all three acquired famous temples and statues. But neither at Olympia nor at Delphi do we have direct evidence of an eighth-century temple, while at Delos the first definite cases arise with the construction, around 700, of temples to Artemis and Hera. The former is much the larger, but even so its area (just over 80 square metres) compares unfavourably with contemporary temples in some other sanctuaries, and is smaller than some domestic structures of the day. By such standards, these were late and unprepossessing developments.

A rather different pattern emerges from the sanctuaries of the individual states. Perhaps the most characteristic of these are sited in the heart of a city-state, on an akropolis or beside the civic centre (Athens, Eretria, Corinth, Sparta, Smyrna, Miletos, Lindos on Rhodes and Syracuse in Sicily all offer well-attested examples); but sometimes the most prestigious sanctuary of a polis was at a short distance outside the main settlement, like the great temples of Hera near Argos and on Samos. An ethnos, too, could boast famous sanctuaries within its territory, sometimes in its towns (as at Tegea in Arkadia or Thebes in Boiotia), but often in open country, as at Aetolian Thermon or Philia in Thessaly, and occasionally on remote mountain-tops (Apollo's sanctuary on Mount Ptoön in Boiotia, Artemis' at Lousoi and Mavriki in Arkadia). These state sanctuaries varied greatly in importance, and few attracted the quality and quantity of dedications of an Olympia. Nevertheless, examples like the Athenian Akropolis and the Samian Heraion show what could happen if the prestige of the state in question was high; and many humbler state sanctuaries at least show an ability to attract dedications from beyond their own frontiers. Sometimes a political importance has been claimed for this; it has been argued that the changing character of the dedications at Perachora near Corinth reflected the struggle for control of the area between the Argives, the Megarians and the ultimately successful Corinthians; and certainly more convincing instances of Corinth exercising her influence in overseas sanctuaries can be found in Ithaka, Delphi, Dodona and later Thermon. But there are many other cases where a different explanation must be sought. Argive and Corinthian pottery, besides Arkadian, is found at Tegea, and the same wares along with Lakonian at Sparta; Spartan bronze figurines, in turn, are dedicated, with many Argive examples, at Arkadian Lousoi. Further afield, there are Argive and Euboian as well as Corinthian finds at the Ithakan sanctuary; Corinthian bronzes at Thessalian Pherai; while Euboian and Rhodian pottery occurs at the Samian Heraion, together with (rather more surprisingly) bronze figurines from the Peloponnese. All of this evidence comes from the later years of the eighth century; when we consider the sanctuaries in the later Archaic period, we shall find richer and better-documented evidence for the cosmopolitan range of dedications. With the monumental offerings of the later period, the explanation is simply that Greek artists travelled widely in search of commissions; with our more portable objects, it may be no more than that other Greeks also travelled – but travelled in almost every case as individuals. At this early stage of Greek society, the religious pilgrimage was more likely to be a private affair than one of official representation; economically- or commercially-motivated ventures were undertaken on one's own initiative and at one's own risk; even diplomacy, in so far as it existed, largely took the form of hospitality and exchange of gifts with one's peers, relatives and guest-friends in other places. It is therefore only when the pattern of extraneous dedications is of a marked and enduring bias that we can begin to infer any deeper political significance.

There is another feature of the state sanctuaries which is of greater significance, and that is the growth of monumental temples. We have already considered this (p. 33) from the point of view of the link between the establishment of the polis and the construction of the temple. If it is accepted that the erection of a substantial and durable cult-building is a natural consequence of the state adopting responsibility for the cult of its patron deity, then the nature of the building may tell us something further about the intentions of the state. The first thing that strikes us is the relative pretension of the buildings, though this will come as no surprise if we are familiar with the pattern of later centuries, when a Greek city was invariably dominated by its temples, and when the contrast with domestic architecture was as obvious to contemporaries as it is from the ruins today. In the eighth century, standards on both sides were lower, and we may even have difficulty in recognizing these early shrines as the ancestors of the Classical temple. There were severe constraints on contemporary building techniques, notably the virtual absence of dressed masonry and roof-tiles, and the apparent limitation of roof-spans to about eight metres, even with internal supports. This last factor meant that the possibilities of enlarging a building were more or less confined to its longitudinal axis, so that considerations of proportion were likely to be overruled. Nevertheless some remarkably ambitious structures were attempted, and in a few cases (as with Anglo-Saxon churches) they were still to be seen eight or more centuries later.

Pride of place may be given to the first temple of Hera at Samos, partly because of its date – it was probably constructed quite early in the eighth century – and partly because it is already a most striking building. With a rectangular plan and a row of columns down the centre, the great length of 100 Greek feet gave it an original ground area of as much as 213 square metres; before the end of the century, the area had been enlarged and the appearance enhanced by the addition of the first encircling colonnade that we know of in Greece, a 'peristyle' of 43 wooden columns. Before very long, a similar-sized temple to Apollo had been built at Eretria, apsidal in plan and lacking an exterior colonnade but again well over 200 square metres in area. Another very large temple-building has been excavated at Gortyn in Crete; its total area, including what was probably an open-air courtyard, was even larger than that of the Samian Heraion; the dedications do not suggest that it was ear-

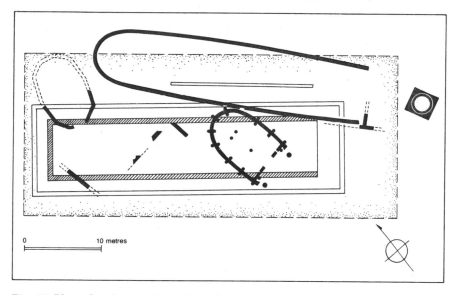

Fig. 10 Plan of early temples at Eretria

lier than the eighth century. A fourth outsize building was erected at the sanctuary of Apollo at Thermon in Aetolia, obscure in date and somewhat hybrid in plan, being basically rectangular but with a distinct convex curvature in its walls. This, too, received an added circuit of external supports (lean-to posts, perhaps, rather than columns). Whatever its original purpose, it almost certainly ended its days as a temple. These are not the only substantial state undertakings of the era: a problematic building at Tiryns, very similar in area and proportions to the Thermon temple, may well be the first temple of Hera on the site, but its date is again a source of great controversy. Smaller temples are known to have been built in this period by several other cities: such as Asine, Mycenae and Sparta in the Peloponnese; Corinth in its outlying sanctuary at Perachora; Smyrna in Ionia and Dreros in Crete; while the still semi-Hellenized islands of Lesbos and Lemnos have also produced what are probably sacred buildings of this date.

In these impressive architectural projects, we can surely see not only the self-assertion but also the incipient rivalry of the new-born states. The correspondence of measurements between the Samos and Eretria temples, and between the somewhat smaller pair in Tiryns and Thermon, suggests at least a mutual consciousness. It was probably very early in the seventh century that one city, Corinth, found the means to put herself beyond the reach of her rivals in this field for several generations. In the centre of the city a temple of Apollo was erected which, even though it apparently lacked a colonnade and despite uncertainty

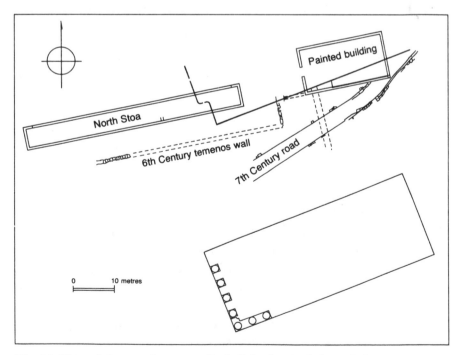

Fig. 11 Plan of the temple area at Corinth in the Archaic period

over its exact dimensions, easily excelled its known predecessors in both length and breadth. What is more, it had walls of dressed stone and a tiled roof, features which for centuries past had not been seen in buildings of any kind in Greece. Not content with this, the Corinthians built, perhaps a generation later, a temple for Poseidon at his nearby sanctuary of the Isthmos, which was in some ways even more imposing. It had a peristyle of wooden columns and its masonry walls carried mural paintings on plaster; the total area, on the foundations and inclusive of the colonnade, was about 560 square metres. Thus began a process which operated throughout the Archaic age and into the fifth century, when all-stone temples had long since become the rule and the introduction of architectural marble had carried the competition onto an even costlier plane. It is clear that, from its early years, the Greek state could command a loyalty that extended far beyond the essential utilitarian functions; and that this loyalty should manifest itself so conspicuously in the religious field is a fact of great significance. There was no factor more important in the composition of the state than the devotion to common cults.

At the same time, the development of the early temple-plan may reflect two successive stages in the establishment of the state sanctuaries. Our difficulty in distinguishing some early temples from private houses may well arise from the fact that, in origin, they were one and the same. Not only did they favour the same two types of plan – rectangular, with the entrance in one of the short sides, and apsidal – but also, as has been observed, many early temples have taken over from domestic structures the feature of a central hearth. At first, it is argued, the main celebration of cult took the form of a ceremonial meal cooked and eaten at this hearth: a survival of the formal entertainment that would have taken place in a chieftain's house. One could well imagine a shrine of this kind serving a smaller community than the whole city-state or ethnos – a kinship-group for example. What finally and irrevocably set off the temple from its domestic antecedents, according to this view, was the addition of an external colonnade, and the introduction of a cult-image of the deity to replace the central hearth; this final step would presumably coincide with the state's assumption of responsibility for the cult. The truth was probably more complex than this: there are many proven temples which never acquired a peristyle, and there are buildings which were from their beginnings unsuitable for housing any sort of communal or social function: the Heraion of Samos, for example, in its earliest phase, with its elongated plan and obtrusive interior colonnade down its central axis. Nevertheless this theory has the merits of offering a credible evolution for the building-form, before it emerges from its obscurity into the familiar shape of the Hellenic temple.

    The discussion of this essentially religious activity may appear to have taken us far away from the economic activities which we were previously discussing. But in fact there are links in almost every direction. The growth of the sanctuaries is connected, *Plate 2* through the medium of the innumerable bronze dedications, with the growth in metal supplies; that the link could be more direct is shown by an inscription of a later period from Ephesos which specifically mentions gifts of gold and silver as contributing towards temple costs, and another from sixth-century Athens which refers to the 'collecting' of bronzes. A more obvious correlation exists between the growth of craft and technology and the rise of the temples: not only did the actual problems of their construction call for techniques which had scarcely been employed in the impoverished architecture of the preceding centuries, but even before the existence of a temple, many sanctuaries were attracting dedications of a specialized and elaborate kind, not found in utilitarian contexts. The obvious example is that of the great bronze tripod-cauldrons, at first cast and later also hammered, which since the earlier eighth century had reached dimensions of a quite unpractical kind (some of them stood over five feet high), and whose ornate relief-work was never to be sullied by placing them over a fire. They must have been the products of specialist craftsmen, perhaps even of a separate branch of industry. Other dedications, from the huge and elaborate dress-pins, nearly three feet long, to the small but often competent bronze and terracotta figurines, are also products expressly designed for the sanctuary.

A less predictable connection existed, on the part of at least one sanctuary, with the Greek expansion overseas. Several ancient narratives of early colonial foundations begin with an account of a consultation of the oracle of Apollo at Delphi. Whether or not this had a practical purpose from the start, in that real and useful geographical information was already in the hands of the Delphic priests, there can be no doubt that after the success of the first ventures, and as a result of the habitual piety and gratitude of the colonists in giving divine credit where it was due (and even where it was not), Delphi must soon have become a repository of such knowledge. Nor was it only colonial voyages for which divine approval was sought, and thank-offerings made in the event of success: we hear of several commercial undertakings that had such backing; Delphi again features prominently, but Hera of Samos also received credit. Both the states and some private individuals were thus implicated in the rise of the sanctuaries.

But the network is much more extensive even than this. Mutual dependence between the sanctuaries and the land, both for arable and for livestock farming, was close. Sacrifices, it goes without saying, commonly took the form of agricultural produce and farm animals. There is a further illustration of this link in the story told by Herodotus (i 31) of Kleobis and Biton, the *Plate 30* Argive twins who pulled their mother in an ox-cart to the Argive Heraion, a distance of over five miles. The story is set in the late seventh century BC, and later writers explain that the mother was priestess of Hera at the time. It is striking that her processional vehicle should have been an agricultural cart, and that the specific occasion for her sons' feat of strength was the fact that the oxen to pull the cart were late in coming home from the fields. A final link which is worth emphasizing is that between the sanctuaries and warfare. Many Greek sanctuaries were in a real sense war museums, and on occasion they served as armouries too. Not only were the portable dedications of arms and armour usually a tithe of the spoils taken from defeated enemies, or else personal offerings of their own equipment by grateful victors; but sometimes the temples themselves were built with the proceeds of successful campaigns. In later times, at least, booty-dedications took other forms as well: we hear of male and female captives being dedicated as temple-slaves, and of plots of profitable land being made over to the sanctuary to increase its revenue. It will be clear by now that the activities of a Greek sanctuary, far from being a detached and spiritual sphere, were very close to the heart of all political, economic and military life. The evidence of the sudden growth of dedications is thus also evidence for a quickening in many aspects of human activity, and we shall continue to use the development of the sanctuaries during the later Archaic period as a kind of index of general growth.

The sites that we have been considering represent only a small, if prominent, fraction of the total number of centres of cult in the Greek world. The reader of Pausanias' *Description of Greece* will be impressed, dismayed and finally perhaps irritated by the seemingly endless catalogue of shrines which the travel-writer visited. In a few pages on Sparta, for instance, where he is describing the town and its outskirts and before he has even arrived at the Acropolis where the main temples were traditionally located, he lists over seventy shrines and cult-centres (iii 12, 4–17, 1). Of most of these no physical trace has ever been found nor, one suspects, ever will be. We have earlier considered (p. 38–40) one small category of these obscurer sanctuaries, the hero-cults centred on prehistoric tombs; but there were countless others consisting of no more than an altar, a statue or an alleged grave. Although some of the shrines were in the care of smaller communities, whether occupational or kinship-groups, it is clear that the state had responsibility for maintaining a vast number of them, including (for example) the great majority of those described by Pausanias at Sparta. Not all of these sanctuaries scattered across Greece were of great anti-quity when Pausanias saw them in the second century AD: the one recurrent feature that they share is that, where archaeologi-cal investigation has proved possible, the date at which cult

1 Model granaries from Athens, *c.* 850 BC

2 Bronze tripod-cauldron
from Olympia,
8th century BC

3 Detail of Late Geometric krater showing bier, *c.* 750 BC

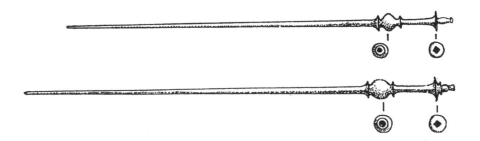

4 Dress-pins from Mycenae, 9th century BC

5  Fragment of Late Geometric krater with battle-scene, *c.* 750 BC

6  Sack of Troy (detail of Attic red figure hydria, *c.* 480 BC)

7 View of tholos tomb at Menidhi, Attica

8 Scene from Protoattic 'Orestes krater', *c.* 650 BC

9 Late Corinthian amphora with scene of Tydeus, *c.* 550 BC

10 Late Geometric stand showing
Siamese twins (left) and Dipylon shield
(right), *c.* 700 BC

11 Protocorinthian olpe with scene of phalanx battle, *c.* 640 BC

12 Hoplite shield, *c*. 600 BC

13 Corinthian alabastron showing arms, *c*. 625 BC

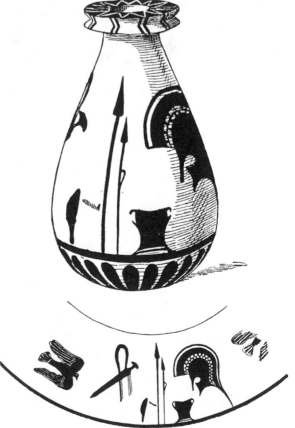

14  Attic black figure cup showing peltast, *c*. 540 BC

appears to begin is most often the eighth century. They thus illustrate the most striking fact about the developments of this era, their relative permanence. Almost all the features which appeared in Greek life at this time, and the total structure which they composed, had come to stay. Very few innovations were abortive, and the more successful of them lasted till the downfall of the ancient world over a thousand years later. One can claim even more for some of them: they enrich mankind to this day. In two prominent cases, it is by the material evidence that we can associate the advances in question with this same eventful century.

Representational art in Greece is not in itself the creation of the eighth century. It had enjoyed a vigorous life during the 500 years of the Mycenaean culture, and a few hesitant works of the ensuing dark centuries – clay figurines, the occasional painted representation on a pot – had kept the spark from being extinguished totally. But, as with so much else, there is a complete transformation towards the middle of the eighth century, accompanied in this case with an important stylistic idea. The principles of the Geometric system of decoration and form – symmetry, proportion, articulation, discipline – had been observed for generations past by every Greek artisan of any real attainment: the bronze-workers who produced the superb dress-pins of the ninth-century Argolid, as much as the potters *Plate 4* of contemporary Athens. The more elaborate products could even claim a certain intellectual content, the precursor of that concern with number and space which later led Plato to inscribe over the entrance to his Academy: 'Let no one enter who is ignorant of geometry'. Against such a background, it is not perhaps so surprising that figure-scenes were slow in appearing: the few early human and animal figures on tenth- and ninth-century vases are isolated, inconspicuous to the point of being apologetic, and not especially 'geometric' in conception. Yet the feeling that man and his actions were the proper subject for the artist can hardly have been entirely suppressed in the Greek mind and, furthermore, there were sometimes figured scenes on the Oriental objects now being imported to Greece, to inspire

emulation. Was there a way of reconciling tradition and innovation? The solution to the problem, obvious perhaps in retrospect
but daring in original conception, was to geometricize the figures too. It was not a lasting solution: within two generations
the vase-painters had become dissatisfied with it and with the
whole Geometric style. Indeed, the Geometric episode in Greek
art left so little overt trace that it was totally forgotten. In the
fifth century BC, there are grounds for thinking that Geometric
pottery, found in some re-opened graves, was judged by the
savants of the day (including Thucydides, i 8, 1) to be Carian;
nineteenth-century archaeologists preferred to call it Phoenician.
Yet the introduction of silhouette-figures into the final stages of
Geometric art was, in its own time, a great success. Not only
was its convention for artistic representation eagerly taken up by
craftsmen in other media but, unlike the abstract motifs which
composed the main bulk of Geometric decoration, it offered a
real basis for innovation and experiment. A silhouette figure can
be geometrically rendered, but need not always be so; it can be
shown frontally, in profile or in a mixture of the two; it can be
grouped in many kinds of composition; and finally it can
develop away from being silhouette at all. In the event, all these
experiments were made, many of them successfully. Much credit therefore belongs to the originators of the convention.

  The development passed through several stages in rapid suc-
cession, all probably within the 770s and 760s BC. One artist,
who dominated the final stage, can be identified by the tradi-
*Plate 3*  tional methods of attribution; some seven major works of his
survive in whole or in part, plus forty-odd others produced
under his close influence; and the best known, a monumental
amphora from the rich Dipylon Gate cemetery at Athens, gives
him his modern name, the Dipylon Master. That he and his predecessors were Athenian is only to be expected; Athens had
produced all the most important advances of the last three
hundred years in Greek ceramics, and it was also a considerable
force in some other artistic fields at the time when his career
began. Some notions relevant to figure-drawing were pioneered
by his immediate predecessors (the dependence on silhouette,

the use of a ground-line on which the figures stand, the enlargement of certain pot-shapes to monumental size to provide a worthy field), and the Dipylon Master himself shows such a conservative tendency in some respects that we can call him a traditionalist at heart. At first sight, his figure-style too might be interpreted as a mere stylization of that of his predecessors, but this would be to overlook the compositions for which he employed it. To judge from works of which only large fragments survive, he was prepared to accommodate well over a hundred figures on a single vase, and forty or more in the same scene; to distinguish men, women and children as well as horses, birds, fish, chariots, warships and funerary biers. As far as action goes, however, he constrains his figures rigidly: they depart as little as possible from a static pose, and he groups them with an eye to symmetry. But this very inhibition gives his scenes a majestic quality; and he shows a steadiness of hand and a sheer physical co-ordination which his predecessors had not achieved, and which his contemporaries strove hard but unsuccessfully to match. We feel the presence of a strong artistic personality.

But it would be a simple anachronism to regard the Dipylon Master as a free agent, in the manner of a great artist of a later age. It was the society of eighth-century Athens which had produced him, which commissioned his works, which required that the most elaborate of them should be funerary in function and, consequently, that the figure-scenes on them should also be funerary in content. It also, at the period in question, approved the use of the large decorated pots as monuments, open to view and providing for the edification of generations yet to come. Since it was the values of his clients which thus determined his subjects, this should offer some guidance in their interpretation – for guidance is sorely needed. The impersonal and timeless quality of the scenes is, at the very least, a barrier to the reading of their narrative content; indeed, in the opinion of many it is a gurantee that they *have* no such content. This may be going too far: what is the point of crowding twenty or more figures, fight- *Plate 5* ing, falling and lying dead, into a single scene if there is no intention to convey a story? But it must be admitted that many scenes, particularly those of the corpse lying in state at a funeral, present less scope for narrative because so little happens in them. Yet even if these scenes could, to a contemporary spectator, carry some of that particularity of message which is the essential part of narrative, the deeper question would remain: what *kind* of setting was intended? Was it the commemoration of recent events, relevant to the deceased? Or was it a more glorified vision of events, either recreating a heroic past or at least idealizing the present on the model of such a past?

A salient fact about contemporary society – and it is essentially *Attic* society which is relevant to the Geometric figure-scenes – is that its interests were actively engaged in the Heroic Age. The cults initiated at Bronze Age tombs, in Attica as much as anywhere, testify to this preoccupation, albeit in a vague and apparently anonymous form. Worship of a more explicit kind was presently established at the official hero-shrines, where the privileges and duties of cult-observance still formed a subject of almost obsessive concern centuries later; but on present showing none of these major cults was instituted quite as early as this. The attention given to the Heroic Age was a reflection of the alarming seriousness with which the early Greeks took it. Let anyone who doubts this consider the case of the Lokrian Maidens (Lykophron *Alexandra*, lines 1141–73). At the sack of *Plate 6* Troy, the legend was that the Lokrian Ajax raped Kassandra as she clung to Athena's statue in the goddess' sanctuary. In atonement for this, the Lokrians continued to send every year, down to at least the third century BC and probably much later, two girls from noted families to serve as temple-assistants at Troy; not only this, but the girls had to run the gauntlet from the moment that they were landed on the coast of the Troad until they reached the safety of the temple; the local people were encouraged to kill them if they caught them. Of all the elements in the Trojan saga, there are few which are less convincing in circumstantial detail than the episode of Ajax and Kassandra; yet for the sake of this legend, the ruling class of Lokris were prepared to sentence their own and their friends' daughters to the alternatives of a possible violent death and a certain lifetime – or at the least a period – of drudgery. We can make some estimate as to when this cruel observance began, for it would have been physically impossible until a settlement and sanctuary were re-established at Troy in the late eighth century. In all likelihood the legend is older than the practice; and certainly a 'ritualist' explanation, whereby a legend was concocted to explain a pre-existing ritual, will not fit this case. If such exacting reverence for the legendary past and the continuity of tradition was possible in the later Classical period, its grip on the Greeks of this period, *a fortiori*, must have been fierce. In a more general way, the 'Heroic Age' is a concept quietly assumed in the poems of Homer, and explicitly described in those of Hesiod.

An interest in heroic questions was thus present in the society of the day; but how would this affect the products of its artists? To begin with, it would be a mistake to imagine that we can draw a clear distinction between 'heroic' subjects on the one hand, and 'real' or 'contemporary' ones on the other, in the art of any early society. Indeed, in the light of some evidence it seems doubtful whether a clear distinction existed even in the minds of the artists. As far as the physical setting goes, neither they nor their public would have found it objectionable for past events to be given 'modern' trappings; this attitude is common to Classical Greece and most eras down to very recent times, and there is no reason to doubt its existence in the eighth century BC. It emphasizes the factor of continuity and common experience between the past and the present, which would appeal to the early Greeks. And yet, some of the effect of such subjects will be lost if their past setting is entirely forgotten. That the artists of the Attic figure-scenes, while feeling their way towards a wholly new narrative art, should have had thought to spare for such considerations may seem unlikely. But anti-quarianism is an attitude amply attested in the contemporary Homeric poems: it is for instance remarkable that three hundred years after iron had begun to replace bronze as the material for swords and spearheads, not one single case of iron being used for these weapons has crept into the battle-scenes of the *Iliad* and *Odyssey*. In the artistic field, evidence for conscious anti-quarianism is generally agreed to exist from the early seventh century BC, and from almost as early a date the converse practice is also attested: that is to say, an artist would render an apparently unexceptionable contemporary scene and then transform its setting by the mere addition of a few heroic names as captions to the figures.

These are all external considerations, drawn from other periods or other aspects of society. Can we relate them more directly to the Geometric figure-scenes of Athens? There is one *Plate 7* point where they at once impinge. The tholos tomb at Menidhi in Attica not only offers a case of dedications at a heroic grave from around the middle of the eighth century, but the dedications there actually include pottery decorated with figure-scenes, including processions of chariots. This single instance should in fairness be set against the much more frequent cases where such vessels stood as markers over the graves of ordinary eighth-century Athenians, but at least it shows that there was no incongruity in using such products in a heroic context. Nor did their use for contemporary burials necessarily exclude a heroic theme in their decoration: early in the following century, for instance, a splendid amphora decorated with scenes of Odysseus *Plate 37* blinding Polyphemos, and Perseus escaping from the Gorgons, was used as the actual container for the burial of a young boy at Eleusis.

The arguments so far deployed would lead us, if not to expect, then at least not to exclude some kind of heroic content in the Geometric figure-scenes. Yet the majority of experts in the field would be against us; at best, such interpretations would be allowed in a few instances and by a few authorities. Why is this? The answer may lie in one presupposition which seems to be shared by both parties in the disagreement. This is, that the main inspiration behind heroic scenes whenever present in Greek art is that of epic poetry. The sceptics who deny all possibility of heroic narrative in the art of the eighth century, when faced with its evident presence in the early seventh, explain the change by appealing to the sudden diffusion of epic poetry around 700 BC. Their opponents argue (or assume) that it was a somewhat earlier diffusion of this poetry which put the notion of heroic illustration in the Geometric artists' minds.

But what if both sides are mistaken in this assumption? It is surely not a regular phenomenon, at any period, for artists to respond directly to a literary stimulus and take their inspiration entirely from it. Here again, we do not have to follow the later course of Greek art very far before we find solid evidence. The number of mythical scenes which were then actually taken from the *Iliad* and *Odyssey*, the two Homeric epics, prove to be a very small minority; by a cautious reckoning of the representations dated before about 650 BC, they number 5 out of 57 pictures from heroic saga as a whole. Far more numerous are those which illustrate moments from other sagas altogether – certain deeds of Herakles and perhaps of Theseus, events from the Theban stories – or those from the sequence of Trojan War episodes which take place before, between and after the actions of the *Plate 8* *Iliad* and *Odyssey*. Others again are characterized as generally legendary by their portrayal of centaurs, sphinxes and monsters; but even so they can be excluded from having a strictly *Homeric* inspiration. Now the episodes which fell outside the *Iliad* and *Odyssey* were certainly described in other early epic poems, and in some cases we can deduce that these were earlier than Homer: for example, an epic on the Argonaut story is presupposed in *Odyssey* xii, 69–72. But can there really have been a complete epic 'coverage' of the whole heroic age so early? In the case of the Trojan saga, the 'missing' episodes were covered by the poems of the Epic Cycle, which survived into Classical times: the *Cypria, Aethiopis, Little Iliad, Iliou Persis, Nostoi* and *Telegoneia.* The verdict of antiquity was that most or all of these were post-Homeric and modern authorities, faced with the rather sorry fragments that survive, have agreed; some recent experts have placed their composition largely in the late seventh century BC, far too late to have inspired the illustrations referred to above. Did they have pre-Homeric antecedents? Very possibly, at least in some cases; but to infer the existence of these from the early illustrations is to beg the whole question.

There is in any case a further difficulty. When, in the later

Archaic period, mythical scenes become ever more frequent in occurrence and explicit in identification, often making use of inscriptions for the latter purpose, they show a tendency to depart from the 'official version' of an episode as enshrined in the epic. This was not from any decline in the status of epic – on the contrary, its prestige was never higher – nor is it likely that alternative literary versions were a significant factor. A more likely, indeed an almost obvious explanation, is that there was a great web of unsystematic, orally-transmitted mythology, which existed all through early Greek history without ever being enshrined in verse form. Some of it can be assumed to have been of great antiquity, old enough at least to be known to the eighth-century artists; some doubtless consisted of later vernacular variants, or even personal versions of an individual artist. Not all of these variants came to be recorded in a written source at any time during the next thousand years of Greek and Latin literature, as we discover when some distinct episode, on which our written sources have virtually no light to throw, is portrayed in a work of art: Jason swallowed by the dragon that guarded
*Plate 9*   the Golden Fleece, or Tydeus murdering the Theban princess Ismene in an obscure context of sexual dalliance. The whole phenomenon was well summed up by the Dutch scholar J. M. Hemelrijk: 'I suspect that the Brygos Painter rather drew what his granny told him as a boy, than what he may have known of our *Iliad*.' If the Brygos Painter, a consummate Athenian artist of the first decades of the fifth century, an age of widespread literacy, could by-pass the direct inspiration of literature, then how much more likely is it that vase-painters would draw on non-literary sources 250 years earlier, when writing was in its infancy in Greece and epic recitations must have been rare and perhaps socially exclusive events? At no time were these craftsmen likely to move among the cultural élite.

If this line of argument is sound, then two conclusions follow for the art of Geometric Athens. First, we cannot use the diffusion of the Homeric epic as a necessary or even a likely occasion for the first appearance of legendary scenes in art. It is questionable whether the artists were dependent on epic of any kind;

and even if they were, their choice of subjects shows that in the great majority of cases the epics in question were quite unconnected with Homer, and could have been composed either much earlier or much later than the *Iliad* and *Odyssey*. Secondly, we cannot presume to dismiss scenes as non-legendary, especially when they occur in the very earliest phases of representational art, simply because they correspond with nothing in our incomplete ancient handbooks of mythology; nor to deny legendary status to an individual scene on the grounds that, although certain features seem recognizable, no literary source tells the legend in exactly this form. All this opens up a much wider range of interpretation. We can approach whole categories of scene and compare them, on the one hand with what is known of Athenian society and life in the period when they were painted, on the other hand with the picture (rather better documented) of what life in the Heroic Age was imagined as having been like. We can consider individual scenes and subjects of a potentially legendary kind, without having to be guided by the epic versions of the stories, still less by their status and prominence within the Homeric epic. Let us try an example of each of these two approaches.

The funerary subjects commonly treated on the front side of the Geometric kraters used for male graves and the battle-scenes sometimes shown on their reverse side, have two conspicuous recurrent features: the use of chariots, and a curious form of shield with two large lateral embrasures, leaving a narrow 'waist' at the middle. Their incidence is variable: the chariots are very common in the funeral scenes, where their occupants are very often armed, but rare in the actual battles; while the shields are at first common in both, but decrease in frequency as the Geometric style nears its end. From contemporary life, we can bring to bear evidence on the chariots only: some points of disagreement exist among modern scholars, but it is agreed that chariot-racing and, less commonly, chariot-processions did take place in Archaic Greece, usually as a part of a festival or programme of games; and they can be traced back almost to the period when the first Geometric scenes were painted. Chariot-warfare, by contrast, is not likely to have existed in Greece proper after the Mycenaean age, when it had been fairly widespread. But races and processions *at funerals* are inherently unlikely to have been a commonplace event. We hear of funeral games for Amphidamas of Chalkis, described in one version as a *basileus* of Euboia, who died around 700 BC. Athens alone has produced about twenty-five examples of chariot-races or processions on vases within two generations, well over half the number of sufficiently well-preserved funeral scenes; and we can guess what a tiny proportion of the original production these twenty-five represent. For funerals of the Heroic Age, on the other hand, such events were thought of as *de rigueur*, as the *Iliad* shows us; while chariot-warfare is the epitome of heroic combat in Homer, who here probably reflects some memory of the Mycenaean practice. From consideration of the chariot-scenes, therefore, the impression emerges that a certain idealization of reality is taking place. When chariots are shown in battle, the model must be that of a bygone society; when they appear at funerals, either the same process, or a more mundane one of unreal social aspiration, would seem to be at work. In neither case do the pictures inspire confidence as literal portrayals of eighth-century practice.

*Plate 10*      The shields are a more controversial subject. The suggestion
*(right)*   was first made in 1955 by T. B. L. Webster that they too have no place in contemporary life, but are a piece of 'heroic property' indicating that any scene in which they appear is thought of as legendary in setting. No one has been able to invoke positive proof that the shield did or did not exist – the argument is conducted in terms of probabilities and logical consistency – but Webster's theory has met with general rejection. A number of specific points have been brought against it, but in my view they can all be answered by an appeal to the external evidence, old and new. The testimony of Homer (p. 69) shows that conscious archaism was not entirely foreign to the spirit of the times. The evidence of the re-discovery of Mycenaean graves (pp. 38–40) suggests one means by which the Athenians of the day could have had access to Mycenaean representations of shields as a

basis for their own imaginative reconstructions. It is no longer necessary to argue, as Webster did, that these strange 'Dipylon' shields in Geometric art were a distorted memory of the Mycenaean 'figure of eight' shield, a view which was open to the valid objection that they bear no real resemblance to it. A much better model has now been revealed in Mycenaean art: a series of representations, ranging in date from about 1400 to 1200 BC, have been found to show the same basic outline, with lateral embrasures, as that of the 'Dipylon' form. In the other direction chronologically, there is evidence that later artists so far misunderstood the 'Dipylon' shield as to represent it turned on one side, with the embrasures now appearing in the upper and lower edges, and an incongruous armband and hand-grip set athwart its long axis. This misunderstood version of the shield was to be used, though haphazardly and without any consistent system, for centuries afterwards as a token of legendary context. The first picture that we have of the shield so misused is on a Corinthian vase as early as about 675 BC; and indeed there is an earlier and rather extraordinary piece of evidence from Cyprus: and eighth-century vase on which the painter was so unfamiliar with the 'Dipylon' shield as not to realize that it was a shield at all, so that he equipped his warriors with an additional small target held in their left hands. Even on the Attic vases, portrayals of the shield vary so widely as to suggest no real acquaintance with it. In these circumstances, it seems very hard to accept the 'Dipylon' shield as a real element in eighth-century warfare. Nor can one go to the other extreme: the shield is not a necessary, but merely perhaps a sufficient, condition for conveying a legendary setting.

I have lingered on this specialized problem because its implications are in fact very wide. Indeed this is, I think, the real reason why scholars have found it so hard to accept the view presented here. For if all the scenes containing the 'Dipylon' shield portray something other than contemporary life, then our whole understanding of the Geometric figure-scenes is affected thereby, so ubiquitous is it in the early funeral and battle-scenes. It will mean that, in effect, the Athenian artists were consistently thinking in terms of another world when they painted their scenes, even when they do not signal them as such. In an era as ill-documented as this, it goes against the grain to reject the most substantial body of representational evidence – the figure-scenes on vases – as evidence for their times. In fact, however, our interpretation is doing nothing of the kind. It is merely changing the *nature* of the evidence that the pictures offer, by bringing them into line with the other evidence that demonstrates an interest in the heroic past in these years. That the Athenians should have committed their dead to the grave in the image, so to speak, of their heroic ancestors may seem less surprising when we consider another practice of the time, that of giving an actual 'heroic burial' to the newly-deceased members of a ruling class. The most spectacular manifestations come from a far-away corner of the Greek world, Salamis in Cyprus, where a whole series of burials, beginning about 750 BC, emulate the great funeral rituals of the *Iliad*: slaughter of animals (including the chariot-horses), offering of jars of oil, human sacrifice, cremation of the dead (a new practice for Cyprus), quenching of the pyre with wine, placing of the ashes in an urn wrapped in cloth, and final heaping-up of a tumulus. Nearer home, a warrior at Eretria in Euboia was given a similar though more modest funeral around 720 BC and his tomb, surrounded by those of a small group of presumed relatives, presently received the signal honour of having a hero-shrine constructed over it, which received votive offerings for centuries afterwards. Other less explicit cases of epic influence on contemporary funerary practice have been detected elsewhere in Greece, including Attica.

To return to the Attic vase-paintings: in four of the funerary scenes, and on six representations from outside Attica, all of them falling within about three generations after 750 BC, there

*Plate 10*  occurs the peculiar theme of a pair of Siamese twins. As it hap-
*(left)*  pens, we have evidence that would give an immediate explanation of this oddity. Twice in the *Iliad* (xi 709–52; xxiii 630–42) Homer tells stories involving a famous pair of twins, the sons of Aktor: once in the context of a battle, once in that of a chariot-race; but he makes only a veiled allusion to their deformity, and

they cannot be said to be conspicuous figures in his story. Not much later, however, Hesiod describes them in more detail (fragment 17B), mentioning that they had 'two bodies, joined to each other'. Later literary sources tell us that they were finally killed by Herakles. One might have thought that this lucky opportunity to explain an obscure theme would be gratefully taken. But no: sceptics have pointed out that the twins are shown more than once in the same chariot-scene and argued, with a perhaps inappropriate application of logic, that they cannot represent the famous twins, but are merely an artist's convention for showing two warriors standing together. The argument that they figure too inconspicuously in Homer to be expected in art has also been applied; we have seen some of the objections to this line of reasoning already. It happens that one of the pictures – not the earliest – shows the helmet-crests of the two warriors joined together at the back, an unmistakable sign that they are Siamese twins; so the argument is that, by a happy coincidence, an artistic convention was taken over and put to new use when the urge to depict the Siamese twins – inevitably, through the diffusion of the epic – first arose. Here I think that the sceptical view flies in the face of probability: one has only to posit the existence of a vernacular tradition involving the twins and their story, independent of and indeed ancestral to the epic version, and the imagined difficulties vanish. But once again, the implications are wide: the earliest picture of the twins is close to the beginning of the Attic series of figure-scenes, on a work by an associate of the Dipylon Master. Once the principle is conceded, that Geometric artists might wish to portray specific episodes as well as the general ambience of the Heroic Age, then other, more doubtful cases (and there are a number of them) begin to appear in a different light.

It begins to look as if this attitude of deference to the heroic past was an important element in the revolution that was sweeping through Greek life. It was not that the achievements of the Mycenaean age could make much practical contribution to progress now. Rather, as in Renaissance Europe, it was the general inspiration which was offered by a conception of the distant past: the more idealized, the better. In some respects the accepted picture was historically very distorted and, again as in the Renaissance, there was a tendency to credit the earlier age with a greater share than it deserved in prompting present achievements. This is seen, for example, in the heroic ancestry which was claimed for some of the religious and political developments of these times. But without such an example, it is doubtful whether the Greek advance would have been quite so swift; and even centuries later, people were still enlisting their heroes for countless purposes of their own.

But of all the achievements of this time, there is perhaps none that impresses the Western world today so much as the recovery of the art of writing – particularly as it took the form of the adoption of an alphabet from which our own is still derived. It is the material evidence on which we mainly base not only our attempts to date this achievement but also our belief in a preceding age of illiteracy. There may still be a need today to justify this latter belief: that a formerly literate society should lose the gift of writing for several hundred years is a notion so foreign to our experience that it is not easily accepted. There is in this case another category of evidence which may help: that of the Homeric poems, whose method of composition has been widely accepted for the past fifty years, since the discoveries of Milman Parry as to the extensive use of formulae in Homer, as being of a kind peculiar to illiterate societies. But if this conclusion is like almost every other one reached about Homer, then it is unlikely to stand unchallenged for ever. We should thus be unwise to depend entirely on the epic as decisive proof of the disappearance of literacy in Greece.

Let us revert to the physical evidence. What it tells us is that the syllabic script known as Linear B was in use (but apparently restricted use) down to the destruction of most of the Mycenaean palaces in the years round 1200 BC; that a fully-formed alphabetic system, modelled on the Phoenician, was adopted no later than about 750 BC; but that the intervening years offer virtually no evidence for the knowledge of either system. The difference between the two forms of writing, and the absence of any influence of the older one on the newer, are so absolute and complete that we should in any event be surprised to find that they were in consecutive use, without any intervening break. After all, even when making the change from a syllabic script, where each single sign is used for an open syllable of the form -*ba*-, to an alphabetic script with a separate letter for *b* and *a*, there are opportunities for assimilation: Linear B, for example, had to have signs for the simple vowels, mainly for use in the initial position. The Greek alphabet entirely ignores these pre-existing symbols, and derives its vowels from Phoenician signs, such as glottal stops, aspirates and the consonantal *y*, for which Greek had no use in their received form.

Then there are the differences in the range of literacy under the two systems. Linear B was essentially an administrative script, used by palace scribes for official documentation, and occasionally by craftsmen for what appears to be communication within a very restricted group: thus one- to three-word painted inscriptions (mostly apparently place-names) were sometimes applied to a pot before it was fired; but these do not seem to have been of general circulation. But graffiti hardly appear, and public inscriptions not at all. We infer that very few people could read the script, and perhaps fewer still write it. If it was the almost exclusive preserve of the palace bureaucracies, as seems likely, then their disappearance will have removed its *raison d'être*. The early alphabetic inscriptions show a sharp contrast. Pottery is again favoured as a writing-surface, but now most of the inscriptions are not painted by the makers, but scratched later by the users. They refer to private matters – ownership, entertainment, personal comments; a striking proportion of them are in verse. Some time later, makers' signatures also begin to appear on pottery; the actual learning process is illustrated by a few abecedaria; and permanent inscriptions on stone follow. Already before 700 BC alphabetic inscriptions are known from a dozen sites – more than have produced Linear B inscriptions from the whole of its life of 200 years or more. It is clear that the conditions of literacy have changed, and that the simplicity of the alphabet was making it accessible to almost everyone.

A completely fresh start had been necessary; and there is no sign, now or later, that anyone in Greece had more than a faint notion that an earlier script had even existed. Homer, too, was able to present his heroes as living in an essentially illiterate society and later Greeks were not disturbed by this. True to form, they nevertheless credited the Heroic Age, in the person of Kadmos, with having brought writing to Greece from Phoenicia; but the legend almost certainly refers to the alphabetic script, not the syllabic. It thus reflects a geographical truth, but perpetrates a major anachronism. Those few scholars who believe in continuity of literacy through the dark age would probably prefer to bridge the gap by extending the use of the alphabet back-

TABLE OF LETTERS

| | N. Semitic | Attica, Sigeion | Euboia | Boiotia | Thessaly | Phokis | Lokrides and colonies | Aigina, Kydonia | Corinth, Korkyra | Megara, Byzantion | Sikyon | Phleious, Kleonai, Tiryns | Argos, Mycenae | Eastern Argolid | Lakonia, Messenia, Taras | Arkadia | Elis | Achaia and colonies | Aitolia, Epeiros | Ithake, Kephallenia | Euboic W. colonies | Syracuse and colonies | Megara Hyblaia, Selinous | Naxos, Amorgos | Paros, Thasos | Delos, Keos, Syros | Crete | Thera, Kyrene | Melos, Sikinos, Anaphe | Ionic Dodekapolis and colonies | Rhodes, Gela, Akragas | Knidos | Aiolis |
|---|---|---|---|---|---|---|---|---|---|---|---|---|---|---|---|---|---|---|---|---|---|---|---|---|---|---|---|---|---|---|---|---|---|
| Alpha | 𐌊 | A | A | Ꜳ | A | A | AA | AAA | AꜲA | A | AAA | A | A | A | A | A | A | AAA | A | A | A | A | A | A | A | A | A | A | A | A | A | A | A |
| Beta | 9 | B | B | B | B | B | B | B | 𐌁 | 𐌿 | 𐌂 | 𐌱 | C | B | B | B | B | B | | B | B | Ͷ | C | C | C | B,P | B | Ͷ | B | B | |
| Gamma | ⅂ | Λ | Γ⊏ | ⊏⊏ | Γ | ⊏ | ⊏,Γ | Γ | Γ⊏ | ⊏ | < | Γ | Γ | Γ | Γ | < | C | ⌣,< | < | < | Γ⊏ | Λ⊏ | < | <ΛΓ | Λ | Λ | Γ | ΛⲤΛꞀ | Γ | Γ⊏ | Γ⊏ | ⊏ | Γ |
| Delta | ◁ | Δ | DD | D | D | D | D | Δ | Δ | Δ | Δ | D | D,Δ | D | D | D | D,Δ | D | ΔD | D | DΔ | D | DΔ | Δ | Δ | Δ | Δ | Δ | Δ | Δ | ΔD | Δ | DΔ |
| Epsilon | ᖷ | Ɛ | Ɛ | Ɛ | Ɛ | Ɛ | Ɛ | Ɛ | B,Ɛ | B,Ɛ | Ȝ,Ɛ | Ɛ | Ɛ | Ɛ | Ɛ | Ɛ | Ɛ | Ɛ,B | Ɛ | Ɛ | Ɛ | Ɛ | Ɛ | Ɛ | HƐ | Ɛ | Ɛ | Ɛ | Ɛ | Ɛ | Ɛ | Ɛ | Ɛ |
| Vau | Y,Ψ | Ϝ | ϜϹ | ϜϹ | ϜϹ | ϜϜ | ϜϜ | − | ϜϜ | Ϝ | Ϝ | ϜϜ | ϜϜ | ϜϜ | ϜϹ | ϜϜ | ϜϜ | Ϝ | ϜϹϜϹ | Ϝ | ϜϹ | − | − | Ϝ,Ϲ | − | − | − | − | − | − | − | − | Ϝ |
| Zeta | ⲍ | I | I | I | I | I | I | I | I | | I | | I | I | I | I | I | I | I | | I | | | I | | I | | I | | I | | I | I |
| Eta | − | − | − | − | − | − | − | − | − | − | − | Ɓ | − | − | − | − | − | − | − | − | − | Ɓ,Ɓ | Ɓ | Ɓ,Ͱ | | Ɓ | Ɓ | | Ɓ | | Ɓ | Ɓ | Ɓ |
| Heta | ᗺ | Ⴌ | Ⴌ | Ⴌ | Ⴌ | Ⴌ | Ⴌ | Ⴌ | Ⴌ | Ⴌ | Ⴌ | Ͱ | Ⴌ | Ⴌ | Ⴌ | Ⴌ | Ⴌ | Ⴌ | Ͱ | Ͱ | Ⴌ | Ⴌ | Ⴌ | Ⴌ | | Ⴌ | | Ⴌ | − | Ͱ | | Ͱ | − |
| Theta | ⊕ | ⊕ | ⊕ | ⊕ | ⊕ | ⊕ | ⊕ | ⊕ | ⊕ | ⊕ | ⊕ | ⊕ | ⊕ | ⊕ | ⊕ | ⊕ | ⊕ | ⊕ | ⊕ | ⊕ | ⊕ | ⊕ | ⊕ | ⊕ | ⊕ | ⊕ | ⊕ | ⊕ | ⊕ | ⊕ | ⊕ | ⊕ | ⊕ |
| Iota | ⌇ | I | I | I | I | I | I | I | Ϛ,I | I | I | Ϛ,I | I | I | I | I,Ϛ | I | Ϛ | ϚϚ,I | ϚϚ,I | I | I | I | I | I | I | I | Ϛ | Ϛ | Ϛ | I | I | I |
| Kappa | Ɏ | K | K | K | K | K | K | K | K | K | K | K | K | K | K | K | K | K | K | K | K | K | K | K | K | K | K | K | K | K | K | K | K |
| Lambda | ∠ | Λ | L | L | Γ | Γ | Γ,L | Γ | Γ | Λ | Γ | Γ | Γ | Γ | Λ | Λ | ∕Γ | Γ | Λ | L,Γ,L | Γ | Γ | Γ | ΛΓ | Λ | L,Λ,Γ | Λ | Γ | Γ | Γ | Γ | Γ | Λ |
| Mu | Ϻ | Μ | Ϻ | Μ | Μ | Ϻ | Ϻ | Μ | Μ | Μ | Μ | Μ | Μ | Μ | Μ | Μ | Μ | Ϻ,Μ | Μ | Μ | Μ,Ϻ | Μ | Μ | Μ | Μ | Μ,Ϻ | Μ | Μ | Μ,Ϻ | Μ | Μ | Μ | Μ |
| Nu | ㄅ | Ν | Ν | Ν | Ν | Ν | Ν | Ν | Ν | Ν | Ν | Ν | Ν | Ν | Ν | Ν | Ν | Ν | Ν | Ν | Ν | Ν | Ν | Ν | Ν | Ν | Ν | Ν | Ν | Ν | Ν | Ν | Ν |
| Xi | ⨦ | XS | ⊞ | X⋕ | + | + | + | XS | ⋢ | ⋢ | ⋢ | ⋢ | ⋣Ͱ | + | X | X | X | X | X | ꞋΜ | ⊞ | ⊞? | ⋢ | ⊓S | X⋢ | ⋢ | KMⵉ | ⵉ | ⵉ | ≡ | X⋢ | X | X |
| Omikron | O | O | O | O | O | O | O | O | O | O | O | O | O | O | O | O | O | O | O | O | O | O | O | O | O | ∩ | O | O | O | C,O,O | O | C | O |
| Pi | ⌐ | Γ | Γ | Ϝ | Γ | Γ | Γ | Γ | Γ | Γ | Γ | Γ | Γ | Γ | Γ | Γ | Γ | Γ | Γ | Γ | Γ | Γ | Γ | Γ | Γ | Γ | Γ | Γ⊏ | Γ | Γ | Γ | Γ | Γ |
| San | Ϻ | − | ⟨Ϻ⟩ | − | − | Ϻ? | − | − | Μ | − | Μ | Μ | Μ | ? | ⟨Ϻ⟩ | − | − | Μ | Μ | Μ | ⟨Ϻ⟩ | − | − | − | − | − | Μ | Μ | Μ | − | − | − | − |
| Qoppa | φ | Ϙ | Ϙ | Ϙ | Ϙ | Ϙ | Ϙ | Ϙ | Ϙ | | Ϙ | Ϙ | Ϙ | | ⟨Ϙ⟩ | Ϙ | Ϙ | Ϙ | | Ϙ | Ϙ | Ϙ | Ϙ | Ϙ | Ϙ | Ϙ | Ϙ | Ϙ | Ϙ | Ϙ | Ϙ | −? | |
| Rho | ◁ | P | PR | PR | PR | PR | PR | P | P | DΥ | PD | P | PR | PR | PR | PR | PR | PR | PR | PR | PR | PR | PR | P | PR | P | P | PR | P | P,D | P | P | P |
| Sigma | Ϡ | Ϛ | Ϛ | Ϛ,Ϛ | Ϛ | Ϲ | Ϛ,Ϛ | Ϛ,Ϛ | − | Ϛ | − | − | Ϛ | Ϛ,Ϛ | Ϛ,Ϛ | Ϛ | Ϛ | − | − | − | Ϛ | Ϛ | Ϛ | Ϛ | Ϲ | − | − | − | Ϛ,Ϛ | Ϛ,Ϛ | Ϛ,Ϛ | Ϛ,Ϛ | |
| Tau | X⋕ | T | T | T | T | T | T | T | T | T | T | T | T | T | T | T | T | T | T | T | T | T | T | T | T | T | T | T | T | T | T | T | T |
| Upsilon | − | Υ | Υ | Υ | Υ | V | Υ | V | Υ | Υ | Υ | Υ | Υ | Υ | Υ | Υ | V | Υ | V | ΥV | Υ | Υ | Υ | Υ | Υ | Υ | Υ | Υ | Υ | V | V | Υ | V |
| Phi | − | Φ | Φ | Φ | Φ | Φ | Φ | ⊙ | Φ | ⊙ | ⊙ | Φ | Φ | Φ | Φ | Φ | ⊙ | Φ | ⊙ | ⊙ | ⊙ | ⊙ | ⊙ | Φ | Φ? | ⌐B | Γ,Ͱ | Φ | Φ | Φ | Φ | |
| Chi | − | X | Υ,Ψ | Ψ,Υ | Ψ,Υ | Υ,Ψ,Υ | Υ,Ψ | X | X | X | X | X | X,Υ,Ψ,Υ | Ψ,Υ | Ψ,Υ | Υ,Ψ,Υ | Υ | Ψ,X,Υ | X | X | X | X | S? | K,Ͱ,KͰ,S | X | Υ,X | X | X |
| Psi | − | ΦϹ | ΦϹ | ΦϹ | ΦϹ | ΦϹ | ✱ | ΦϹ | Ψ,Υ | Ψ | | Ψ | | ΦϹ | ✱ | ΦϹ,✱? | | ΦϹ | Ψ | Ψ | ΓϚ | | ꞀΜꞀΜ | ꞀΜΨ,Υ | | | Ψ | |
| Omega | − | − | − | − | − | − | − | − | − | − | Ɓ? | − | − | − | − | − | − | − | − | − | − | − | − | − | O | Ω | − | −? | O | Ω | − | O | −? |
| Punct. | ⦙ | ⸭ | ⸭ | ⸭ | ⸭ | ⸭ | ⸭ | ⸭ | ⸭ | ⸭ | ⸭ | | ⦙ | ⸭ | ⸭ | ⸭ | ⸭ | ) | ⸭ | ⸭ | ⸭ | ⸭ | ⸭ | ⸭ | ⸭ | ⸭ | ⸭ | ⸭ | ⦙⨳ ⦙ | ⸭ | ⸭ | ⸭ |

Fig. 12 The early Greek local alphabets

wards in time, rather than that of Linear B forwards; but even they must concede that it was not the script of the Mycenaean age. When one adds to these arguments the weight of negative evidence, the case seems well established: for 450 years, not so much as a letter of Greek alphabetic writing is known. About the only apparent survival of Linear B in Greece proper is on the stones of a building, probably of eleventh century date, at Iolkos in Thessaly, where a single symbol which resembles a sign of that script is used as a mason's mark; but such practices have a history in Greece which goes back well before the first writing-system was known there, and in no sense imply real literacy.

Present evidence thus suggests that the alphabet was introduced to an illiterate Greek world, probably not very long before 750 BC. The common features between the various local Greek alphabets – all of which from the very start add four or more vowels, with other letters, to the vowel-less Phoenician alphabet – further suggests that the innovation was originally diffused through a single Greek source. There is room for some disagreement as to the geographical setting of this event, between the Levant on one hand and some part of the Aegean on the other; and as to the identity of the first Greeks involved – Euboians perhaps or Athenians, with Cretans a less likely possibility. But nevertheless the transmission of the alphabet to Greece is relatively well understood, in comparison with another and ultimately more significant problem: the motives for its adoption. The evidence here is perplexing. Since the alphabet unquestionably came from Phoenicia, and since Greek relations with the Phoenicians appear to have been largely commercial in nature, it is only natural to infer that the *initial* impetus for the adoption of this writing-system was in some way connected with commerce: that Greek traders, for example, saw the commercial advantages which their Phoenician counterparts were deriving from recording and even transacting business in writing. This may be true of the very first steps in the process; and the likelihood increases if (according to the currently prevailing view) these steps were taken somewhere on the Levantine coast, since the Greek settlers known to us at this time were largely traders. Another argument in favour of this view is that the script chosen as a model for the Greek one was the cursive North Semitic version, used for business activity. On the other hand, it must be observed, first, that none of the early surviving Greek inscriptions has anything to do with commerce, and second, that the commercial explanation does not satisfactorily account for the distinctive feature of the Greek alphabet – one which in the view of some purists makes it the first *truly* alphabetic system: the addition of the vowels. The Phoenicians and other Semitic peoples had long conducted their activities, including commercial and religious transactions, with a consonantal script, and continued to do so; the Etruscans, who presently adopted an alphabet based on the Greek, complete with vowels, later became indifferent to the value of the vowels and began to omit them; the Cypriots remained largely satisfied with their syllabic script, whose unbroken survival from its Bronze Age forbears one is tempted to ascribe to pure chance. What gave the Greeks the urge to develop, before the date of the earliest surviving alphabetic inscription, a complete set of six vowel-signs (including both a long and a short *e*) and to retain and even add to this range in later years?

The answer should lie in some peculiar feature of Greek society at this time, but it is not easy to see which. The most important features, the rise of the state with its need for an official system of recording, and the proliferation of religious cult with its attendant dedications, rituals and contributions, though both would benefit from the availability of writing, do not seem specific enough as explanations; and anyway it is some time before we know of the Greeks using the alphabet for either purpose. We might ask, too, whether either of them marked a sufficiently radical departure from the earlier practices of the Phoenicians. If one looks around for a unique feature of Greek society, there is no doubt as to which is the first to offer itself: the epic. To many, the suggestion that the peculiar features of the Greek alphabet were designed as a notation for epic poetry appeared far-fetched, when it was first voiced by H. T. Wade-Gery in 1952. The best arguments in its favour might seem to be the frequency of verse-inscriptions in early Greek writing (see p. 79), and the fact that vowel-notation does indeed serve the purpose of poetic communication – as will be apparent to anyone who compares a critical edition or translation of the *Iliad* with one of, say, the Psalms of David. It seems to me just possible that this was the decisive factor in the Greek modification of the alphabet, but only after commercial motives had inspired the original desire to use alphabetic writing at all. If so, it offers an illustration of the central place in eighth-century life that epic poetry had now assumed and, indirectly, of the pervasive concern with the Heroic Age. This explanation of the rise of the Greek alphabet (and for that matter most others) presupposes a vastly more extensive use of writing, both in length of texts and in range of writing-material, than is reflected by our tiny sample of early incised sherds and stones. But since a literary purpose was best served by writing on perishable materials, especially papyrus, the theory seems more plausible than, for instance, those which would posit an extensive use of stone for public inscriptions, none of which happens to have survived.

What is much clearer is that the alphabet, once adopted, proved an enormous asset to the progress of Greek society. By making the art of reading and writing widely available, it enabled organizations to communicate beyond the close circle of those actually operating them, and individuals beyond their immediate acquaintances. Governments could write down procedures and law-codes, cult-associations could record forms of rituals and names of officials, sanctuaries could list their property and record information of wider interest, as the priests of Apollo may have done at Delphi (see p. 63). At the same time, merchants could record payments, craftsmen sign their products, property-owners publish their claims against potential usurpers, poets set down their compositions. But permanency did not necessarily mean immutability: on the contrary, once a thing is set down in writing, it becomes inherently more open to analysis and criticism than when it is secreted in the memories of a specialist group. In this way alphabetic writing, despite the fact that in our view it was adopted with no such intention, must have made a considerable contribution to the speed of development in the institutions of Archaic Greece. It provides a final illustration of the way in which a discovery in one field can precipitate advances in quite another. But only in the full Archaic period, which forms the subject of the following chapters, were the full effects to be seen.

# The Just City?

The choice of patterns is made clear
Which the machine imposes, what
Is possible and what is not,
To what conditions we must bow
In building the Just City now.

(W. H. Auden, *New Year Letter*, iii)

By the seventh century BC, most of the decisive steps that were to shape Greek civilization had already been taken. After the tremendous structural changes of the later eighth century, several generations were needed to absorb their full implications; but because it was this process of absorption which carried Greek civilization visibly ahead of its rivals and into uncharted territory, its period is often styled the 'Age of Revolution'. The facts seem hardly to support such a description, which should embrace as a central feature the idea of *political* revolution; and that we do not really find in Archaic Greece. Experiment rather than revolution is what distinguishes these years; for all their undoubted vitality and originality, the developments took place within certain accepted norms.

Of these last, one is of paramount importance: the fact that the forms of state in Greece were now accepted. The implications of this were wide. The state was the whole basis of society, the society which in turn created every aspect of the Greek achievement. Henceforward, few questioned that the proper medium for true civilization was a network of small independent states, and few could yet envisage the notion of a Panhellenic culture. Once the multifarious pattern of polis and ethnos came into being – the numbers ran into hundreds in Greece and the Aegean alone, not counting colonies – then relatively little occurred to alter it during the Archaic period. Occasionally a small polis was swallowed up by a more powerful neighbour, or a town within an ethnos would aspire to the status of an independent polis, or even to the subordination of its fellow-nationals; but as a whole the framework remained at least formally secure, down to and beyond the end of Archaic times. The early developments, the differences and the struggles took place almost entirely within this framework: they concerned the form of government, not the form of state. Of course there was inter-state warfare as well; but its aim was much more often that of an advantage, an ascendancy, even a hegemony for one's own state, rather than the complete eclipse of another one. Attempts in this latter direction, as for example by Corinth against Megara and later Epidauros (below, p. 92), usually ended in failure. It is significant that the biggest successful war of outright conquest of Greek by Greek was fought just before the general acceptance of this political pattern: the Spartan conquest of Messenia, which may even have resembled a traditional tribal conquest, in that the later traditions about it show a certain lack of geographical concentration, and make vague references to feuds and cattle-rustling. Most other cases of the conquest, destruction or merging of independent states, by contrast, belong not to the Archaic but to the Classical period.

There can be no doubt that much of the variety and richness of Greek civilization arose from just this multiplicity of political units. There were many different directions in which a state and its constitution could develop and in Archaic Greece the choice between these rested with the citizen-body, independent of outside pressure; probably no two states followed exactly the same path. But who composed the citizen-body? This was the first critical question, one so fundamental that it seems reasonable to make it the basis of any classification of Archaic states. Already there were many different answers to it in the different states; but it should be frankly admitted that the largest group consists of those for whom we have no reliable evidence at all.

We can, however, make a beginning by distinguishing first an important group of states where there was a permanently subjected population, excluded from citizenship and many other rights, and broadly to be described as serfs. It is interesting to find that they include states of every form, from an extremely scattered and even primitive ethnos like that of the Thessalians, to the island of Crete which in many opinions carried the polis principle to excessive lengths. Predictably, the status of the serfs was not identical in all these communities. We may begin with Thessaly which, if only because we know less about it, appears to be one of the more straightforward cases. A sizeable proportion of the population, known as the *penestai* ('toilers' or 'poormen'), seem to have been dependent peasants, contributing a part of the produce of their land in return for certain minimal rights. They occasionally served in warfare along with other Thessalian troops but, at least according to Aristotle (*Politics* 1269 a 36), they were also repeatedly in revolt against their masters. That is virtually all that is known about them, although there was some ancient speculation as to how they came to find themselves in this posture of subjection: generally it was believed that they represented an earlier stratum of population overlaid by the arrival of the conquering Thessalians. Politically, Thessaly was unusual in other ways, too – governed by a warrior aristocracy who, at least on occasion, elected a war-leader called the *tagos*; and surrounded by a population of outlying subject allies or *perioikoi*, in addition to the serfs. There were numerous substantial towns in Thessaly but instead of being independent they were incorporated in a tribal state which was loosely-grouped, huge by Greek standards, and at first entirely dominated by a landed aristocracy.

These features, together with the subjugation of the *penestai*, are foreign and indeed repugnant to the accepted vision of the civilized Greek state. Yet there is another side to the story. Thessaly might be culturally backward, but she was politically a major force in early Archaic Greece. Her institution of serfdom might be offensive, but it can be shown to have acted, here and elsewhere, as an effective deterrent to the growth of another

equally unpleasant practice, chattel-slavery, which at the beginning of the Archaic period was a more or less negligible factor,
but by its end had become a mainstay of many Greek states,
particularly those of the polis type. The warrior-characteristics of
the ruling element, the existence of *perioikoi* and of agricultural
serfs, also at times liable for military service, are paralleled in the
most powerful polis of the Archaic period, Sparta. All of this
may cause us to reflect critically on the traditional dichotomies
between polis and ethnos, 'enlightened' and 'primitive', 'central'
and 'peripheral', in whose terms Greek history has often been
interpreted. The ethnos of the Thessalians is far less well-
documented than the polis of the Athenians, but both alike are
part of Archaic Greece and there may have been moments when
the prospects of the former would have looked the more favourable to a contemporary.

     For all the greater complexity of the state and institutions of
Sparta, there can be no doubt whatever that the serfdom of the
Helots was equally essential to its existence. The difference here
is that the process of subjugation, or at least its later stages, had
happened recently enough to become a matter of historical
record rather than pseudo-historical surmise on the part of the
Greeks. Militant resistance and brutal repression are both recurrent and well-documented. In Thessaly we can only dimly
envisage the composition of the citizen-body: it obviously
excluded *perioikoi* and *penestai*, yet though dominated by the aristocrats its scope was in due course extended to allow of a federal
assembly and subordinate bodies, which had their own special
centres of civic and political activity set aside in the towns. In
Sparta we can be much more precise: the system that emerged
there, although not without internal struggle and not earlier
than the seventh century BC, provided for an exceptionally
homogeneous citizen-body, the *Spartiatai* or *homoioi* ('Equals'),
who were defined by the criteria of military function and peculiar life-style as well as the expected one of landholding, and who
comprised a small minority (probably less than a fifth) of the
adult male population of the state. The excluded parties comprised, again, *perioikoi* and Helots, and some more obscure

groups of temporarily or permanently disenfranchised 'Equals': the 'Tremblers' who had shown cowardice in battle and the 'Inferiors' who had failed to keep up with the property qualification. But the status of these groups did not correspond exactly with those in Thessaly: the Spartan *perioikoi*, in particular, formed part of the Spartan state and enjoyed powers of local government under it, rather than being mere external allies as in Thessaly. For about three centuries, the Spartan system displayed a quite exceptional stability, helped in a marginal way by the provisions which existed for promotion into (as well as demotion from) the citizen body.

Argos, Lokris and the numerous cities of Crete may provide further examples of what we may call the exclusive pattern of citizenship. In Argos, once again, we hear of *perioikoi* and of an additional tribe, composed of a different stock from the main Argive citizen body and perhaps not admitted to citizenship until the fifth century; and again there is what may be a serf or, perhaps more probably, another under-privileged citizen class, the *gymnesioi* or 'Light-armed'. But the organization of the state is obscure here, and even more so in the ethnos of the Lokrians. Only the Cretan cities offer further detailed information. Here we find the whole gamut of non-citizen groups: the disenfranchised, the *perioikoi*, and not just one but two classes of serf, the public- and the privately-owned. All these cases – Thessaly, Sparta, Argos, Lokris, Crete – show a high correlation with some further important features: first, they were 'conquest-states', in that their main population spoke the Dorian and north-western dialects of Greek which were held, rightly or wrongly, to belong to the last great immigrant groups which had occupied their homelands at the end of the Heroic Age. Thus the differential treatment of 'indigenous' peoples could be explained if not justifed. Secondly, they all had deep-rooted and lasting aristocratic tendencies in their government, often with leanings towards militarism too. The great ruling clans of Thessaly, with their baronial estates, retained their grip on the country into the Classical period; so did the 'Hundred Families' who ruled Lokris, with the aid of an assembly of the entire Lokrian citizen-body, revealingly named the Thousand. In Argos, there was an all-powerful oligarchy until near the end of the Archaic period, and it elected from its number a small executive of magistrates called *demiourgoi* or 'public workers'. The Cretan cities had a similar practice, with annually-elected *kosmoi* ('Marshals') chosen from the ruling clan (*startos* or 'host') – both of them significantly military titles. Only in Sparta was there even the show of internal egalitarianism among the 'Equals'; indeed, although by Classical times it had come to look restrictive, at the time of its first institution this will have appeared an unusually broadly-based citizen body; in the seventh century even the cry for redistribution of land, that ultra-radical slogan whose implementation was normally only possible under a tyranny (below, p. 97), was raised in Sparta. The trouble was that the reality did not for long match even this limited ideal; and ever wider discrepancies, both in wealth and in political influence, appeared within the body of the 'Equals'. The third recurrent feature is the survival of some notion of monarchy – again, usually with explicit military overtones. The famous dual kingship of the Spartans and the elected war-lord of the Thessalians are clear examples. But in Argos, too, a hereditary monarchy survived later than in most places; and, even when it was abolished, a system of elective kingship took its place for a time. In some of the cities of Crete, also, there are signs that kingship lasted well into the Archaic period. The correlation of all these phenomena may be inexact, but the group of states which exhibits them is an important and distinct one, offering a model of conservative political development. As such, it shows what might have been the general result, had the more radical developments in other Archaic states never happened. There might have been considerable political and military achievements, on this hypothesis, but not many cultural ones; much of the impact, one feels, would have been of local and short-term significance only, particularly if exclusiveness shaded into xenophobia, as at Sparta: just a few ideas would have attracted wider notice. The total achievement might have compared with that of the Etruscan or Phoenician cities.

The exclusive pattern of citizenship is repeated, in a slightly different form and with different origins, in another distinct group of states: those of colonial type, including the settlements of the Ionian migration which were, strictly speaking, pre-colonial. The pattern is widespread, though not universal, among these cities, and it derives from the fundamental fact that they were planted among alien populations. Theoretically (although this first alternative was seldom taken) the indigenous peoples could be assimilated entirely into the state; they could be excluded from citizenship but allowed to remain within the state's territory on terms of peaceful intercourse; they could be allowed to remain as dependent serfs; or they could be expelled altogether. The second of these alternatives was common, but a significant number of Greek colonial settlements is known to have taken the third, reducing the native element to serfdom and sometimes even empowering the citizens to buy and sell them. We hear of this relationship most explicitly at Syracuse (with the Sicilian Killyrioi), at Byzantion on the Bosporos (with the Bithynians) and at Herakleia on the south shore of the Black Sea (with the Mariandynoi); it is probably not significant that these, and others such as Gela where the policy was also based on force, were all colonies of Dorian Greeks; certainly there is little sign of an internal political system such as existed in the group of homeland Dorian states that we have just considered, and anyway there is more than a suspicion that similar methods were used in some of the cities of Ionia too, such as Miletos with its native Gergithes. More probably, the truth was simply that non-Greeks were seen as, by definition, unsuited to partnership in any form of Archaic state, the polis most of all.

On the other side, we can define a large group of Archaic states where the citizen body was allowed to become much more broadly-based. The clearest test of citizenship was membership of the Assembly, and it was characteristic of the progressive states that they allowed the Assembly to increase in size and, eventually, in powers as well. Inevitably it is at Athens that we find our best example of this group; but there are glimpses from other states, showing that there too the citizen body was growing. There was nothing in the least inevitable about this growth:

the starting-point of development was in some respects quite close to that of the 'exclusive citizenship' states and, as time went on, there could have been assimilation in other respects too.

To give examples: in early Corinth, under the rule of the Bacchiads (*c.* 747–657 BC), citizenship was strictly confined to the adult males of the Bacchiad clan, which probably included some 200 families. Here was an aristocracy as exclusive as almost any of those that we previously considered (p. 89). The numerous body of outsiders, increasingly resentful as the years passed, eventually brought about its downfall by means of a tyranny. But things might have gone the other way, with the aboriginal, non-Dorian element in Corinth reduced to serfdom on the model of Sparta or Crete. Much later, with the fall of the tyranny (*c.* 585), we find an oligarchic régime in control; but it is broader-based than the aristocracy of the Bacchiads had been and, although the effective power remained concentrated in relatively few hands, there was at least a full citizen body now in existence too. For this, Corinth probably had her tyrants to thank; certainly Kypselos, the first of them, was credited with having re-distributed land, and the equation of landownership with citizenship will have given this wider implications. Two other neighbours of Corinth, both of which had undergone tyrannies and both of which had also suffered brief periods of actual subjugation to Corinth, show similar developments. Epidauros had an extremely narrow ruling-class of 180 men (or perhaps families); sometimes this is interpreted as the number of the Assembly and thus of the total citizen body, but it seems more likely that our defective evidence has preserved memory only of a smaller Council, with whom the real power resided and who called a full Assembly only when they chose to. That was the usual arrangement in oligarchies and, as at Epidauros, it could be even more restrictive than in an 'exclusive citizenship' state like Sparta. But the point is that, unlike Sparta, it had the *potential* for reform, by re-allocation of powers, in the direction of liberalization and even democracy. So, too, with the other neighbour, Megara: here we learn from the poetry of the diehard

Theognis that, in the second half of the sixth century at least, the citizen body had been enlarged to a degree repugnant to him, and political power was temporarily in the hands of non-aristocrats.

The case of Athens, however, is sufficiently well documented to show us, not only what happened, but also what might otherwise have happened. The foundation of the Athenian state and the expansion of its population in the later eighth century (pp. 23, 24) proved to have been in some respects premature. The ruling aristocrats had behaved like men of their time in terminating the monarchy during the eighth century; while the far-sighted unification of the state, and the extension of citizenship to the free male population of all Attica, were actions well ahead of the times. By the seventh century, the same aristocrats, presiding oppressively over a more or less stagnant society, have an air of living in the past. The opportunity to participate in the great wave of western colonization had, rightly or wrongly, not been taken. The evidence of the graves gives reason for thinking that the rise in population had stopped, rather abruptly, after 700. Only when the second wave of colonial ventures, in the north and east, was far advanced did Athens make her small and almost posthumously late intervention, with the foundations of Sigeion and Elaious at the Hellespont. There was little overseas trade: the great natural harbour of the Piraeus, almost unbelievably, had not yet been brought into use; and Athens relied on the open roadstead of Phaleron. An attempt at setting up a tyranny, by Kylon in 631, was a fiasco because the people, instead of supporting him, united in suppressing the coup; but the fact remained that the disparity in wealth among the population was now acute: trouble in some form was bound to erupt. Large numbers of poorer Athenians were reduced to the state of debt-bondage: some at least were *hektēmoroi*, compelled to pay over one-sixth of their produce to their creditors, on pain of being sold into slavery (often abroad) in case of default. Many had fled into exile to avoid this fate. It seemed that Athens was regressing into the pattern of the serf-based states.

What prevented this happening was the inspired decision,

which must have been formally taken by the ruling aristocracy, but probably under pressure from the citizen body as a whole, to appoint one of their number, Solon, as annual magistrate (*archon*) with special powers of arbitration. Solon was an exceptional man for his class and epoch: a thinker, a poet and a businessman with widespread foreign connections. It was his decisions which set Athens on the path to the exceptional achievements of the next two hundred years. He saw that the strength of Athens lay in the number and potentialities of her citizens, and that at all costs their individual rights must be restored and protected. This was done by the abolition of the debts, by the redemption of the Athenians sold into slavery, and by the prohibition of such practices in the future. He is also said to have introduced (or more probably restored) the right of the poorest citizens to vote in the Assembly. At the other end of the scale, he introduced a major reform of the Athenian ruling class: eligibility for the highest magistracies (and thus also for the Council of the Areopagus which was made up of retired magistrates) was now decided on a basis of agricultural wealth, not of aristocratic descent. Lesser privileges were allocated on the same criterion but at a lower level, and among these were the power to elect to a second Council, the Four Hundred, and to hear appeals against the legal judgments of magistrates. We shall consider something of the economic effects of his reforms in the next chapter. Posterity has come to regard Solon as a man of peace and a gradualist, and he did suffer the fate of so many 'moderates' in being attacked from both sides. His own image for his plight, however, was that of a wolf at bay among a pack of hounds; we need not doubt that the crisis in Athens had been a desperate one.

That his solution could be thought of, in some quarters, as insufficiently radical is a tribute to the progressive acts of his predecessors in other cities, some of them unknown to us, others paradoxically familiar in the guise of the tyrants, to whom we shall turn presently. Meanwhile, let us note two other cities where measures reminiscent of Solon's are attested at much the same epoch, and thus betoken similar conditions. Mytilene, on

the eastern Aegean island of Lesbos, was in one of the regions of
Greece where non-Greek serf- or slave-labour was available; her
citizen body is therefore unlikely to have been reduced to the
same straits as that of Athens. Many other things had gone
wrong, however: aristocratic feuding had torn the city apart and
two short-lived tyrannies had been set up. When the citizens of
Mytilene, perhaps following the recent Athenian example,
elected Pittakos with powers of arbitration, they did so for a
ten-year term instead of one year. Pittakos, lacking Solon's literary gifts, has been commemorated largely in the testimony of his
political enemy, the poet Alkaios. Despite this hostile bias, he
emerges as a peer for Solon. Alkaios's gibes of 'tyrant' and
'low-born' are contradicted by other evidence: like Solon, Pittakos was an aristocrat who could see the limitations of aristocratic politics; like Solon, he introduced legislation against the
extravagance of the rich, and then peacefully abdicated his
powers, leaving his city still an oligarchy but a more settled one.
Both men were rewarded by being later numbered among the
Seven Sages. We know far fewer details here but, judged by
the results, Pittakos may have been, on his own terms, at least
as successful as Solon in the long run. Chios, the next island to
the south of Lesbos, furnishes evidence of a quite different kind:
a famous inscription, dating from *c.* 575–550 BC, fragmentary but
tell-tale, which provides for an elected Council of the Assembly,
and lays down its duties as, among others, to meet monthly, to
transact the affairs of the people, to exact penalties and to hear
appeals against the magistrates' verdicts. If there was an element
of Athenian influence on Chios here, then the next episode may
have seen a reversal of the influence; for the tradition was that
the men of Chios were the first to practise chattel-slavery on a
large scale, and it is not long before the men of Athens were
following suit.

That political progress should result in an increase of
enslavement is shocking to modern notions; but in the eyes of
most Greeks, the important feature of this kind of slavery was
that it mainly involved barbarians and foreigners, and was thus
clearly preferable to the reduction of fellow-Greeks to serfdom

or slavery. For the historian, every institution should be judged primarily against the effective alternatives available at the time. So too with tyranny; we shall return to this topic later (pp. 111–16), but at this point a few basic facts about the Archaic tyrants can be appropriately stated.

First, the institution of tyranny took its name from a foreign language, probably Lydian; at the very beginning it may have been used simply as another word for kingship, but the first sense that we can definitely identify is that of a special kind of monarchy, one that was usurped by force and not inherited. Monarchy did not have the unacceptable overtones in the Greek states that it did in, say, republican Rome: for one thing, the extinction of the early kingships in the various states had been gradual and, it seems, usually peaceful; for another, monarchy of a kind still persisted in a number of the more conservative states, as we have seen (p. 90). 'Tyranny does not exist in the order of nature,' says Aristotle loftily (*Politics* 1287 b 39); it is certainly a pity that we do not have more guidance from him over this vital new development. For the truth is that it was through tyranny that most Greek states had their first taste of radical policies and, conversely, there were few leading progressive states which had not passed through a phase of tyranny at some stage in the Archaic period, though usually it was of fairly brief duration. There is a strong modern tendency to regard tyranny as a widespread but not a very positive phenomenon. This is partly because it had no specific constitutional framework associated with it (hence Aristotle's lack of interest), but was simply superimposed on whatever constitution the state in question currently had. That said, however, one must go on to acknowledge that the tyrants used their power to enforce changes which, in good time, transformed societies and even constitutions. We have already seen the example of Kypselos of Corinth (p. 92): by redistributing the land of the now-exiled aristocrats who had hitherto monopolized the government (and, one suspects, much of the territory too) he not only averted potential serfdom but made possible the growth of a class of prosperous smallholders, who made up Corinth's notable citizen-army. His son and successor, Periander, besides completely reversing the foreign policy of the earlier aristocracy, is represented in one episode (Herodotus v, 92) as seeking to undertake a reform of government, before resorting to more drastic methods.

Other tyrants too, such as Periander's father-in-law Prokles of Epidauros, Theagenes of Megara and even Peisistratos of Athens a century later, are vaguely associated in our sources with such questions as land-reform and grazing-rights. In several cities, the tyrant's desire to increase the numbers of his adherents may have led him to extend citizenship more widely – to the landless, to the disenfranchised, to foreigners. Certainly, by Solon's time, redistribution of land in particular had become tarnished by its close association with tyranny, and was therefore to be avoided by a man who wished himself to avoid the charge of despotism. Thus Solon in the 590s was seen to be acting less radically than Kypselos sixty years earlier. Politically, the tyrants were not initiators so much as catalysts for forces which would have erupted in some form anyway; it is the high incidence of tyranny *per se* which is the most significant political phenomenon, emphasizing as it does the utter dissatisfaction with the methods of the ruling aristocracies, in state after state, on the part of those citizen bodies who had some means of expressing their feelings.

There was at least one common element in the make-up of every Greek state, which had a bearing on every distinctive feature, not excluding the form of the state itself: this was warfare and the armed forces. We can detect its operation in countless incidental names and phrases. The ruling-class in some aristocratic states was known collectively as 'Knights', 'Horse-rearers' and by other such names. The magistrates and the ruling families could have revealing titles in conservative societies like Crete, as we have seen (p. 90), but not only there: in many states the word for the assembly of the people was the same as that for the army (*stratos*). The word for 'tribe' (*phylē*) also served for 'regiment' on the battlefield. The kings of Sparta were called not only 'kings', but also by the old title 'war-lord' or 'commander' (*archagetas*). When the Delphic oracle wished to insult Kleisthenes, tyrant of Sikyon, it called him a 'skirmisher' (literally, 'stone-thrower'). All of this suggests the underlying presence of a military hierarchy, which indeed was the case; but there was more than that. The original and most important raison d'être of Greek kingship had been for the king to lead the tribe and (where he survived in existence long enough) the state in warfare. What brought this role to an end was probably – although this is an obscure and controversial matter – the general rise of equitation, which was at all events an episode that took place during the dark age and becomes detectable at its end.

Once the ownership of horses offered a man the chance of actually riding on horseback – in place of the more costly, cumbersome and unreliable practice of chariotry – then military and social conditions were transformed. It is a debated question whether a phase of true cavalry warfare, in which a warrior actually *fought* from horseback, ever existed in early Greece; the balance of recent opinion is against it. But even without this, the advantages conferred on the rider were enormous. Strategically, he could travel further, faster and with less effort than the footsoldier; tactically, he could hope (in the words of a famous American cavalry commander) to 'git thar fust with the mostest men', even when he dismounted for the actual fighting. Further differentiation existed in the horse-owning classes: spare mounts were needed and with horses (as aristocrats still meaningly observe today) breeding really counts. So, in Aristotle's words, 'we ask how many horses a man keeps' (*Politics* 1289 b 35): and, he goes on, 'horse-rearing is always expensive'. For a time, warfare seems to have become almost the preserve of those who fulfilled these conditions, and they were of course the aristocrats.

But their phase of supremacy is not well-documented, and was probably a short one, except in some outlying regions where it survived almost indefinitely. Homer, who must have witnessed it in part, almost entirely excludes it from his story, no doubt because it was too recent a development to be appropriate for his heroic society; indeed, a recent theory holds that his suppression of the ridden horse in warfare, though systematic, is so conscious and artificial that we can detect tell-tale traces of it in what purport to be descriptions of chariotry. Hesiod, another presumed witness, is not concerned with the battlefield; and by the time of the military poets of the seventh century, such as Archilochos and Tyrtaios, we find that Greek warfare has entered its next stage of development – one in which cavalry indeed persisted within the restraints imposed by dismounting to fight, but where the developments in infantry warfare had seized the military initiative, permanently as far as Archaic Greece was concerned, and so exposed the limitations of a cavalry which could not similarly develop.

This last change was the most momentous in early Greek warfare, even (in some opinions) in Archaic Greek history as a whole. Since it involves a substantial and costly product, bronze defensive armour, it also puts us back into contact with the material evidence, thus imposing a check on the very indirect written testimonies as well as offering a number of insights which would otherwise escape us altogether. The first archaeological fact to emerge is that the introduction of the new armour almost (but not quite) coincides with the discontinuation of burial with arms (p. 53), a fact of some social significance. It means that the time-honoured and individualistic desire to give a man the distinctive attributes of a warrior, in death as in life, had given way to something more practical and broadly-based: the realization that the self-esteem of the dead is less important than the needs of the living, especially when costly materials and long hours of craftsmanship have gone into the products in question. If a man's arms could be handed on, to remain in the service of the state, then all alike would benefit; thus the needs of the community were given preference over those of the family, and above all of the aristocratic family, which had particularly subscribed to the warrior ethic. A new spirit was abroad; if I may again quote from a poem of Auden's:

> Nobody I know would like to be buried
>    with a silver cocktail shaker,
> a transistor radio and a strangled
>    daily help, . . . .

> *About the House*, ii, 'Thanksgiving for a Habitat'

There may be another factor as well: aristocrats may no longer have seen themselves as warriors before all else, but rather as leaders of the new community in all its functions. They certainly appear to have dropped the practice, at about this time or shortly after, of going about their ordinary daily business armed.

The coincidence between these two changes is not quite exact,
Plate 15 however. Shortly before 700 BC we have two graves at Argos in which pieces of the new bronze defensive armour were included in graves, and there may have been one or two others excavated long ago elsewhere. After 700, as one would expect from the social systems involved, burial with arms continues sporadically in the more conservative states of ethnos type: we have fully-fledged panoply-burials of the seventh and sixth centuries in western Achaia and Lokris, and we have what look like more economical compromises in several regions – Crete, Thera in the Cyclades, Cyprus – where men who may have worn a bronze panoply in battle are buried with the more expendable offensive weapons only. This evidence suggests that the new bronze armour began its life in the more advanced states, and continued in the less advanced ones, in association with the aristocratic warrior-ethic. If this were so, we should expect to find some association with the horse as well; and so we occasionally do, although it was not until ten years ago that one of the vital pieces of evidence came to light: a late eighth-century Attic vase, on which a rider is shown clad in the metal cuirass of the newly-adopted shape, and leading a second horse behind him. He is presumably an example of the aristocratic 'cavalryman', who will in practice dismount to fight while his mounted squire (symbolized by the second horse) will look after both horses. Already it had been seen that a number of other contemporary Athenian vases show mounted men wearing helmets, which were easier for the painter to indicate. In later centuries, when styles of painting became more expressive, we see numerous portrayals of these panoplied riders, often explicitly attended by an unarmed squire; doubtless they attract the painters' attention for their social, not their numerical prominence, for by this time it is clear from our historical sources that cavalry were seldom

the decisive arm in Greek warfare. The specialism of a few regions like Thessaly and Macedonia kept alive the art of true cavalry and the associated breeding techniques, but seldom applied them successfully away from their home ground. At least two Thessalian attempts at southward expansion were defeated by the Phokian and Boiotian infantry. On a famous occasion in 511 BC, Thessalian allied cavalry won a decisive victory for the Athenian tyrant Hippias over the invading Spartan army (Herodotus v 63); but, significantly, only after the plain of Phaleron had been specially prepared and cleared for the charge – an attempt to repeat the experiment a year later met with total disaster. Elsewhere, the use of 'mounted infantry' was continued, and at times combined with true cavalry; a few further states – certain Ionian cities, Boiotia, Chalkis and Eretria in Euboia – had a reputation for higher standards than the average.

How was it that the mere development of bronze defensive armour brought about such a dramatic shift of power on Greek battlefields? On its own, it could never have done so. What gave such effect to this change was, first, the social and economic position in which the more prosperous Greek states were already placed and, secondly, the growth of a new form of military tactics. The former point becomes clear once we realize that the primary aspect of bronze armour was its costliness; the number of people who could afford it turned out to be very considerably greater than the number of people who had hitherto been engaged in warfare and since landownership was overwhelmingly the most important category of wealth, this means that there were numerous substantial landowners who were not aristocrats. But substantial they had to be: the making of a bronze panoply required days of work, done to close specifica- *Plate 13* tion, on the part of a highly skilled artisan using expensive raw materials. That the state did not normally equip a whole army with panoplies is both a tribute to their cost and a sign of the low level of taxation or other revenue in the early states.

But what incentive can have existed to bring these landowners out to war? The ultimate answer is that it was one of the conditions of the survival of the state and one of the burdens of citizenship, that all should serve who could; but were those the terms in which the proposition was put in the mid-seventh century BC? Much more probably the ruling aristocracies, who had themselves (as we have seen) tried out the equipment, decided to broaden their military base by calling on the help of men who, while they could not afford to mount themselves, could turn out on foot, sufficiently protected with armour, alongside the aristocrats. The Council would decree the necessary property census; then the word would go out that all men who were above a certain qualifying level were to find themselves a suit of armour. Reluctance could be overcome in several ways: most obviously, by ruling that certain rights of citizenship, hitherto taken for granted, would in future be restricted to those who complied with the military requirements. To this, those who qualified would have a very strong counter-condition: it must be the *state* that they served, not an aristocratic grouping and not for some purpose of civil strife. But different arguments would apply in different cases. Where development had been slower and there were fewer privileges to withdraw, then aristocratic disfavour might serve instead: a man who could truthfully say 'I am your landlord, judge, priest and commander; in future I shall require your help to defend my property; and (assuming that you agree to serve) your own will be looked after too' – such a man could offer persuasive arguments. They could also, indeed, be applied in the interests of other groups besides the state as a whole, and we do find cases of armoured infantry taking part in the civil wars of aristocratic factions.

The other main factor is that of tactics. Here we must appreciate that, ever since infantry had existed, some kind of primitive tactical formation, usually in parallel ranks, must have been desirable. It is ranks of this form which Homer presumably denotes by his repeated use of the word *phalanges*, for the largely passive and ineffectual infantrymen of the *Iliad*. What was now developed was a real 'phalanx' in the sense in which we under-
Plate 11  stand the word today: a close-order formation, several ranks deep. The offensive weapon was the spear which, whether used

for throwing or thrusting, requires the minimum of lateral space; the main defence, more important even than body-armour, was a shield large enough to form an almost continuous surface when the men closed up; it was round, with a double grip, for the left fore-arm as well as the hand. The individual infantryman took his name, *hoplitēs*, from the *hoplon* or shield. But at this *Plate 12* point we enter an area of controversy: was the shield invented with phalanx tactics in mind? Or, in other words, do the tactics of the phalanx go back to the very earliest appearance of this type of shield? We cannot answer this question from the external evidence, which merely tells us that the form of shield had been invented before 700 BC – almost as early as the metal breastplate and helmet, and taking us back into what we would otherwise judge to be the era of supremacy of the mounted aristocrat. The tactics, on the other hand, are not unmistakably to be seen in representations until some way on in the following century, when they appear on Corinthian vases with a frequency which suggests that they were an innovation. One might add that the arrangement of double handles, which is the most distinctive feature of this type of shield, appears (at least in later art) on the shields of many other types of soldier than the heavy infantry-man in phalanx formation; it is even seen on the arm of the *Plate 14* Greek *peltastēs* or skirmisher, who by definition operated in loose array. It cannot therefore be said to be incompatible with individual combat, as is often claimed.

These are less than conclusive arguments. But a different line of argument leads to similar results. The phalanx tactics can hardly ever, for reasons of numbers, have been used in *exclusively* aristocratic forms of warfare. So the crucial modifications of the shield – adding the arm-band and increasing the size and weight of an existing type of round shield – were either designed to improve the aristocrats' equipment or else brought into immediate mass-production with the specific aim of equipping a whole infantry phalanx, drawn from the lesser land-owners as well as the aristocrats. This latter alternative would posit a triple coincidence: of the political will to broaden the *corps d'élite* of the army; of the military insight to devise a new formation that would promote the strength of the new force; and of the technical skill to invent a shield-type that would in turn promote the formation. The other explanation, which involves no such coincidence, therefore seems the more plausible, especially as there is positive evidence so much earlier for the shield than for the phalanx.

If this is right, then we have to make sense of the shield and the rest of the bronze panoply as a series of technical improvements, initially adopted by the ruling aristocracies to strengthen their domination of the battlefield. There were cultural reasons why these steps were taken now and not earlier: not so much the availability of bronze, for the dedications of the giant bronze *Plate 2* tripod-cauldrons – at Olympia, Delphi, Delos, the Athenian Akropolis and Ithaka – had been going on in considerable numbers and for about a century beforehand; more probably, it was the encounter with other peoples who were making sporadic use of the same ideas, both to the west and to the east of the Greek world. Chieftains in Iron Age Italy were wearing bronze helmets and probably breastplates when the first Greek settlers arrived there, and it has been recently shown that a few of their accoutrements ended up as dedications in Greek sanctuaries; while whole armies of Assyrians, equipped with bronze-faced shields and metal helmets were now appearing on the eastern Mediterranean seaboard. Sometimes it may have been actual clashes of arms which brought home to the Greeks the advantages of bronze armour. At some point, too, a contribution may have come from the unlikely source of their own collective memory, as enshrined in epic poetry. Two rarer additions to the panoply, bronze greaves and metal ankle-guards, had been worn by Mycenaeans, are mentioned in the epic, and were presently revived in Archaic Greece. There are no likely outside sources in this case, and a purely Greek transmission seems more probable.

None of the pieces of armour was unthinkingly borrowed; there was always some intelligent modification, whether by the invention of the double shield-handle or merely by the elimination of unnecessary surface-decoration on breastplates and shield-facings. Helmets developed a more close-fitting and less top-heavy contour, thus again putting function before ostentation. A developed Greek helmet, of the Corinthian type especially, has that same extraordinary combination of economical form and organic-looking curves which we can recognize in a masterpiece of sixth-century Attic pottery: in the modern sense of the phrase, it 'has style'. More significant, perhaps, are the economic implications of the new armour. Where was the bronze to come from? The main answer seems to have been through the abandonment of production of the great tripod-cauldrons which had been piling up in Greek sanctuaries since the beginning of the eighth century.

*Plate 16*

Towards the end of that century, the variety and quality of these objects reaches a peak, but then production tails off rather rapidly and two new phenomena make their appearance: firstly, from shortly before 700, imported Oriental cauldrons, on separate stands, are found in quantities large enough to replace, in part, the native Greek products; and secondly, the dedication of helmets, shields and other armour begin to appear in force. Finds in graves or settlements are extremely rare (cf. p. 53 above), and it is the sanctuaries which provide the overwhelming bulk of the evidence; of these, Olympia is easily the most prolific site for this kind of dedication. It may be worth giving some figures of the finds there, dividing the material into arbitrary periods of equal length since the chronology, being based on style, is imprecise:

| | c.800–725 | c.725–650 | c.650–575 | c.575–500 | (Date of latest publication) |
|---|---|---|---|---|---|
| Tripod-cauldrons | c.280 | c.240 | – | – | (1957) |
| Oriental cauldron-attachments | – | 58 | ? | – | (1966) |
| Early conical helmets | – | 31 | – | – | (1967) |
| 'Illyrian' helmets | – | 30 | 7 | 13 | (1967) |
| Corinthian helmets | – | 17 | c.65 | 30+ | (1964) |
| Hoplite shields | – | 8 frags. | c.90+ | c.80 frags. | (1964) |
| Breast- and back-plates | – | 2 | c.10 | 1+ | (1960) |
| Decorated Hoplite shield arm-bands | – | – | 35+ | 40+ | (1950) |

Although the available publications are not equally up to date in all cases (right-hand column), the picture is reasonably clear. From a date in the region of 675 BC, the dedications of the monumental tripod-cauldrons seem to come to an abrupt end. By that time, the role that they performed had been partly taken over by Oriental imports, while the practice of dedicating bronze helmets (but not other armour) had become quite common. Not until the mid-seventh century did the main wave of armour-dedications begin, with the appearance *en masse* of breastplates and other armour such as greaves (not show here), of the improved helmets of Corinthian type, and above all of the characteristic hoplite shields, the most important single item. If Olympia is a reliable guide, it would seem that these years at the mid-century witnessed the widespread appearance of the hop-lite phalanx, as was argued above. It must be conceded, how-ever, that experiments in the handling of massed infantry had been undertaken before this: an observant critic has recently drawn attention to the presence, in a battle-scene on a Corin-thian vase of about 675, of a piper – an indispensable participant in the later Spartan phalanx where his music kept the men in step, and therefore perhaps a sign of incipient phalanx tactics, although the moral-boosting effect of military pipers, as modern parallels show, is not confined to those operating in close forma-tion. What, though, is the significance of the dedications of bronze helmets of earlier types, shown in the second column of the table? Surely they are examples of just that sort of improve-ment in equipment which the traditional warrior class would adopt, and to which the isolated earlier shields and breastplates from elsewhere in Greece (above, pp. 100, 103) also testify. Both the conical and the so-called 'Illyrian' helmets are open-faced types, suited to men operating independently; whereas the Corinthian type, encasing the whole head except for small aper-tures for the eyes and mouth, bought greater protection at the price of restricting the wearer's vision and hearing, besides con-ferring on him an anonymity that was, in turn, partly relieved by the use of individual devices on the shield. After a time, it seems that this price was found to be acceptable, if the disadvantages could be offset by the solidarity of the phalanx. It is not in the nature of military innovation for essentially defensive devices such as these to outpace the offensive capacities of the enemy; so we may see these developments as reactions, originally to the attacking power of the long swords and spears of the eighth century, and perhaps to that of cavalry as well; and later, to the vulnerability of the individual man-at-arms.

This change, great in its implications, must not be regarded as revolutionary in intention: as it was defensive militarily, so it was politically neutral as a conception. By calling on others to join them on the battlefield, the aristocrats can have had little notion that they were thereby jeopardizing the structure of society: it was only a small sector of the community, after all, who could afford the equipment necessary for that kind of warfare. Their assumptions, too, could well have been correct: elsewhere in the ancient world, phalanx-tactics were adopted without any apparent disturbance of the old order, and even in the Greek world the new military system was sometimes harnessed to a political régime which then underwent little change. But in other cases it was a very different story: the military reform came to be associated, at least by Aristotle, with the earliest steps on the road to democracy. Yet we cannot regard it as the *very* first step: that place must be given to a purely intellectual development, the realization that there were alternatives to unsatisfactory aristocratic rule. The military reform, as has been well observed, merely provided a means for bringing such alternatives into effect, when a hundred war-hardened aristocrats suddenly found themselves in confrontation, not only with their opposite numbers in a neighbouring state, but with a thousand well-armed commoners in their own. A possible solution lay in compromise; but in some cities events had already moved too fast for that. The military reform falls close in time to another, more notorious phenomenon of the age: the rise of tyranny.

Before we consider the complex relation between these two developments, there are other results of the military reform to be mentioned. First, the inter-state and even the international balance of power was transformed by the military change. There

was no reason why the states with a prominent military aristocracy should be the same as those which could put into the field a
powerful yeoman force of heavy infantry; and events show that
it was otherwise. Chalkis and Eretria in Euboia, with their aristocrats whose traditional names of 'Horsemen' and 'Horse-
grazers' were still remembered by Aristotle, begin to decline
from the status of major powers in Greek politics from about this
time; despite the copper-mines which allegedly gave Chalkis her
name, there is little sign that she was a major producer of bronze
armour. The cities of Ionia, which had displayed precocious features in some aspects of the development of the Greek state and
were to continue to do so in others, make a poor showing in
land-warfare from now on; they too had been famed as centres
of horse-breeding, but they offer significantly little archaeological evidence for armour, and they later proved unable to defend
their independence for long against invaders. Thessalian cavalry
were a name to fear in the eighth century and later, but Thessaly
simply lacked the social structure which would have made it
possible to field a hoplite army: her aristocrats were too few, her
farmers too impoverished.

Instead, new powers came to the forefront, especially in the
Peloponnese. Two cities, Corinth and Argos, claim pride of
place because they gave their names to staple components of the
hoplite panoply. 'Argive' was the common name for the big
two-handled round shield which was to remain the standard
arm of the hoplite for over three centuries; here literary evidence
can be supported by art-historical arguments, which show excellent grounds for connecting the regular decoration of the
shields, and particularly of their arm-bands, with Argos. Somewhere about this time, too, a low lens-shaped hill on the edge of
the city of Argos may have been re-named 'Aspis', the shield,
for its profile closely resembles the newly-adopted shape. Similarly, 'Corinthian' was almost certainly the name by which the
commonest and most protective form of infantry helmet was
known in ancient Greece; here, too, there is some confirmatory
evidence in the frequency with which it is shown on Corinthian
vases and in the signs of Corinthian workmanship in at least one

group of the surviving examples. What this must mean is that these two cities, taking a serious initiative in military innovation, either originally pioneered or else later specialized in the mass-production of the respective pieces of armour. If the former, then the relevant date in both cases was the years shortly before 700 when each type first appeared; if the latter, then we should think rather in terms of the middle and later seventh century. Since this is in any case when the material evidence for the connection with Argos and Corinth appears, the second is perhaps the more likely alternative; certainly the two were major powers within Greece by then.

Inexorably, however, they and other states were coming to be overshadowed by Sparta. Late and perhaps reluctant in their acceptance of the new military order, the Spartans – perhaps under the duress of a desperate struggle in the Second Messenian War – came to adopt it with an obsessive intensity. For their unusually restricted concept of citizenship (pp. 88–90) permitted a unique relation to exist: the citizen body, instead of comprising a far wider group than the hoplite army, was actually a narrower one. Citizens who defaulted on their obligations could be relegated to the ranks of 'Tremblers' and 'Inferiors', but they still seem to have kept their places in the phalanx; non-citizens – the *perioikoi* regularly, the Helots on occasion – could be used to augment the hoplite army when heeded. Sparta may well have instituted another unique feature in that the state and not, as elsewhere, the individual soldier may have furnished the panoply, at least on occasion. (When non-citizens were enrolled, it certainly did so.) This was only one step in the long process that converted Sparta into that strange phenomenon which was to attract such admiration, envy or disgust on the part of other Greeks and moderns alike; but militarily it was the most important one. Together with their educational system, it enabled Sparta's citizens to make an almost total identification between a uniform military role on the one hand and citizenship on the other. Trained from birth as full-time infantry soldiers, insulated from agricultural and other labour, they came to see the defence of the state as an honoured privilege. On top of all this, the enrolment of the *periokoi* meant that for a long time the Spartan phalanx was actually bigger than that which any other single state could put in the field. No wonder that by 500 BC the Spartan infantryman was a figure whose repute extended even to the Persian capital, a thousand miles to the east.

This mention of the outside world raises a second point: as the internal balance of power in Greece was changed by the reform, so too was the external relationship of Greeks with other peoples. A few foreign powers acknowledged the breakthrough by adopting the heavy armour and the tactics of the Greek infantryman themselves; in one case, that of the Carians of southwestern Asia Minor, they did this so early that the Greeks charitably credited them with having invented some elements of the panoply; in another a little later (the Etruscans), the historical result of their having done so was momentous, since the Romans borrowed the idea from them in turn. Most foreign states, however, lacked the appropriate social system and did not attempt to follow, though some pieces of the Greek hoplite's equipment proved to be adaptable, as mere hardware, to the traditional practices of warfare. But it was the Greek infantryman himself who was found to be more widely exportable than either ideas or objects on their own; in particular his services were keenly sought in the role of mercenary. It may be significant that the earliest Greeks whom we find serving as mercenaries abroad came from areas where the new military system, though known, seems to have fallen short of full fruition, whether military or political: that is, Ionia and the islands of the Aegean. The poet Archilochos of Paros at least envisaged serving as a mercenary; a group of Ionians and Carians who actually did so in Egypt around 664 BC established a major precedent by their action, for they played a leading part in bringing about a change of dynasty and the new Pharaohs took to employing them on a permanent basis. Their prestige may have spread from Egypt: early in the next century we find Antimenidas of Lesbos (brother of another poet, Alkaios) serving with distinction in the army of the king of Babylon. Mercenaries seldom enjoy a favourable reputation, nor are they a good advertisement for the health of society in their homeland; but the fact remains that in the prowess of Greek heavy infantry, we have the very earliest proof of recognition by foreign peoples of the achievements of Archaic Greece.

Nor was this an entirely eccentric feature to choose. To a great extent, the strength of an Archaic state *was* the strength of its citizen infantry, and thus of the landowning middle class who provided the infantry. There is certainly a loose correlation between the political achievements of the Greek states and their prowess in the new form of warfare. For example, when we seek to explain the surprising fact that Athens, so prominent in the preceding and succeeding epochs, passes through a long period of eclipse during the seventh century BC, we may note the evidence for a deepening agrarian depression, and eventually of a crisis, during these years (p. 93), and infer that the non-aristocratic landowners of Athens were ineffective politically. But they also appear to have been backward militarily, and Athens' indifferent military fortunes continued (notwithstanding the laboured performance of an alliance of Thessalians, Athenians and Sikyonians in defeating the little city of Kirrha in the First Sacred War in the 590s) until her successful attack on Megara in about 565; and the commander in that campaign, Peisistratos, was eventually to be rewarded with the first tyranny in Athens.

But what exactly was the connection between the rise of the new military class and the establishment of the first tyrants? For, a hundred years before Peisistratos, tyrannies had begun to grow up in Argos, Corinth, Sikyon, Megara, Epidauros and Pisa – all probably within a generation – and many other states presently followed suit. This long-drawn-out resurgence of monarchy in Greece thus had its origins in the same period as the military reform. But if the latter was itself a lengthy process as I have argued (pp. 100–7), then it is difficult to disentangle cause and effect here. At the date when the very first tyrannies arose, a self-confident middle class of trained infantrymen is still, so far as we can see, only just emerging. On the other hand the early tyrannies, once established, generally lasted long enough to witness a very considerable advance in this respect. It seems a reasonable conclusion that the new military class and the tyrants found some interests in common: that the tyrants seized power with the acquiescence of the citizen soldiers and finding, then or later, that some support could be mustered among them, they accelerated the process of enlarging and training the citizen army. The more positive inference, that the new armies actually precipitated the coups d'état which brought the tyrants to power, seems less likely: not only would such a revolution be improbably precocious, but the whole episode of the rise of tyranny appears to have been conducted on the level of aristocratic power-politics. The tyrants themselves were almost always dissident aristocrats, who exploited the unpopularity of their fellows in the ruling class, killed or exiled those currently in power, and often recalled to favour other recalcitrants. Thus far they were dealing entirely in the traditional units of politics – aristocratic families and their followings. It was their policies once in power that were innovatory; and there is no reason why these should not have included the furtherance of the military reform. This last suggestion is supported by a further fact: all the early tyrannies listed above arose in or close to the Peloponnese, between about 675 and 640 BC. This is the same epoch in which the sudden upsurge in dedications of armour at Olympia begins (p. 106) and the style and workmanship of the new dedications, in almost all ascertainable cases, proclaim them as Peloponnesian too: Argive in the case of the shields and probably a group of the helmets, Corinthian for the broader class of helmets, probably Corinthian for the breastplates, more generally Peloponnesian for some other items. Of course, Olympia was itself a Peloponnesian sanctuary; but this does not detract from the fact that the major Peloponnesian states were producing large quantities of infantry armour at just the period when they had recently been taken over by tyrants.

Whether or not this sequence is correct, there is certainly an important difference between a Greek tyrant's and a modern dictator's seizure of power: the absence of a standing army in the Archaic state. There could be nothing to correspond with secret indoctrination and the rolling of tanks: instead, the 'army' was everywhere, in the more substantial town-houses, villages and farms, its weapons hanging on the walls of private rooms. To mobilize it was the supreme and weightiest duty of the state. To the aristocrat launching his coup, the first question was whether the army would mobilize at all, and the second, on which side if so. It happens that the first instance where we have a detailed account is one in which the citizens opposed the prospective tyrant. This is the coup of Kylon at Athens in 631 (p. 93), which received military support from one of the Peloponnesian tyrants whose recent successes Kylon was emulating, his father-in-law Theagenes of Megara (not to mention the moral support of the Delphic oracle). But the citizens, under the command of the current magistrates (also of course aristocrats) mobilized and besieged him on the Akropolis. Kylon's use of foreign troops shows that the citizen army was, at best, an unknown quantity to him. Even eighty-five years later, when Peisistratos made his successful bid for the same objective, he used the same methods, landing with a force of foreign mercenaries. This time a sufficient proportion on the citizens joined him to bring victory, but only after a pitched battle between two armies of Athenian infantry. It would be easy to reconstruct the course of further successful coups in these terms; very much harder to do so in terms of a spontaneous move by the scattered citizen-soldiers.

Tyranny was, for better or worse, a form of monarchy. Further, the earliest tyrant of whom we know, Pheidon of Argos, is said by Aristotle (*Politics* 1310 b 26) to have been one of several hereditary kings who exceeded their constitutional powers and so became tyrants. In his person, therefore, the oldest form of government extant in Greece reached out to touch the newest. Again, a symbolic factor of some importance was the tyrant's place of residence: just as Kylon's attempt on Athens began with the seizure of the Akropolis, so later Peisistratos, after his final and successful attempt, resided permanently on the Akropolis. (It has even been suggested that some of the sculptures found there may have decorated his palace.) By so

*Plate 23*

doing he gave the people an inescapable reminder of the royal line of Erechtheus who had been the last human occupants of the citadel, and even challenged comparison with the gods and heroes who had held it undisputed since then. He also followed most of his predecessors in trying to establish a hereditary dynasty: it lasted 35 years in his case, but the record was held by the Sikyonian tyrants who survived for just a century. With the second and third generations of hereditary tyrants succeeding, we may well ask whether such a tyranny could be distinguished from the monarchies of the traditional kind, several of which still survived elsewhere in Greece. Indeed, at no time in Greek history, even if one leaves Sparta out of account, was monarchy entirely extinguished.

How much does all this imply? Doubtless a ruler like Pheidon will have invoked his time-honoured authority (in at least one context he posed as the heir of Herakles) to justify his policies. But more important is the nature of those policies, and in the particular case of Pheidon we know little of them. Elsewhere, however, there are recurrent features: a number of tyrants, after an initial flurry of violence, settled down to a rule that was in many respects constitutional, leaving the operation of internal politics almost unchanged and placing themselves partially under the rule of the laws; this, as Aristotle grudgingly admits (*Politics* 1315 b 14) was the secret of the long life of the tyranny at Sikyon. Other tyrants, he says, came to the fore as 'leaders of the people', including two of the greatest names, Kypselos of Corinth and Peisistratos of Athens: such radical measures as property-tax and the institution of circuit-judges, as well as redistribution of land, are attributed to these rulers. Then there is their exercise of propaganda through religion and myth, which was relentless. Sometimes it was blatant to the point of absurdity, as when Kleisthenes of Sikyon drove out the cult of the Argive hero Adrastos (p. 38); or when Peisistratos, on his second bid for power, dressed up a tall and beautiful girl in full armour, stood her beside him in a chariot, and drove into Athens proclaiming that she was Athena, endorsing his right to the tyranny (Herodotus i 60, 3–5).

Behind all these stories, we can detect a deeper theme: in Archaic Greece, the policies of the tyrants, as of other reformers like Solon, could be presented as a reversion to older ways. In due course, the narrowly restricted egalitarianism of Sparta and the radical democracy of Athens alike came to acquire ancient pedigrees. The object was to reach back far enough into antiquity to achieve precedence over those who had wielded the effective power in more recent centuries; that is, over the aristocracies. Sometimes it was enough to reverse policies which had taken effect almost within living memory; we can imagine, for example, that this was how Solon would see his cancellation of debt-bondage (p. 94), restoring the position before the excesses of the aristocrats had taken their toll. Sometimes it was necessary to go back much further: in many Peloponnesian states, for instance, the ruling aristocracies were recognizable as the speakers of the Doric dialect, who were believed to have immigrated at the end of the Heroic Age. Thus reformers and dissidents looked to pre-Dorian (or at least non-Dorian) heroes for inspiration and patronage. Pheidon of Argos claimed sovereignty over the 'Heritage of Temenos', a territorial concept going back five hundred years; Kypselos of Corinth actually claimed non-Dorian descent on his father's side; Kleisthenes of Sikyon, grandson of a cook and also apparently non-Dorian, pursued an all-out propaganda war against the hitherto dominant Dorian element, adopting derogatory tribal names for them and an honorific one, *archelaoi* ('Leaders of the People'), for his own tribe. Even the very king of Sparta, Kleomenes I, was prepared to play the anti-Dorian card when it suited his convenience (Herodotus v 72, 3).

Another general tendency of tyrants was the institution and enlargement of state cults and festivals, to the detriment of the exclusive, family-based cults which widely prevailed: this is especially recorded of Peisistratos, while Pheidon and Kleisthenes both went so far as to interfere (at Olympia and Delphi respectively) with the running of major inter-state festivals. The main losers in every case were the local aristocracies. The time-honoured associations of monarchy were also exploited to the full: a 'good king' from the Heroic Age like Theseus could be credited with having given Athens democratic institutions. It helped greatly that he was supposed to have won his kingdom by defeating an aristocratic clan, the Pallantids; the fact that the aristocrats also claimed Theseus's patronage for their exclusive council, the Areiopagos, was no serious obstacle. It recalls the way in which, in seventeenth-century England, the imaginary statutes of Edward the Confessor were invoked against the subsequent legislation of the upstart Normans, whose usurpation dated from a mere six hundred years earlier. Religion and myth, then, could be enlisted on either side in Greek political controversy, and very often it was the more radical party which searched the more diligently through the legendary past to find respectable precedents.

All of this is part of the process whereby religion, along with much else, was now being pressed into the service of the community as a whole; that is, of the state rather than of any one faction, class, family or individual. Part of the strength of the tyrant lay in his ability to pose as representative of this whole community, and at the time of the rise of the first tyrannies the appeal would still have been a fresh one. The military reform likewise put the ultimate sanction in the hands of men who would be reluctant to fight in any cause but that of the state as a whole. Nothing was more natural, in Archaic Greece, than that religion should be enlisted too. There are innumerable examples which one could give, and if a disproportionate number of them is taken from Athens this reflects merely the familiar Athenian bias of our evidence, not the historical reality. But Peisistratos does appear to have been most assiduous in his centralizing of cults. It is to his tyranny that we can date either the foundation or a major expansion of the Great Panathenaia, the four-yearly festival of Athena (the heroes Erechtheus and Theseus were, predictably, enlisted as forerunners). Another festival with an even greater cultural future, the City Dionysia, was probably founded in his time; significantly, this involved transferring a cult of Dionysos from the border-town of Eleutherai to Athens itself and, even more significantly, that act was symbolic of the political incorporation of Eleutherai into Attica, detaching her from the Boiotian confederation. He intervened at Eleusis in the area of his own first military successes (p. 111), and very likely established Athenian control over the Eleusinian Mysteries for the first time. He gave a great stimulus to the festival of Artemis at his own birthplace, Brauron, and probably also created a pre- *Plate 17* cinct for the goddess on the Akropolis itself. Nor was it only divine cults which engaged attention; heroes too, associated with outlying districts where they could prove a troublesome focus of local aristocratic prestige, might find themselves transplanted and installed at shrines in the middle of Athens; this is what probably happened to Eurysakes the son of Ajax, at some time in the Archaic period; and his father followed him in 508 BC when he was needed for 'tribal duty' under the new constitution of the Athenian Kleisthenes. Peisistratos was neither the first nor the last to manipulate the festivals of Athens. Already in Solon's reforms we find the institution of an annual state festival in honour of the dead, the *Genesia*; as far as we can see, this was a stroke aimed at the Athenian clans, whose celebrations of the funeral rites of their aristocratic leaders were an occasion for ostentatious and divisive demonstrations (we know that Solon also legislated against excessive expense on funerals).

There were many less obvious ways in which religious events entered into the state's calculations. We might hardly expect, for instance, that one of the main supports of Corinth's economic prosperity would be the revenue brought by the crowds attending the Isthmian Games; but this is the factor singled out for special emphasis by Strabo (viii 6, 20) and there is no reason to reject his opinion. The atmosphere of Greek athletic festivals is above all enshrined in the victory-odes of Pindar, and here too one notices how persistently the poet stresses, not merely the noble lineage of his patrons, but their attachment to their home state, and the glory that their victory will bring to it. That the construction of temples should form a major element of state finance is understandable, but one might not guess that expenditure on sacrifices would become the substantial public concern that it did – that is, until one appreciates the general truth that religion was perhaps, apart from war, the biggest single factor in political and economic life. For the Classical period, it has been estimated that (to quote a leading authority) 'sacred administration absorbed . . . probably a fifth of the total internal revenue'. This statement, it is true, applies to Athens, which by the fifth century BC was notorious among Greek states for the frequency and costliness of its festivals; nor did all this expenditure have to be found by the state, since financial patronage was by then imposed on rich private individuals. In the Archaic period, the total will have been less but the state share of it probably greater. As for the material evidence, whichever test we prefer to apply – the incidence of stone-cut inscriptions (themselves laborious to execute) with religious content, the religious predominance in the content of stone sculpture (even more costly), the frequency of divine scenes in art – we shall find a resounding confirmation of a verdict suggested in the previous chapter: that the heart of an Archaic Greek state was in its sanctuaries.

In the formation of the city there is one element – some would say a central element – which has so far been mentioned only indirectly, and this is the law-code. It was indeed a fundamental need, sometimes consciously felt but more often, one suspects, unconsciously at first: as by Hesiod, who protests against the injustice of his rulers but can invoke no remedy and, except on a supernatural level, no sanction either. Law-courts and litigation can exist and flourish for centuries without a codified set of laws (Hesiod is again a clear witness of this stage), so long as the absolute power rests in the same hands inside the court-room as out of it: that is, in the hands of a monarch or narrow ruling-class. If a set of laws is published, and inscribed on stone, then the same conditions can continue to exist for a little while, but not for long: sooner rather than later, the general result of having an accessible writing system (cf. pp. 78–84) will show itself here too. The mere fact that the laws exist outside the prejudice of an individual magistrate is the first and greatest check on his power. But hard on its heels follows another effect: the public exhibition of the laws, where they can be pondered at leisure by anyone who can read, may be designed to compel deference, but will inevitably also invite criticism. It is now open to citizens to notice omissions, anachronisms, inconsistencies and absurdities; ultimately there will be pressure to improve the laws. Reform of the laws may then provoke a third step: reform of the bodies that administer them. In some cases, the court became no less than the full assembly of citizens. In Classical times, control of the law-courts was still an important and central issue for progressive politicians, and the strength of the opposition to such changes is an equally strong hint of its seriousness. Yet the first of these steps is still the greatest: the existence of a publicly accessible law-code – *any* law-code – is a direct, if long-term, threat to the survival of absolutism. Perhaps this fact was already understood in Archaic Greece, almost from the time of the first experiments in this line. This would explain why the names of the early law-givers were still revered centuries later, often to the complete exclusion of any memory of the content of their codes: which was as well, for posterity would have been shocked by their primitive brutality. But the instinct was sound: to bring a law-code into existence was a greater achievement than merely to improve one.

Our evidence for the earliest Greek law-codes is defective, but fundamentally consistent. Everything suggests that, during the seventh century BC, city after city followed the example of adopting or commissioning a code of laws. The incidence of borrowed doctrines and codes, and even of borrowed law-givers, shows how diffusive this process was (Crete was said to have been exceptionally generous here). But who was the first in the field? The literary tradition is strong in favour of the western colonies. Zaleukos of Lokroi, said by one authority to have compiled the very first written code, lived around 660; while of the travelling law-givers, few could rival the fame of his pupils Charondas of Katane and Androdamas of Rhegion. This may remind us that at a yet earlier stage, when the state itself was coming into being, there were grounds for thinking that the western colonies may have acted as pacemakers (pp. 40–2). It has been well observed that the colonists, some of them constrained in one way or another to emigrate, may have had a keener sense of injustice than their contemporaries in the homeland. Yet there is another strong tradition giving primacy to Crete, and here we can call on the surviving evidence. Early law-code inscriptions exist from *Plate 18* several Cretan cities, and that from Dreros is the earliest extant one of all (rather before 600 BC). Even before this, Archilochos of Paros (see below, pp. 169–73) had made a sarcastic reference to 'cretan lands'. The early presence of Phoenicians and other Levantine craftsmen in Crete has been invoked to suggest a potential source of inspiration, for Semitic law-codes had existed over a thousand years before this (here again, there is a reminiscence of an earlier suggestion about the formation of the state (see p. 32)). A third view, based on modern inference from ancient sources rather than any direct statement in them, gives priority to Sparta and the reforms later attributed to Lykourgos. One law-giver, though hardly a codifier, belongs not in the seventh century at all but in the later eighth: Philolaos of Corinth, an exiled aristocrat who devised a law on adoption for the Thebans.

To decide between the claimants is difficult, and really not very important, so swift was the diffusion. Wherever we look, the notion of the demand for order and codification springs up: at Corinth, where the tyrant Kypselos receives encouragement from the Delphic oracle to 'put Corinth straight'; at Sparta, in the contemporary references of the poets Terpander and Tyrtaios to constitutional advance in the years before 650; at Athens, in the proverbially severe code of Drakon (*c.* 621), which follows significantly closely after the abortive Kylon coup (pp. 93–4); at Mitylene, where the rise of Pittakos (p. 95) saw the publication of a code of laws – all but the last of these, and many others too, are to be dated well before 600. Like the rise of the Archaic tyrannies with which it partly overlapped in time, this was a seemingly irresistible movement which swept across the Greek states. That it was the stronger wave of the two is shown by the studied policy of many tyrants to leave the laws intact and express their power by other means; and it was also ultimately the more productive of progress in later generations.

In the last three chapters, the rise of the Greek state has been presented as a series of great steps forward, several of them unprecedented in history, and most of them in some way paradoxical in that they appear to have been contrary to the interests of the group that initiated them. There was first of all the establishment of the state itself, which can only be explained as the action of the leaders of the aristocratic groups in a locality. It is in the polis that this paradox appears in its most intense form; indeed it has proved too intense for one modern school of thought, which has questioned the reality of the aristocratic groupings of the preceding era. Denis Roussel, in his brilliant book *Tribu et Cité* which was referred to on p. 25, writes that 'Without doubt, the city would never have come to birth if such systems had been implanted everywhere in Greece' (although he allows of their operation in the area of an ethnos like Thessaly). But it is unsafe to rely on such 'laws' of historical necessity, when we have so much evidence from all phases of Archaic Greek history that the aristocrats were political innovators on a large scale. Nor were the Greek aristocrats less enterprising than their counterparts in areas like Phoenicia and Etruria; and small independent states grew up at the initiative of aristocracies there. But the fact was that neither they nor anyone else could predict the results during the next two hundred years of their experiment in Greece. They saw only the advantages to be gained from greater cohesion among prominent families; and some of them may have hoped, with reason and subsequent justification, to continue their former dominance on the higher level offered by the formation of the new state.

So, too, with the later processes of founding colonies, enacting military reform and accepting law-codes: it is easy to see, with hindsight, that these steps would ultimately circumscribe the power of the aristocracies, but much harder to reconstruct them as they appeared, in prospect, to the aristocrats of the seventh century BC. But if we are confident as to where the power to take action lay, we should not allow our necessary uncertainty as to the possible motives for that action to get the better of us; and everything suggests that these steps were taken on aristocratic initiative. The colonial founders, the early tacticians and the early law-givers will have been drawn from the aristocracy, just as inevitably as the early tyrants were. The crucial difference is that the rise of the tyrants, and their acts once in power, were the first moves *consciously* directed against the interests of the aristocracy as a whole. In the tyrants, the swing of the pendulum of power towards a wider community of the state gains new pace, and this is their ultimate importance.

There is also a more general argument, which may apply to all these more surprising developments. The pressures exerted by economic factors, about which we know particularly little in the earliest stages and which have played a minor part in the discussion so far, could be responsible for many otherwise improbable changes. It is time to turn and examine them.

# Economic Realities

Serious historians care for coins and weapons,
Not those re-iterations of one self-importance
By whom they date them, . . .

W. H. Auden, 'Makers of History'

In the past three chapters, our main problem in discussing the development of Archaic Greece has been lack of evidence, and especially the absence of any contemporary historical writing. That shortcoming will persist; but to it we must now add a new one. If we were able to summon a well-informed early Greek from the grave, he would readily understand our desire to find out about the political history of his culture, and could doubtless offer an answer to many of our questions. But as soon as we began to question him about economic developments, a gulf of incomprehension would open. Neither economic history nor economic theory was a field of study among the ancient Greeks (or indeed anyone else until the eighteenth century of our era). That does not preclude us from trying to write the economic history of Archaic Greece today; but it makes one pause to ask why the intellectual achievements of the Greeks did not extend further in this direction.

There are several established answers to this question, and between them they do convey much of the truth: that in the Greek scale of values, commercial and industrial activity were rated so low as to be thought unworthy of the expenditure of any intellectual effort; that the economic structure of Archaic Greece (though this is more controversial) was in any case simple to the point of being almost primitive, and so attracted little attention from contemporaries. Especially significant, now that linguistics has educated us into understanding more of the relationship between language and thought, is the fact that the Greek language was not then equipped with a proper economic vocabulary: *oikonomia* itself was a common Greek word, used in more than one sense; but not in one that corresponds to the meaning of the modern term which we have derived from it. Its original and most frequent sense was that of management of a household in all its respects, from budgeting to the treatment of slaves; indeed one ancient author, probably a disciple of Aristotle rather than the master himself, states in quite specific terms that *oikonomia* is to the household as politics is to the state (ps.– Aristotle, *Oikonomika* i, 1). When its use was extended, it was extended across this whole broad front to mean management of some larger unit up to and including the state – but again, in all its aspects. The term was thus applied, first to the province which we might mentally assign to Mrs Beeton, later to that covered by Machiavelli, without at any time specifying that of Adam Smith.

None of this prevented individual Greeks from recognizing specifically economic problems or, on occasion, applying economic remedies; what it did was to discourage any kind of economic analysis, and practically to exclude the growth of economic theory even in the Classical period (to which the linguistic evidence mentioned above belongs), let alone the Archaic period. The truth seems to be that all Greeks regarded what we call economic activity as an inseparable part of a larger whole, the operation of a community big or small; just as economic history was merged into political history. Few economic decisions were consciously taken by Greek states; most economic change came about as the incidental result of political decisions or, even more indirectly, as the result of a general shift in moral values. Yet it is obvious to us today that social and political changes, as radical as those which came to pass in Archaic Greece, will have created acute economic problems, many of them foreign to all previous experience. It also happens that a substantial proportion of the evidence that has come down to us has a potential bearing on economic problems. This is true of many of the classes of material objects studied by archaeologists: of coins, almost by definition; of a few official inscriptions recorded on stone and of a number of unofficial ones preserved on other materials; and even of a surprising proportion of the poetic literature of the period (one thinks especially of the surviving works of Hesiod and Solon). But, having said this, one must at once add that this evidence is not *only* economic in implication: the point about the Greek view of economics cuts both ways. If the Greeks did not divide economic activity from social and political activities, then neither can we study it in isolation from these.

So there is not necessarily a conflict here; only a gulf. Whether the ancient Greeks could not see that the state was in part an economic enterprise, creating effects which were not controllable by purely political instruments, or whether they saw it but did not think it worth recording their observations, the result is initially the same: we must try to investigate those effects without their help. The danger comes when we start to make inferences from those effects, back to the nature of their economic structures and even to hypotheses as to their economic policies. On the latter question, I have already implied my view, which is today almost an orthodox one: that the Greek states, especially in the Archaic period, did not really *have* economic policies, in the sense of allocating the state's resources, and so did not directly bring about the effects which we can see in the evidence by any kind of communal design. The most that they are likely to have done is to realize that these would be among the results of their social or political policies; and even that, one suspects, only rarely. By the Classical period, for example, there are examples of Greek states adopting, as a policy, the importation of grain from overseas. How such a policy would be implemented in the Archaic period is a difficult question; the important thing at this stage is to realize that, even when achieved, it carried no implication whatever of any corresponding state direction of exports. The grain would have to be paid for by the individual private carrier, but it was not found necessary for the state to control or facilitate the means of payment and there was a considerable choice of regions – the Black Sea littoral, Egypt, Sicily – where surplus grain was apparently freely available. In any case, in the Archaic period there were very few places where the ratio of population (and particularly urban population) to arable land was high enough to necessitate even such rudimentary economic planning.

Economic structures are another matter. It is easy to say that they too were bound up with social and political structures; but we seldom have a sufficiently detailed knowledge of the latter to make this an enlightening statement. Our written historical sources, concerned above all with political history, can pass on traditional generalizations about Boiotian agriculture or Arkadian pastoralism; but our knowledge of populations and land-holdings would have to be greatly increased before we could begin to reconstruct the economic development of these areas. Even for Athens, it is only in the Classical period that we can build up a tentative picture of the state's economy from a combination of written references, inscriptions and environmental studies.

There is thus a natural tendency to turn, with some degree of expectancy ranging from optimism to sheer desperation, to the archaeological evidence as an alternative source of knowledge which has a considerable bearing on economic life and which differs from our documentary evidence in being almost infinitely extendable. But here there are fresh pitfalls: attempts at economic reconstruction have been beset, above all, by a special form of 'positivist fallacy', which assumes that the importance of a class of evidence for antiquity stands in some relation to the quantity in which it survives to be studied today. The obvious example is painted pottery, by far the richest category of ancient artefact from which economic inferences have been drawn. When fragmentary material is taken into account, the quantity of Greek painted pottery retrieved by excavation and now more or less available in museum showcases, storerooms and basements, or still under scrutiny by its excavators, or even thrown away and re-buried by exponents of an earlier archaeological ethic, must be greater than most non-archaeologists would imagine in their wildest fantasies. Also, the quantity of Greek painted pottery that has survived is certainly large enough to form a valid statistical sample of the total original production: at least in one class of vessel, the Panathenaic amphora, there are grounds for thinking that it represents rather more than one five-hundredth (equivalent to 70,000 voters in an opinion-poll in modern Britain). Furthermore, Greek pottery-fabrics have been studied to the point where their geographical provenances are better established than those of any other common kind of uninscribed artefact, and their chronology even better than that of inscriptions and coins. Pottery was in antiquity a material of exceptionally wide use, extending over a range that would have been covered jointly in more recent times by fine porcelain, glass, wood, basketry and leather, and comparable with that of the stouter forms of plastics in our own days. Potentially, therefore, the study of painted pottery would be expected to release a flood of basic information on economic and other aspects of ancient life.

But, the more one thinks about it, the more objections spring to mind. In the first place, painted pottery plays a smaller part in the broad economic activities – that is, the exchange of the commodities contained in it – than does unpainted pottery, which has been immeasurably less well studied and is, in its nature, less susceptible to identification from photographs or descriptions. The production of fine pottery was, by comparison, almost a luxury industry, and trade in it had little connection with the essentials of life. Again, there is some evidence that indirect trade in fine pottery, whereby the carriers (who would absorb much of the profit) belonged neither to the state which produced the ware in question nor that to which it was exported, was quite common. Next, much painted pottery consists of shapes like cups, bowls and jugs, which cannot be used for the transport of commodities, but can only be transported for themselves. Here too it must be remarked that a fine pottery industry simply did not exist in the majority of Greek states; and in those where it did, it seems to have been a very minor component of the economy. In Athens in the fifth century BC, when rival industries elsewhere had been virtually eliminated and Athenian production was at its peak, it is doubtful whether the whole industry employed more than 500 people; productivity must therefore have been extremely high, but this was hardly a 'commanding height' of the Athenian economy. The comparison with metalwork is a chastening one: here the surviving material is far sparser, and it is much harder to give either a date or a geographical provenance to it; yet the economic significance of the industry, both for the fundamental importance of its applications and for the intrinsic costliness and relative scarcity of the raw materials, must have been vastly greater than that of pottery-production. The non-specialist reader of works on ancient Greece should therefore look somewhat warily at the economic conclusions he is often asked to accept, and in particular ask himself how far they depend on the evidence of painted pottery alone. 'Trade leagues' and 'flourishing mercantile cities' appear less often in the literature nowadays than they once did, but caution is still sometimes needed.

It is in fact the increasing sophistication achieved by pottery-studies which has made possible the revision of some views which had been based on earlier interpretations of the same kind of evidence; the new insights have sometimes been quite unexpected. Take, for instance, the location of centres of production. By the 'thirties of this century, it was believed that most of the major problems of determining geographical provenance had been solved, though a few wares remained 'homeless'. The identification of the main fabrics by visual methods was almost universally accepted and it did not encourage belief in multiple centres of production for one and the same fabric. Western colonies, for example, were normally thought to have imported virtually all their fine ware. Then, in the early 1950s, the excavators found a sixth-century potter's kiln at Megara Hyblaia in Sicily, which prompted reflection; by 1964 they were able, in their publication, to distinguish by visual methods a substantial component of the painted pottery as locally made, even if in overall proportions it remained fairly small. By a different line of reason-

15 Bronze panoply from Argos, *c.* 720 BC

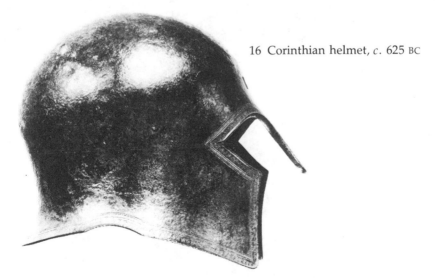

16 Corinthian helmet, *c.* 625 BC

17 View of Brauron sanctuary

18  Law code inscription from Dreros

19  Attic black
figure cup with
agricultural scenes,
*c.* 525 BC

20 Bronze lion dedicated by Eumnastos, from Samos, *c.* 550 BC

21 Early coins from Aigina (left) and Miletos (right), *c.* 550 and *c.* 575 BC

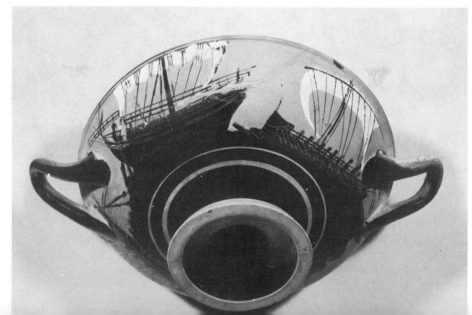

23 Athena from Archaic pediment, Athens, Akropolis, *c*. 525 BC

22 (Left) Attic black figure cup with merchantman and galley, *c*. 520 BC

24 View of the diolkos at the Isthmus of Corinth

25 View of Eupalinos' tunnel, Samos

26 Late Archaic coin (Syrakuse)

27 Attic red figure amphora with arming of Hektor, *c.* 510 BC

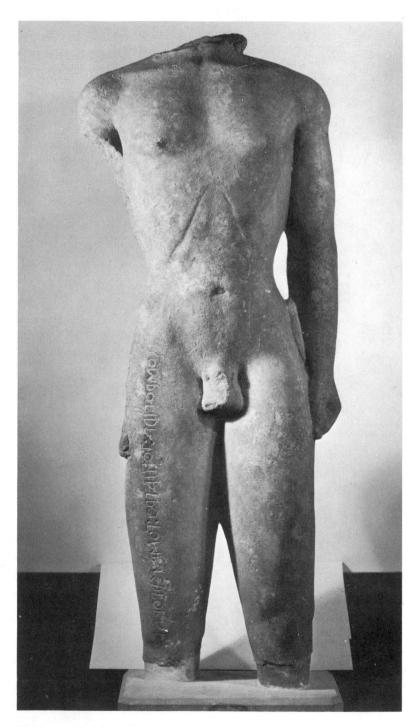

28 Torso of statue of doctor from Megara Hyblaia, *c.* 550 BC

ing, similar conclusions have been reached for Marseilles and other Phokaian colonies founded in southern France and eastern Spain. Here, a large element of the early pottery of the colonies consisted of the unpainted 'Aeolic grey bucchero'; this was assumed to have been brought initially, and imported subsequently, from the mother-city of Phokaia in Asia Minor, which lay within an area where pottery of this general type had long been characteristic. But now the total *absence* of this ware from contemporary levels at another Phokaian colony, Elea in Italy, has led to reconsideration: is it possible that much of the ware found in France and Spain was made locally after all? More startling still have been the results of applying the technique of trace element analysis at an eastern site, Istria in Roumania, a colony of Miletos. For here a new and in many ways more objective method was applied to material which could hardly be distinguished, by any visual test, from the imported Ionian wares from Miletos and her neighbours; and this time the finding is that a very substantial proportion of the painted pottery was probably locally made. The implications are becoming steadily wider; the more local centres of production emerge, the less the part played by long-distance trade.

When we take the evidence as a whole, from written sources, from inscriptions and from archaeological evidence of all kinds and all contexts, the same conclusion is insistently forced upon us: that the economic life of Archaic Greece was dominated by a very few activities. First place among these activities must go not to commerce but to agriculture. Its importance, impossible to quantify accurately, nevertheless becomes obvious almost by elimination: as soon as we consider the small scale and relative lateness of urbanization in early Greece and contrast it with the number and spread of small settlements, as soon as we compare the country's poverty in minerals with its modest sufficiency (often underrated in modern studies) of viable farming-land, then it becomes difficult to see this as other than an agrarian society. Centuries later, urban intellectuals still hankered after these conditions and looked around the obscurer states of Greece for instances of their survival: the agrarian type of democracy, Aristotle held, was the oldest and the best (*Politics* 1318 b 6–9).

Next in significance, perhaps, is warfare, as much an economic activity in Archaic Greece as it was a political one. It was through the medium of war that the individual expressed his economic status as well as his political loyalty, thanks to the form of military organization that the Greeks adopted (pp. 100–7). More practically, however, warfare was seen as an instrument which could be applied directly to the essential elements of economic life, food, wealth and labour. Aristotle describes it, with cold-blooded simplicity, as 'a way of acquiring property' (*Politics* 1256 b 23). It was by warfare that Greek states increased their agricultural potential and threatened the livelihood of their neighbours, through the acquisition or devastation of the farming-land; it was wholly appropriate that Archaic Greek battles should be fought by tactical methods operable only on a fairly level plain, and between armies composed of farmers. But there was also the element of movable property: successful armies could expect to acquire booty and, to judge from the later evidence of the Classical period, they did so on a surprising scale. We hear of numerous cases where, even after the introduction of state pay, whole armies maintained themselves more from booty than from official sources. The proportion of the booty which found its way back to the homeland was often sufficient to have significant economic effect there. Some of it (often the traditional tithe) ended up in the sanctuaries, in the form of private or state dedications; and here at last we can pick up its trail by means of the contemporary archaeological evidence.

Only a small proportion of the innumerable dedications in Archaic sanctuaries was inscribed, and some of it has nothing to do with war; but the evidence of these surviving pieces opens up a wide vision of military and diplomatic activities, and it is reasonable to extend our inferences to the great majority of uninscribed dedications, which may also convey less explicit information of their own through their provenance, use, condition or value. At an exceptionally rich site like Olympia, we learn of the wide geographical area from which dedications were attracted, from the colonies in Italy to fairly remote mainland sites like Tanagra in Boiotia, embracing non-Greek states (notably the Etruscan cities) and including peoples such as the Anaitoi, Akroreioi or Serdaioi, so obscure that we are uncertain of their identity and location.

The sheer numbers of these dedications give them a significance in their own right, quite apart from the activities that they represent. Of course we cannot estimate accurately the original quantities of objects dedicated: to take the multiplier suggested for the Panathenaic amphorae (above, p. 127) and apply it to the bronzes recovered at Olympia (p. 105) would give startling results. Few would countenance the idea of 250,000 tripod-cauldrons dedicated at Olympia alone in rather more than a century, or of 100,000-odd helmets in the two hundred years between 700 and 500 BC; and it would be easy to think of arguments against such a calculation. Yet bronze in general does not have a high survival-rate; and when we read in Herodotus (viii 27, 4) that on a single occasion in the late Archaic period, the Phokians dedicated as many as 2000 captured shields at Delphi, then we may fairly believe that, over the centuries, the major inter-state sanctuaries amassed vast quantities of war-booty. All of this serves to emphasize that the third great field of economic activity was simply religious cult itself. We have already seen some illustrations of this fact (p. 118); and we may also take into account the wide range of religious activity which would leave little if any archaeological trace: communal meals, festivals, dedications of 'first-fruits', dancing, processions, initiations – some of them quite expensive events which would have to be financed by the state or some smaller body.

Each of these main activities – agriculture, warfare and religion – thus occupied a much more important position in Archaic Greece than it does in a modern developed economy, which can only mean that, correspondingly, commerce and industry were assigned a lesser role. We must also pay heed to a further important argument: that out of those who *were* occupied full-time in industry and commerce a high proportion in any case appears to have consisted of slaves, or non-citizens of other categories like the metics of Attica. The implications of this fact are mainly political and social, whereas economic processes affected the population of the state as a whole; but in as much as it was the interests of the citizen-body (or some part of it) which were likely to play the main part in determining the state's decisions it was so much the less probable that consideration would be given to commercial-based arguments in reaching those decisions. So it is unrealistic to make too much of Archaic Greek commerce. In passing, too, we may note another fact about the three other spheres of activity just discussed: with the first two of them, agriculture and warfare, pottery has almost nothing to do, and it plays a very subordinate role in the third. Pots do, of course, occur as religious dedications, and they also featured in some festivals and as prizes in games; but at the major sanctuaries they are uncommon compared with the surviving bronzes, even though their value is *pro rata* so much less. Pottery studies, however thorough, must therefore inevitably reflect only a partial picture of Greek economic activities.

We should, finally, remind ourselves that even exchanges of goods, which we naturally identify today with the exercise of commerce, did not necessarily have that character in antiquity. Even if we leave out the whole category of gifts to sanctuaries as being essentially one-sided in material terms, there was a further field of transaction in Archaic Greece which could hardly be called commercial: this was the whole network of gift-exchange, guest-friendship and hospitality. In the Homeric epics, this network is so prevalent that it has reasonably been called the life-blood of Homeric society. It has also been argued that such a society must have existed at a comparatively remote epoch of Greek history, some time earlier even than Homer's own day. Yet this element in it, the phenomenon of gift-exchange and hospitality, particularly with foreigners, remained entirely familiar in the Greek world long after Homer. We can find only occasional direct references to the practice, as contrasted with their frequency in Homer, but that is mainly because the subject-matter of Greek literature is no longer that of the epic narrative with its capacious appetite for detail. But when Herodotus, for example, turns to the actions of kings or tyrants, it emerges as quite an important element in their foreign policies. Amasis, Pharaoh of Egypt, sends gifts not only to Greek sanctuaries but to the Spartan state; while in the reverse direction, the same Spartans – and, somewhat earlier, Periander of Corinth – are found sending presents to the kings of Lydia (Herodotus iii 48, 2; i 70, 1). Nor did these activities take place only on the level of 'affairs of state'; a surviving fragment of Solon (fr. 13) reckons as an essential condition of happiness for the man of means the possession of 'a friend in foreign parts', and he legislated about gifts of property. Even at the close of the Archaic period, the odes of Pindar, which again belong to the world of the well-to-do, are pervaded by the same spirit. How far down the social scale such transactions extended, and what proportion of all exchanges of goods they represented, are harder questions. But their role may have been larger than one would expect. To take just one instance, the first Herodotus passage mentioned above was concerned with an episode of Spartan military intervention in the island of Samos in the 520s. It has been remarked in this connection that an unexpectedly large quantity of Spartan painted pottery (that is, in relation to its thin distribution elsewhere) has turned up in the sanctuary of Hera on Samos, from approximately this period. Such humble dedications are not likely to represent official gifts from state representatives, so what was the process which brought them to a Samian sanctuary? It is easy to assume that the initial stage of their journey was a commercial one, but there are a number of other possibilities. They could have been brought by Spartan soldiers or – perhaps more likely since the Spartan military presence was a fleeting one – by individual Spartans on peaceful errands, as was evidently the case with a fine bronze lion offered to the goddess by the Spartiate Eumnastos on some occasion a little   *Plate 20* earlier than this; equally, they might have been taken back home by the Samian exiles who had called at Sparta to seek her military help. In most other cases where Greek pottery has 'travelled', we do not have even this glimpse of the context in which such a process took place, but this may serve as a warning against attributing it, without argument, to the operation of commerce.

A similar warning may be needed with early coinage, since its economic application, though obviously in one sense real enough, is hardly that which modern analogy, or even the analogy of the Classical period, would lead one to suppose. Recent numismatic studies have produced broad agreement on three conclusions, each of them negative in its implications for the commercial use of coins. First, the dates of the earliest Greek coin-issues have had to be lowered by a considerable margin from the dates which were widely accepted when many studies of early Greek economic history were written. It now seems doubtful whether the very beginning of the development, when *Plate 21* the cities of Greek Asia Minor adopted from the Lydians the *(right)* idea first of standardizing the weight of small nuggets of precious metal and then of stamping them with designs, occurred before about 600 BC. For the preceding stage, a recent find at Gordion in the interior has yielded what seems to be the earliest known group of Lydian coins; they are dated to the years *c.*625–610, and would thus belong in part to the reign of king Sadyattes. For the ensuing stage, it now appears most likely that *Plate 21* Aigina – agreed to be the first state in Greece proper to issue a *(left)* silver coinage – did so only after 575. Any possibility of connecting a reform of coinage with historical figures such as Pheidon and Solon seems therefore to be excluded on chronological grounds.

Secondly, there is the question of the *value* of the earliest coin-issues. The first specimens in Asia Minor were of electrum, an extremely costly alloy at any period and one which, even in very small denominations, gave values too high to be useful in retail trade. Only later were they joined by silver issues, and bronze came in generations later still. In any case, the incidence of small denominations in the early finds is very low; some states seem to have had no regular supply of anything smaller than a drachma (a modest day's wage for an artisan). Thirdly, Archaic Greek coin-issues, with very few exceptions, show a tendency not to travel far beyond the vicinity of the state where

they were minted. Very late in the Archaic period, a few silver-
producing areas (notably Athens and the Greek colonies on the
coasts of Macedonia and Thrace) seem to have hit on the idea of
using their coinage for overseas trade, and their high-
denomination silver coins are found dispersed over a wide area.
But this serves only to draw attention to the absence of this practice elsewhere and earlier. Even the view that Archaic coinage
was intended for *internal* trade is open to the second objection
mentioned above.

Greek coins, in nearly all ascertainable cases, were minted by
governments and heads of state, and there is no reason to doubt
that this was true of the first issues. From what has already been
said, it will be clear that a commercial motive for the early issues
is unlikely in these circumstances. There has been no shortage of
suggestions for alternative uses: from the state's point of view,
income in coin might be expected from fines, harbour dues,
leases and taxes; while likely heads of expenditure would be
public works, the payment of mercenaries, the retention of
services of specialists and the distribution of surpluses among
citizens. Some of these practices are attested by more or less contemporary evidence: the first-named, for instance, on a fragmentary legal inscription from Eretria which belongs as early as
c.550–525, and which prescribes that penalties be paid 'in legal
tender'. Distributions among the citizen population may appear
unexpectedly in the list, but that this too was an established
practice, in some form, is shown by two passages in Herodotus,
one referring to Siphnos in the years before 525 (iii 57, 2) and the
other to Athens in 483 (vii 144, 1).

In Archaic Greece, all these activities had in common the official involvement of the state; and the prime function of early
coinage was the political one of emphasizing the authority, or
merely the independence, of the body that issued it. Economic
functions were secondary and even incidental to this political
one; least of all did the invention of coinage transform the
Archaic world into a 'monetary economy'. Indeed, in many
respects it merely streamlined the processes which were already
in operation with the use of pre-coinage 'currencies', more cum-

bersome and susceptible of variation, which had for centuries existed in Greece. Just as in ancient China, which adopted coinage a few centuries later, we hear of 'knife money' and 'spade money' in the preceding era, so in Greece finds of unmarked gold, silver and electrum 'dumps' occur, perhaps as early as 800 BC in Crete; while in written sources we read of oxen, tripods and above all iron spits (*obeloi*) as pre-monetary units. Archaeological evidence from the late eighth and seventh centuries has confirmed the significance of the *obeloi*, for they occur both in graves and as sanctuary-dedications. Most revealing of all is the fact that, centuries after the first coins were struck and not only in the consciously conservative society of Sparta, these primitive 'currencies' still enjoyed a fairly wide circulation. It is clear, therefore, that as sources of information for economic history neither the adoption nor the early development of Greek coinage fills quite the expected role; only further work can reveal what their precise significance was.

The object of these remarks is not to eliminate trade and industry from the economy of early Greece, but to keep them in proportion. Of course there was a commercial element, in this as in many earlier and more primitive cultures. What is strikingly absent from Archaic Greece is any kind of widespread professionalism or concentration in trade. There are many illustrations of this: other civilizations had their commercial class, often established in a commercial quarter of a city, or even comprising the main population of a trading settlement – what the Greeks called an *emporion*. But in Greece we have to look hard to find any of these elements; and indeed we may say that the first of them, a commercially-based social class, shows no sign of having existed. It has also been noted that real trading-posts were few, remote from the Greek homeland and usually inhabited at least in part by non-Greeks. In eastern Spain and on the Sea of Azov, there were places actually named 'Emporion', but they were not founded until the second half of the Archaic period. Naukratis in Egypt was somewhat earlier, and the settlement at Al Mina on the Syrian coast very much earlier, having been frequented by Greeks since about 800 BC. It may also be recalled that the foundation of the early Greek settlement at Pithekoussai on Ischia seems to have had an element of commercial motivation, quite exceptional for a colony (pp. 40–1). The Greeks also traded with ports which were entirely in foreign hands, and often called them *emporia* too. This is implied in a rather mysterious passage in Herodotus (vii 158, 2): Gelon, tyrant of Syracuse, makes a speech, set in 481 BC, to a group of envoys from the leading states of mainland Greece, whom he castigates for their failure to support him in an otherwise virtually unknown earlier war against Carthage – a war whose partial aim had been 'to liberate the *emporia*, from which you have derived great profits and benefits'. We do not know where these lay – in western Sicily, or more probably in North Africa – but the profitability of the *emporia* does not seem to have been impaired by their being in foreign and potentially hostile possession.

Most of the Greeks living in such places were probably occupied full-time with commerce. In this, they were hardly typical of their age, but their counterparts at home, though harder to detect, must have existed. The notion that all trade within the Greek world was conducted by non-citizens and foreigners is exaggerated. What is much more persuasive is a recent suggestion that it was often carried on by men who were agents or dependents of the ship-owners and exporters, rather than being self-employed merchants. This finds support of a kind in the evidence of the types of ships used. The written sources and the illustrations alike suggest that, down to the later sixth century *Plate 22* BC, Greek and even Phoenician maritime trade was mainly carried on in the same oared longships which were used for naval warfare. This implies rather more than that trading-vessels had to be able to defend themselves; it shows an emphatic weighting of priorities, in which sea-going and cargo-carrying capacity and economy of manpower were largely sacrificed to speed and battle-worthiness; Homer himself (*Odyssey* ix, 127–9) refers to 'ships which would serve all purposes, travelling to the cities of men, as so often men cross the sea to visit one another'. One may reasonably speculate that other motives besides commerce, and other kinds of men than professional merchants, were involved in these voyages. Only in the late sixth century do we begin to see pictures on Greek vases of large, sail-driven and purpose-built merchantmen; by the very end of the Archaic period, it is no longer so surprising to find Gelon (see above, p. 137) using the incentive of the profitability of sea-trade to encourage the Greeks of the homeland to participate in a war against Carthage.

By this time there were certainly independent ship-masters, and a few of them became famous for the fortunes that they made. The greatest name known to Herodotus was Sostratos of Aigina (iv 152, 4), a figure who has suddenly come to life in the past few years with the discovery of an inscribed stone *cippus* set up by him at Gravisca on the Etruscan coast as a dedication to Apollo, and with the persuasive suggestion that a series of trade-marks scratched on fine Attic black-figured pottery of c.530–510 BC are abbreviations of his name, implying that this was one of the commodities in which he was trading. His patronymic hints that he may have been an aristocrat; and some lines ascribed to Theognis of Megara (1165–6) certainly raise the possibility of aristocrats embarking on such ventures at this period. Sostratos's nearest rival in good fortune was Kolaios of Samos, whom Herodotus (rightly, it seems) places more than a century earlier, in the context of a curious episode on the coast of Cyrenaica (iv 152, 1); Kolaios, also described as a ship-master, is on his way to Egypt carrying a cargo of unspecified nature (though some archaeological evidence suggests that it may have included ivories), and with enough spare food to supply a guide from Crete, marooned on an off-shore island, for a whole year. At this date, there seems to have been no permanent Greek settlement in Egypt, although mercenaries had already found employment there. Kolaios ended up on the Spanish coast beyond Gibraltar, where his luck turned good and he found a market (Herodotus again uses the word *emporion*) hungry for his wares. The resultant profits were evidently shared by the whole company of the ship, who made a joint dedication at Samos which Herodotus appears to have seen with his own eyes. There is room for speculation as to what their original aims had been;

they hardly look like that of short-term commerce, what with the initial destination in Egypt (where there are actually no signs of Greek imports so early), the ample provisioning and the collective nature of the enterprise.

Tackling the question from the opposite end, we may take two heavy commodities which, we may be absolutely certain, were transported over considerable distances in the Archaic Greek world: metal ores of various kinds, and marble. The evidence in both cases is mainly archaeological, apart from the elementary fact that neither substance is universally distributed geologically: they run, in descending order of frequency in Greek lands, from the relatively plentiful but unevenly distributed iron ore, through marble, copper and silver, to the rare gold and the non-existent tin. The mere presence of artefacts in all these materials, over virtually the whole area settled by Greeks, thus proves that there was an extensive network of distribution, which in some cases though not all could be described as trade. Small objects in precious metals, for example, may very often have changed hands in the form of gifts. But these materials are alike in requiring the medium of special skills and equipment before they reach the final form in which they are attested for us by the evidence.

As far as base metals are concerned, there are theoretically at least three stages of transportation involved: from the point of extraction to the smelting location, from there to the craftsman's workshop, and from him to the ultimate owner, with or without the intervention of a retailer or distributor. In fact, however, we have grounds for thinking that in Archaic Greece the second stage was commonly eliminated: evidence for the iron-foundry and the blacksmith's forge lying side by side was found in two early sites on islands, Pithekoussai on Ischia and Motya off the western end of Sicily. In both instances the ore must have been brought from some distance away – in the case of Ischia, we know that it was from the mines of Elba nearly 250 miles to the north-west – and worked locally, probably for local customers. Even at so remote and inaccessible a site as the sanctuary of Apollo at Bassai, 3,500 feet up in the hills of Arkadia, traces of iron-smelting in the Archaic period were found on the spot: here, the destination of the objects must have been as offerings in the temple a few yards away. Such a procedure, if widely followed, would have reduced the element of profitable trafficking to a minimum: an occasional voyage by the ore-shipper might be all that was involved, with the diffusion of the finished metal objects, often over very wide distances, being accomplished *after* they entered the final owner's possession. Even the most remarkable cases of this last phenomenon would often fit this kind of explanation better than one of long-distance sea-trading; some of them are exceptional in the remoteness of the find-spot: the early seventh-century Greek helmet found in the River Jerez in south-western Spain, the gigantic bronze krater in a princess' tomb at Vix in Burgundy, the gold harness-plate in the shape of a fish from a Scythian tomb near Vettersfelde in northern Germany. Others are notable more for the proportion of extraneous (but still Greek) finds among the total of objects found: the early Cretan bronzes at Delphi, the Athenian tripod-cauldrons and the armour-dedications from the Italian colonies at Olympia, the Ionian fibulae at Perachora. At the same time, there are other groups of finds, such as the 132 Egyptian bronzes at the Heraion on Samos, which do admit of an explanation at least partly commercial, since a major influx of Egyptian visitors to Samos is unlikely and we know that Samians were commercially active in Egypt in the sixth century. It will be noted that the last four are all sanctuary-sites; and behind all studies of Greek metalwork the old theme of religion (together with war) looms insistently.

The traffic in marble has a rather different pattern, but it shares this last feature with metalwork: any material primarily employed for monumental sculpture and architecture, as marble was, must inevitably gravitate towards the major sanctuaries before anywhere else. A degree of scepticism about the scientific basis for determining the origin of the various Aegean marbles is no doubt proper, but need not impede us here; for the plain fact is that several regions of Greece contain no deposits of marble (even more have none of *white* marble), and some of the major sanctuaries lie within these regions. The early statues and, beginning in the later sixth century, the marble-built treasuries and temples at these places had therefore to be made from material brought over considerable distances. Periklean Athens was fortunate in having to transport the huge quantities of marble for the new Akropolis buildings no further than the 18-odd kilometres from the Mount Pentelikos quarries.

It is thanks to inscriptions and historical sources that, in this last case, we can state quite categorically that such *was* the source of the Akropolis marble. The same kind of evidence throws light on one or two occasions in the Archaic period as well. At Delphi, so Herodotus tells us (v 62, 3), the exiled Athenian family of the Alkmaionidai won the favour of the oracle by paying for a new marble-fronted temple of Apollo, with much sculpture, to be built in the years between 513 and 510 BC. The marble, he says was brought from Paros. This is an early attested example of a laborious feat of transport, over a route that probably included three land-portages and two seapassages, of many tons of heavy materials. Even without such evidence from explicit literary sources, we may nevertheless safely infer the execution of similar projects on a smaller scale well before this. The construction of the treasuries of Knidos and of Siphnos, also at Delphi and also of marble, took place in about 560–550 and 525 BC respectively. Both buildings show a mixture of stones, but the main component in each case is a marble closely allied to that of the Apollo temple and reasonably classed as Parian, the more so because, in the later case, Herodotus tells us that the people of Siphnos had their meeting-place and town-hall fitted out with Parian marble at about the same period (iii 57, 4).

All over the Greek world, Archaic marble statues have been *Plate 28* found which do not, however, carry comparable written evidence for the source of the stone of which they are carved. What they do offer nevertheless is some very valuable epigraphic evidence on another question: the origins of the artists who carved them. There is enough of this to make it likely that the common practice of Archaic marble-sculptors was to travel to the places where they could find commissions for work. This must have been especially true of the craftsmen from the Cycladic islands, which were mostly too small to offer a continuous livelihood, but which were rich sources both of artistic talent and of fine marble. It is impossible to prove that, in every case, the two quite literally went together, sculptor and raw material, rather than the sculptor receiving the commission at home and exporting the finished product; but for the Archaic period, most considerations favour this conclusion. We have a body of written testimony to the effect that sculptors often travelled far from home: Cretans in Tegea, Sikyon, the Argolid and even Aitolia; an Aiginetan in Argos and Samos; Corinthian exiles in Etruria; an Ionian from Magnesia at Sparta; Spartans at Olympia; an Athenian in Ionia; a Sikyonian in Miletos. In all these cases, either we are told in so many words that the artist travelled to carry out the commission, or the size and elaboration were such as to make execution on the spot essential. The sources of information are often relatively late and not entirely reliable; nevertheless, inscriptions and other evidence give us much general support, and in one or two cases more than that. There is, for example, an unfinished female statue, in imported Greek (probably Parian) marble, at Taranto in Italy, which seems at any rate not to be of local workmanship. If the artist did not go to the site himself, there was the risk of damage to a fully finished statue in transit (many Archaic statues were carved from a single block, and some were more than life-sized); there was also the problem of ascertaining the client's desires, and securing his approval of the final product. In the rather better-documented case of Archaic temple-builders, the incidence of non-native architects speaks for itself as to the readiness of craftsmen to travel.

It looks, therefore, as if it was the general practice of the Archaic marble-sculptor to travel to the site of his commission. Sometimes, perhaps, he would be accompanied by a marble block, chosen by himself, from which the statue was to be worked, or else by an already roughed-out version of the statue. Some interesting traces of this latter practice have been found in or near ancient quarries: three statues, at least two of them of Archaic date, are still to be seen around the quarry-sites on Naxos, and another was found close to one of the Mount Pentelikos quarries. The remarkable thing about them is the degree to which they have been worked: some have been carved to within about an inch of their final surface. What does this mean? Clearly, either that the sculptor had visited the quarry to give detailed instructions to the mason, or else that sculptor and mason were the same man; so the sculptor was often closely involved at one end of the operation. But since even a short journey would be dangerous to a fully-finished statue of stone, he must often have had to be present at the other end too, to bring the work to completion. For the execution of a work in imported marble, the likeliest picture that emerges is of the journey from quarry to final site, which might involve a sea-passage hundreds of miles long, being made by the artist and the material in company. The necessary transactions would be, first a payment by the sculptor to the quarry-owner (who might in some cases be the state); then a further payment to the shipper, for passage and freight; and finally the artist's fee, which would have exceeded the sum of the first two, *plus* perhaps a year's keep for the artist while he did the carving. Marble must have been one of the very heaviest commodities which Archaic ships were asked to transport over long distances; yet in all of this, at least for the Archaic period, nothing emerges that could be called precisely a 'marble trade'.

So two kinds of 'trade' or 'commerce', when examined more closely, have shown themselves to be in reality no such thing. Rather, they speak for a range of other operations, some purely social, some yet again religious or warlike, and only seldom motivated by considerations of profit. It is time to consider the economic implications for Archaic society. What we have discovered so far suggests that, for this society, such an eventuality as a falling-off in trade would be very much less significant than, say, a run of poor harvests; that a successful war might have a deeper economic impact than the growth of a new industry; that the amassing of great wealth by a sanctuary could happen more

easily than a rise of the general standard of living within a state.
If we look for signs of economic tension, we are accordingly
more likely to find them in other than purely commercial
spheres. The causes of inter-state wars provide an illustration of
these tensions in extreme form: of the three earliest for which we
have a clear explanation in ancient sources, the Spartan conquest of Messenia and the Lelantine War in Euboia were
brought about by the desire of one or more states to extend their
agricultural land, while the 'First Sacred War' was fought, a century later than the other two (c. 595–586), for the control of one of
the great sanctuaries, Delphi. All three were big enough to draw
a number of states, not all of them adjacent geographically, into
the fighting. So we may infer similar causes for other, more obscure early conflicts: a sea-battle between Corinth and her colony,
Corcyra, dated to c. 664 BC by Thucydides (i 13, 4), is more likely
to have been fought for political reasons than for control of the
western trade-routes, especially as somewhat later we find
Corinth trying, successfully, to seize political control of Corcyra;
a battle between Argos and Sparta at Hysiai in 669 BC is suspiciously close in time to an episode of interference, plausibly connected with Pheidon of Argos, in the Olympic festival of 668.

To turn from greater conflicts to lesser and more local tensions, we should be wise to begin with the best-documented
economic crisis of Archaic Greece, the one which faced Solon of
Athens in 594. We have seen that his solution to it was in part
political and only partly economic (p. 94): in this at least he was
characteristic of his age. But where had the crisis arisen? Predictably, in the agricultural sphere. It was the concentration of land-
ownership in the hands of an unacceptably small minority and
the dispossession, debt-bondage or even enslavement of many
smallholders which had brought Athens to the brink of civil war.
We are also told that Solon's system of constitutional class-
divisions, which henceforth decided eligibility for offices of various kinds, was based on a criterion which was not merely
economic but specifically agricultural: namely the yield of a citizen's land-holding in terms of produce. It is true that this is not
one of the Solonian measures which is attested by the surviving

fragments of his own poetry; other legislation which is mentioned only in much later sources includes one episode – a reform of coins, weights and measures – which cannot be regarded as entirely historical, for reasons of chronology (above, p. 134), and other episodes – such as those giving encouragement to industrial crafts, and forbidding all agricultural exports but olive oil – which are to be treated with a little scepticism. But the distinction of land-based classes still survived in Aristotle's day, and seems then to have been generally credited to Solon; we have no serious reason to reject it, and we have Solon's own word for his having supported the policy of conquering the off-shore island of Salamis, which looks like an act of pure land-acquisition.

Solon the agricultural reformer, it is fair to conclude, is better attested in the primary evidence than is Solon the 'industrial revolutionary'. Even Plutarch, our main source for the latter kind of initiative on Solon's part, presents him as motivated by the *lack* of maritime trade and of exportable commodities in Athens hitherto; and this underlines the fact that, at the mid-point of the Archaic period, Athens had become an economically backward state. But there is at least one category of independent evidence to support the idea that Solon did *something* about the industrial aspect of the Athenian economy, and it is again that of painted pottery. Both the production and the export of Athenian pottery show an upsurge in about the 580s, which is maintained throughout the remainder of the Archaic period; furthermore, there are strong indications of Corinthian influence and even a hint of actual Corinthian participation in this production, which recalls another act credited by Plutarch to Solon: the encouragement given to foreign artisans to immigrate to Athens.

Another indication of a rather different kind is given by Attic marble statues. Our judgment here is to some extent coloured by subjectivity and weakened by chronological uncertainty; but on a reasoned estimate of the dating evidence it seems that there begins, rather after 600 BC, an unprecedented series of both male and female figures. Some were dedications at sanctuaries, some acted as grave-monuments; all appear to be made of imported marble. In quantitative terms, the Attic group comprises rather over a third of the surviving Greek stone statues of this early phase, between about 600 and 570; qualitatively, they can only be described as outstanding. All of this is in dramatic contrast with the previous century, which had not seen many notable achievements by Athenian artists, in this or most other media, and which had not produced comparable signs of ostentatious prosperity. It is a reasonable inference that Solon's economic reforms had something to do with these new phenomena; but where exactly their impact was effective is another question. Since the agricultural potential of Attica had strict and permanent limits, which no mere reform of land-holding could overcome, it is tempting to assume that there were great advances in the non-agricultural spheres. But the evidence of sculpture, in its very nature, tends to throw its main light on the prosperity of those rich enough to afford monuments; and here the relevant point in Solon's reforms was his substitution of a criterion of landed wealth for one of birth, which admitted a new group of families to the ranks of the politically prominent and the socially self-assured. The sudden appearance of the Attic sculptures, executed for private individuals, looks more like a reaction to this new situation than a result of a slow-working economic process. In a similar way, the presence of several funerary monuments among them, in the face of Solon's reputed legislation to limit expenditure at funerals, must mean that this kind of commemoration lay outside the scope of his law, and was maybe even stimulated by the wish to compensate for the ban on ostentation of a more ephemeral kind.

If Athens is an example of an economically backward state, then the obvious choice for an advanced counterpart in the mid-Archaic period would be Corinth. 'From an indefinite time', writes Thucydides (i 13, 5), she had been a commercial emporium; even Homer had called her 'rich', and Herodotus observes that it was her citizens who 'despised craftsmen least' (ii 167, 2). This is an impressive range of testimony, and it is supported by the undoubted vitality of the Corinthian pottery industry between about 725 and 575 BC. But closer examination of the evidence, particularly that of Thucydides, shows that it does not quite yield the conclusion which is often drawn from it. It is clear that, for Thucydides, the wealth of Corinth is derived from the duties imposed on traders from *other* states who use her unique amphibious facilities: overland trade from the Peloponnese must pass the Corinthian isthmus, while sea-trade from the Aegean to the western Mediterranean, by using the same isthmus as a land-portage in the transverse direction, can escape the dangers of the passage round the Peloponnese. Similarly the most impressive piece of physical evidence, the *diolkos* Plate 24 or causeway for haulage across the isthmus which was constructed around 600, probably at the behest of the tyrant Periander, had been studied for some time before the observation was made that it can have served little purpose for Corinth's own trade, and not much more for her naval dispositions. Since the diolkos measured some 6 kilometres in length, and Corinth had a harbour on either gulf at Kenchreai and Lechaion, about 10 and 4 kilometres respectively from the city, her import- and export-trade gained nothing by use of the diolkos, while naval contingencies were best met by keeping a fleet on each sea. It was the traders of other states, particularly neighbouring ones, who gained most advantage by using the isthmus, and Corinth who stood to gain in revenue. This process may have begun long before the construction of the diolkos: we may recall that the conspicuous and at first isolated occurrence of temples of dressed stone at Corinth (p. 60) belongs nearly a century earlier than this. But it is also a fact that the quality (though not the quantity) of agricultural land in the Corinthia far excels that of Attica, and the legendary wealth and power of the Bacchiad aristocracy seems to have begun improbably early for it to have been founded in commerce. Corinth was also a noted naval and military power and, under her tyrants, went to the unusual length of forcibly subduing some of her own colonies and reducing them to political dependence. Nor should the profitability of her Isthmian Games (p. 117) – the only great inter-state festival under the territorial control of one of the major powers – be forgotten. Even Herodotus does not say that artisans were actually *admired*

in Corinth; and the direct contribution of commerce and industry to her wealth, though probably far greater than in most
Archaic states, was hardly overwhelming.

If this disparaging general estimate of Archaic Greek trade is
to gain some credibility, it requires a supporting explanation on
one level or another. The favoured practice as we have seen (p.
123) is to seek a cause, for this as for other phenomena in Greek
culture, in ideological factors. It is true that the manufacturing
and trading occupations were regarded as a social and even
more as a political disqualification in Greek society. In the words
which Xenophon put into the mouth of Sokrates (*Oikonomikos* iv,
2), anyone whose occupation forced him to work 'seated and in
the shade' was liable to be weakened in soul as well as in body.
Such attitudes would not encourage industrial growth; instead,
they harmonized with the progressively stronger assumption
that activities of this kind were better allocated to slaves. But
possibly another level of explanation may serve to complement
this, even though the ideological one may prove to underlie it as
well: I mean the consideration of technology in Archaic Greece.

There has been a marked absence in these pages of any great
technical advances, to match the breakthroughs in ideas and the
feats of organization, many of them without precedent, which
were surveyed in the earlier chapters. Though I have drawn
attention to such things as the growth of maritime communication and shipbuilding in the eighth century (pp. 54–5), the construction of temples in dressed masonry shortly afterwards (pp.
60–1), or the development of sheet bronze armour (p. 99), these
events should always be seen as part of a longer perspective of
ancient achievement. Masonry of similar quality had been common in Egypt two millennia earlier; bronze defensive armour
had been developed by the Mycenaeans 700 years before; while
sea-travel, at much the same period, had reached the point
where twenty-eight different classes of ship were recorded in
the documents of Ugarit in the Levant.

A feature of these phenomena in Greece is their early date
within the Archaic period. In technology as in much else, one
has the impression of a spate of advances in the years around

700 BC which was not, indeed could not be, maintained. Another Greek tendency, well illustrated here, was that of borrowing devices, technological as much as any other, from the older civilizations to the east. But what differs very markedly is the sequel to such borrowing, according to whether it lay in a purely technological field or not. Again and again we find that, if a borrowed idea had an application to intellectual, political or artistic life, it was soon modified out of all recognition after the Greeks had inherited it. This is the pattern which we have already found with the possible inspiration of the city-state (p. 32), with the borrowing of the alphabet (p. 82), with the revival of representational art (pp. 65–6) or with the taking-over of military devices from the powers of the Near East (pp. 104–5); and we shall encounter perhaps the classic instance of it in the relationship between Egyptian and Greek sculpture later. In contrast, the technology of Archaic Greece was, by and large, an assemblage of borrowed and inherited processes which had not undergone much change once they reached Greece.

A good recent illustration of this was given by J. J. Coulton in the field of constructional methods. He noticed the remarkable fact that the weights of single blocks used in the early phases of Greek architecture and sculpture extended, at the upper end of their range, to some 70 tons or more, with many specimens in the bracket of 20 to 40 tons; but that from about 515 BC, and for two centuries thereafter, the maximum weight of block drops, with virtually no exceptions, below 20 tons. Conversely, signs of cutting for lifting-tongs and lewis-irons, and of channels for rope-slings, are largely or entirely absent in the earlier period, but become suddenly and widely prevalent in the later. The logical inference from these two observations is that, in the late sixth century BC, the Greeks began using a system of hoists and pulleys which had not been available (indeed had probably not been invented) until then; that this meant operating with moderate loads only, since the system was at an early stage of its development; and that the preceding era must have used methods in which the direct lifting of blocks played no part, and the strict limitation of size was not yet the overriding concern.

But what were these methods? We have a piece of literary evidence which is, however, from such a relatively late and unreliable source that archaeologists had hesitated to accept it. The elder Pliny (*Natural History* xxxvi, 96–7) describes how the upper works of the Temple of Artemis at Ephesos were raised into place by means of a ramp of sandbags; he seems to be describing the Archaic temple built in the 550s BC, although there is some confusion in the account. The Ephesos temple was one of the very largest built in the Archaic (or any other) period and the biggest block of its architrave may have weighed over 40 tons; but there are other huge Archaic buildings, and there are several smaller temples where opportunities are taken to introduce fewer and larger monolithic blocks (for example, in columns), where later builders used more and smaller ones. Since we know that both the Egyptians and the Assyrians had long been using ramps of earth and mud-brick, supplemented by levers, for constructing large stone buildings and erecting obelisks, it seems highly likely that the Greeks had learned these methods from them in the seventh century when, for the first time for at least 500 years, they had occasion to apply them. In the course of that century, we find them graduating from the half-ton building-blocks of the early stone temple at Isthmia to the colossal statue, now only fragmentarily preserved but originally weighing over 20 tons, erected by the Naxians on Delos.

Methods like these are instinctively associated in modern minds with authoritarian régimes and with massed, unskilled (and therefore presumably slave) labour. This may in part explain the reluctance to accept Pliny's account as typical of the practices of the Archaic Greek states. But they are technological methods, without any very serious implication for the intellectual world, and this is just the sphere in which we find Archaic Greece to be least original and inventive. Indeed, some positive attraction may have been found in the spectacular nature of the physical feats which were possible only with such laborious techniques. Pliny's account of the Ephesos temple (or rather, that of his source) is characterized by pure admiration, and some similar response must have been sought by the Naxians who inscribed on the base of their colossus: 'I am of the same stone, statue and base.' (The statement is not literally true and may constitute a deliberate attempt at deception; otherwise, and less interestingly, it is best interpreted as meaning 'of the same *type* of stone', that is fine marble.)

A question remains as to where the ultimate invention of the hoist and compound pulley took place, which brought this era of antiquated constructional methods to an end. The presumption that it was in Greece is based on the monumental evidence surviving in Greek buildings; if this is right, then it shows that the Greeks were not indefinitely satisfied to cling to inherited methods; and it also coincides in time with some other evidence, suggesting that in the late sixth century BC a second, if lesser, wave of technological advance swept over the Greek world, 200 years after the initial revolution which we discussed in chapters 1 and 2. The appearance of purpose-built sailing merchantmen (above, p. 137) is probably another feature of the period in Greece. We shall return to the remarkable developments of the final Archaic epoch in the last chapter.

Meanwhile the evolution of military technology, on which we touched before (pp. 101–7) can be shown to follow a similar path. In the late eighth century, there is a series of radical innovations: the adoption of bronze plate-armour, the invention of the two-handled shield, the development of the Corinthian form of one-piece helmet and, then or shortly after, the revival of the greave. With the evolution of a new form of tactics to accompany the new hardware, things were then allowed to rest essentially unchanged for well over 150 years. Greeks outside Crete ignored the art of archery. Little was done to improve the quality of cavalry, despite the possible introduction of a stronger breed of horses in the seventh century. Infantry armour and tactics saw only marginal modifications: a hoplite of 700 BC could have fought a hoplite of 550 BC on more or less even terms. But then towards the end of the sixth century we sense an air of unease and renewed experimentation. It is in the nature of military technology to be more than usually sensitive to external developments, since they present a potential threat. From the

late 540s onwards, the cities of Greek Ionia were falling one by
one to the besieging armies of Cyrus of Persia; while the sea,
about 535 a fleet manned by Phokaian refugees who had settled
in Corsica was worsted by the Etruscans and Carthaginians. In
c.520–510 a Spartan colonial venture in the West was first
repulsed in Tripolitania and then defeated in Sicily, its leader
Dorieus being killed in battle with the Elymians and Carthaginians. Greek military and naval prowess had for long appeared
supreme in Mediterranean warfare; was it now to pay the pen-
alty for its seeming complacency? Cyrus himself had
threatened Sparta with retribution for intervening in Ionia;
though he still lacked the naval power to implement this, it
probably seemed only a matter of time before he acquired it.

At all events, some change in Greek military thinking is
*Plate 27* detectable. Around 530 BC, a new type of composite cuirass,
leather-based with metal reinforcements (often including scales),
begins to appear on Greek vases, in place of the plate-armour
which had been universal for the past two centuries. Its most
obvious advantage was its relative lightness, and the resultant
mobility that it conferred on the infantryman. Then we hear
(Pausanias v 8, 10) that in 520 a new event made its appearance
at the Olympic Games: the *hoplitodromos* or race in armour, in
which the runner covered nearly a quarter of a mile wearing a
helmet and carrying a shield. In later years, when it had outlived
its military application, this event became something of a joke;
but its original institution suggests an interest in the training of
mobile infantry. A new type of one-edge sword, very possibly
itself of Persian inspiration, is seen in battle-pictures of the same
period. Next, we learn of two experiments on the part of tyrants,
both around 530, in the field of archery: Polykrates of Samos
recruited a special corps of a thousand bowmen (Herodotus iii
39, 3 and 45, 3) which formed an important part of his land
forces; while a series of Athenian vases, from the later part of
Peisistratos's reign and that of his son Hippias, shows archers
(who appear in this case to be Skythian mercenaries) operating
in close concert with the heavy infantry. All of these measures
point to a general concern with tactics, and a specific desire to

confront on equal terms enemies who were strong in the handling of light-armed infantry – such as the Persians, and perhaps also those Greek states who had been swiftest in emulating the Persians. In the event, the increased mobility of the Athenian troops was to be triumphantly vindicated at Marathon in 490; while by the time of Plataia in 479, it is clear that Athens had an effective corps of archers of her own (Herodotus ix 22, 1 and 60, 3).

More momentous than any of these advances in land warfare was a naval change, the invention of the trireme, a warship with three banks of oars; but the difficulty is that scholars cannot agree as to its date. There are two main schools of thought: those who, with the somewhat ambiguous support of Thucydides and the explicit testimony of some later writers, make it a Corinthian invention of the seventh century BC, whether early or late in that century; and those who believe that it was first adopted in the Aegean in the time of Polykrates around 530 BC, relying partly on the negative evidence of our main historical accounts of naval warfare and on the corresponding absence of artistic representations of triremes before that date. The second view at least leaves open the possibility of an important corollary: that the trireme was actually invented by the Phoenicians at some earlier date, and then taken over by Polykrates and other Greeks. The arguments are extremely complicated and the choice between them correspondingly difficult. But, in different ways, each view would conform fairly well to a pattern that appears in other technological aspects of Archaic Greece: the early invention by the Corinthians would be admitted, even by its supporters, to have been followed by a long period of relative inactivity in which the triremes are not built in quantity and do not dominate Greek sea-power; the late adoption by Polykrates would correspond neatly in time with the evidence of military innovation under the threat of new enemies (for it was the acquisition of the Phoenician fleet which was shortly to convert Persia into an amphibious power). It also recalls Herodotus' great enthusiasm for Samian technology (iii 60): for him, the three greatest feats of Greek engineering were

the building of the Heraion, the construction of the tunnel of
*Plate 25* Eupalinos and the construction of the harbour mole – all three of
them to some degree visible to this day on Samos, and all datable between about 540 and 520 BC.

The development of technology illustrates neither the steady
advance nor the 'compulsory originality' which observers have
rightly detected in may other aspects of Archaic Greek history.
But how does this relate to the other 'explanation' for the relatively slow development of the commercial sector of the Greek
economy which we cited earlier (p. 148), namely the low prestige
of manufacturing and trade? Did ideological prejudice discourage
technological progress, or was the relative stagnation of Greek
technology a reason for the low repute of those whose work
depended on it? For several reasons the first alternative is to be
preferred, though it does not contain anything approaching the
whole truth. Greek technology proved itself capable of swift
response when society, in the cause of growth or survival, pressed it hard enough or when, for reasons of prestige, it valued
sufficiently highly a particular contribution that technology
could offer. But for long periods, Archaic society made no such
demands. Technological activity, like economic activity, had
proved to be merely a subordinate part of the social and political
system; the modern notion of technology positively shaping the
development of human society seems not to fit Archaic Greece.

It is indeed to the economic life of Greece generally that the
word 'archaic', with all the force of its implications, seems to
apply most closely. The physical form of the Archaic 'cities' is
another case in point. Throughout this book, the repeated use of
the word 'polis' and its common translation as 'city-state' have
probably allowed a picture of a fairly well-developed urbanism
to form. Such a picture would be utterly misleading for a good
part of the Archaic period. The very fact that we found the first
glimmerings of urbanism as early as the ninth century at Smyrna
(p. 32) in a way adds force to the claim that this was a late and
hesitant, if not an almost unconscious development. For when
we look at the physical evidence of the period around 600 BC, we
find a disconcerting lack of progress. That Athens at this time

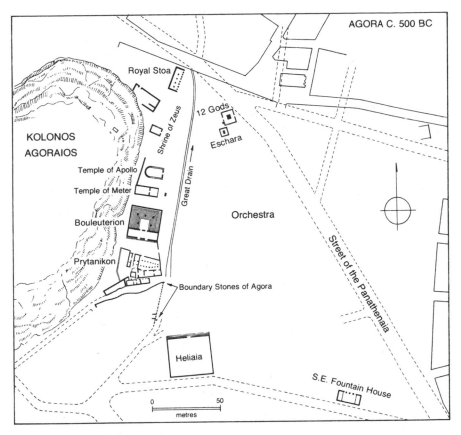

Fig. 13 Plan of the civic centre of Athens *c.* 500 BC

should correspond so little to the modern conception of a city (or
even of a town) may not seem so surprising after what was said
about its lack of economic development (above, pp. 144–6). But
it is certainly true that, down to Solon's time, the site which was
to become the market-place and civic centre (or *agora*) of Athens
had not yet been designated as such: wells are found to contain
domestic débris, burials had ceased not very long before and recognizable public buildings are virtually non-existent. There may
have been an earlier nucleus on the upper slopes of the
Akropolis, but if so the nature of the terrain excluded anything
in the direction of urban planning. The recognizable centres of
habitation, indicated by cemeteries, are numerous, small and

widely scattered; we have once again the choice of regarding Athens either as a very extensive settlement or as a collection of separate villages. Many considerations, and above all the absence of any physical trace of a city-centre, support the latter alternative. But soon after Solon, things appear to change: in the agora area, the domestic deposits cease, the area is cleared, buildings of political function begin to appear and are presently joined by monumental sanctuaries. (By a curious coincidence – or it may not be entirely coincidental – another city with a great cultural future, Rome, was undergoing a similar development at a similar date, with the laying out of a monumental forum). In Athens, Peisistratos and his sons are predictably prominent not only in establishing cult-centres, but also in providing facilities like water-supply and drainage. A fortification-wall was possibly constructed before the end of the Archaic period. By 500 Athens would at last have been physically recognizable as a city, albeit a modest one, by an inhabitant of Memphis or Tyre.

It is fortunate that Corinth, in this as in much else the first place that one would look to for a contrast with Athens, provides some of the best evidence for Archaic urbanization, or the lack of it. For in fact this evidence shows that there was no contrast at all: on the contrary, evidence for an early civic centre at Corinth is even more negative than at Athens. Not only are the centres of population equally widely separated, but there are signs that one of them, a potters' quarter about a mile away from the ultimate city-centre, was disposing of its products at the place of manufacture, a strong pointer to the absence of any central market. There is even a hint that it may have had its own private fortification-wall. This state of affairs apparently continued to exist long after Athens had taken its first steps towards centralization. The remarks which Thucydides made about Sparta in the late fifth century (i 10, 2) are an object-lesson as to how far the political development of the polis, the growth of its power and the extension of its cultural and even its commercial activity could be combined with an absence of urbanization: from 'scattered villages after the ancient fashion of Greece' there emanated a mystique which has been with us ever since.

It was not necessarily the same story everywhere in the Greek world. Greek communities which settled either within the sphere of influence of older urban cultures, or on colonial sites where they found themselves surrounded not by their own rural citizens but by indigenous and potentially hostile aliens, naturally proceeded to a more concentrated form of urbanism. As we saw, fortification-walls may appear much earlier at such sites; so, too, may urbanization and even rudimentary forms of town-planning. The excavators of Smyrna found seventh-century housing wherever they dug within the fortification-circuit; the fact that this was not true of earlier periods, together with the very early date of the wall, shows that here too we have a sequence of developments attested elsewhere (cf. p. 31): the wall-circuit is first built and then, with greater or less delay, urban growth takes place inside it. Smyrna by now had its main sanctuary and perhaps an agora as well. The reconstructed drawing of the late seventh-century city has become familiar, and may well be fairly representative of certain types of Greek settlement overseas; but it should not be taken (as it often is) to illustrate the typical early polis in the Greek homeland.

Away to the west, the excavators of Magara Hyblaia in Sicily have dated the creation of the agora to the middle years of the seventh century – about three generations after the first foundation of the colony. A roughly parallel development, just a century later, can be seen at Selinous, founded itself as a colony of Megara Hyblaia; here some scheme of organization must lie behind the arrangement of the sanctuaries of the various divinities, beginning about 550 BC, in carefully-aligned rectangular blocks. With urbanization, as with an earlier stage of state-formation (pp. 41–2), it is not impossible that the overseas settlements exercised some reflexive influence on the homeland; in fact, if one includes Ionian foundations like Smyrna, this becomes positively likely. In this way, for instance, western colonial experience could have effect both on a non-Greek community such as Rome, which lay within its circle of contact (p. 156), and on a mainland city like Athens. But we are bound to conclude that, whatever factors made possible the achievement of Archaic Greece, an advanced urban culture was not one of them.

And yet, despite everything – despite their own low social standing and exclusion from any informed intelligentsia despite the framework of a backward economic structure in which they had to seek employment, despite the slow growth of urban centres and industrial technology – the craftsmen of Archaic Greece consistently achieved things which still command our unqualified admiration. It is only thanks to their workmanship that one can begin to write a study of Archaic Greece such as this, based on the material culture of the age. But because of the shortage of literary celebration of their products and the virtual absence of any kind of historical reference in the subject-matter of their art, it is extraordinarily difficult to relate their activities to those of their better-known or more articulate contemporaries. Later ages remembered the names (and little more than the names) of only a handful of Archaic artists. It is almost as if they were working in a milieu like that of Etruria or Phoenicia, where no literary and little historical record survives; we have to judge their products on their own merits, and they pass the test triumphantly.

Almost every characteristic type of artefact which we associate with the Greek achievement was pioneered and brought to maturity in the Archaic age: temples of the Doric order, Ionic buildings ranging from the miniature treasury to the gigantic temple, polygonal masonry jointed with a perfection that later Greeks never surpassed, beautifully executed *stoichēdon* inscriptions, studies of the human body at its ideal best and in a variety of actions, figured coin-dies with the familiar symbols of
e 26  Athena's owl, the Arethusa-head of Syracuse or the Corinthian Pegasos, hollow-cast bronze statues of life size, hammered bronzes of an expertise that has been the despair of imitators over the next two thousand years, grave-reliefs that manage to combine reticence about death with poignancy, functional objects from water-jars to dress-pins with real beauty of design – the list could be almost indefinitely extended. There are even classes of handiwork in which the Archaic accomplishments

greatly overshadow the Classical, such as mythical and legendary scenes on vases, or decorated armour. The anonymous
executants of these triumphs must inevitably live in the shadow
of their fellow-countrymen who operated in the sphere of the
mind rather than with the hands, and whose achievement we
shall consider in the next chapter; but they live none the less.

Yet it has to be admitted that the hope expressed at the end of
the previous chapter remains unfulfilled. Economic factors have
*not* sufficed to explain the more paradoxical developments in the
political history of Archaic Greece. The truth seems to be that
the economic realities are not especially remarkable, let alone
unique. Our search for really distinctive features and decisive
causes must be pushed further.

# The Rise of the Individual

Have you heard of someone swifter than Syrian horses?
Has he thrown the bully of Corinth in the sanded circle?
Has he crossed the Isthmus already? Is he seeking brilliant
    Athens and us?

W. H. Auden, *The Orators*

For us today, it is perhaps the intellectual advances, and the things that they made possible, which transform the achievements of Archaic Greece from a series of precocious and small-scale innovations into something timeless and indestructible. For this reason alone, it would be an act of cowardice to omit all discussion of them; yet such discussion, in a book by an archaeologist, may be suspected of possible pretension or even hypocrisy. It is the *written* word which, in the form of extant original texts and later descriptions, gives the proof positive of the reality of these advances. Luckily, however, they are also reflected in other fields besides that of the written word. Indeed, they are probably inseparable from the material record, and certainly we can use the material evidence as one aid in following them. Nor are the literary texts always impossible for the non-specialist to penetrate.

To describe these discoveries as *intellectual* advances perhaps disguises the most important single fact about them: that they were accessible to many people besides intellectuals, and in time affected the lives of almost everyone in the Greek world. (This is also the reason why they came to be reflected in physical and durable form.) It is the distinguishing characteristic of Greek culture that, long before the notion of democracy had been conceived, there was an established sense of rights of the individual citizen; one of these rights was that of a degree of free communication and, on some issues at least, of criticism. It is this 'openness' of Greek society which is its most precious single legacy and, as with so much else, we detect it coming into being in the Archaic period. There is little doubt that a close link exists between the intellectual speculations of the few and individual freedom among the many: it is not so much that the operation of the first encouraged the growth of the second, as that the second, once it existed, encouraged the first. If we begin, therefore, by examining the progress of intellectual speculation, it is because of the wider freedom of society as a whole that this activity implies, and which it expresses in unusually articulate form.

It is difficult to identify a unifying thread running through the intellectual activities of the Archaic Greeks which were remembered by later ages; they covered a wide variety of fields and they differed greatly in the length of time that elapsed before they were supplanted by new theories, or even entirely new methods. The most that we can do at first is to isolate certain common features. First, a prerequisite for nearly all of them was leisure; few of the discoveries were of the kind which can arise from consideration of working problems, encountered in a man's pursuit of his trade, and even these required a period of withdrawal for contemplation. The majority were not of this type, nor did they allow of profitable material application afterwards. It follows that the Greek intellectual of the Archaic period was usually a man of independent means. This in turn has a chronological implication; it means that prosperity had to reach a level adequate for the support of such a group, broad enough to include the very highest range of intelligence, and in many states this level was simply not reached until some way into the Archaic period. It is very difficult, for example, to see any room for a group of this kind in the worlds of Homer or Hesiod.

Next, there is a geographical concentration to be observed. Perhaps the six greatest names in the philosophy of the sixth century BC – Thales, Anaximander, Anaximenes, Pythagoras,

Herakleitos and Xenophanes – were all Ionians, the first three
from Miletos, the others from Samos, Ephesos and Kolophon
respectively. Of these, Thales also acquired a sufficiently lasting
reputation for practical wisdom to be later included among the
'Seven Sages', men who applied their brains to political and
especially to legislative problems. The list of the Seven Sages
was not quite unanimously agreed, but it certainly included four
men – Pittakos of Lesbos, Bias of Priene, Kleoboulos of Lindos
(in Rhodes) and Thales – who came from the coastland and
islands of the eastern Aegean. To an earlier generation of modern scholarship, the great reputation of the thinkers of eastern
Greece implied a truly dominating role for this region in the
growth of Archaic Greek culture generally. This impression is
hardly borne out by the evidence we have examined in the previous chapters; and in fact the inference was always essentially
false, for two main reasons. First, there is the chronological
point made above: none of the 'great Ionians' was active much
before 600 BC and by then Archaic civilization had essentially
taken shape. The second reason is one of geography and politics: its easterly location might give Ionia the advantage in those
fields (such as the intellectual ones) where there was much to be
learned from the civilizations further east, but it also meant that
it was particularly exposed to military threats from the same
quarter – from the kings of Lydia, from the Kimmerian raiders
and above all from the Persians. Already by 540, we find mass-
emigration of communities of Ionian Greeks in the face of the
Persian threat. The intellectual élite not only advocated this policy (we hear of Bias advising the Ionians to emigrate *en bloc* and
settle Sardinia), but in several known cases followed it themselves, if for more personal reasons: both Pythagoras and
Xenophanes became political exiles in the west. Thus after a life
of little more than fifty years the flowering of Ionian culture
began to be cut short by a progressive draining of human
resources. It was Ionia's misfortune, and the Greek mainland's
salvation, that a further fifty years separated the onset of the
Persian threat in the two areas.

The other great common feature of early Greek intellectual

speculations was that they dealt in observation, rational thought, theory and explanation, but seldom in experiment or application. To some contemporary Greeks, this will doubtless have seemed as serious a shortcoming as it does to many moderns, for whom 'theoretical', 'abstract' and 'academic' are mainly pejorative words. Thus the Seven Sages were largely distinguished from, and on many counts preferred to, the philosophers of Archaic Ionia. Even in the thought of the one man who combined membership of both groups, Thales, the striking thing is the lack of connection between the theoretical and the practical.

This said, it must also be stated that in Ionia, during the sixth century BC, the essential foundations of modern philosophy, astronomy, mathematics and geography were all laid. That is a very large achievement, even though the Ionians did have some predecessors in other cultures on whose work they could in part build. Observations of the sun, stars and planets, for example, had been made for thousands of years before this. It is an inescapable conclusion that these had occurred (though to what degree of sophistication is highly debatable) among the megalith-builders of prehistoric north-western Europe. More relevant to Thales' circumstances is the fact that some astronomical observations of the Babylonians may actually have been available to him. In the same way, geographical knowledge had already, before 2000 BC, reached the point where a crude map of northern Mesopotamia could be drawn on clay. But the achievement of Thales in astronomy and of Anaximander in geography was still original and, one is tempted to think, would hardly have been possible at this stage outside Greece. Thales probably appropriated some Babylonian knowledge (astronomy being a subject in which the building-up of observational data is a very long-term process), but without adopting Babylonian astrology and religion; instead, he used it to forecast an eclipse of the sun (probably that of May 585 BC) at a moment when military fortunes were affected by the portent. Anaximander collected geographical information in order to draw a map, not of his own homeland but of the known world, and his Ionian successors built on his work. Around 500 BC, Aristagoras of Miletos was able to impress the king of Sparta by showing him a map of the world engraved on bronze (Herodotus v 49, 1), which gives an inkling of the Ionian pre-eminence in this field. In a similar way. Pythagoras and the other Ionian mathematicians had a basis of Egyptian geometrical work to build on, but the perfection of the procedure of pure deduction, whether in geometry or in arithmetic, was largely their own achievement.

Most original of all (though also, one suspects, most difficult of general access) was the Ionian adventure in physical speculation. Here our own age should be better placed than many of its predecessors to appreciate, without a feeling of patronization, the enterprise of the early Greek thinkers. A common feature of both our era and theirs is the growth of a new crop of far-reaching, intellectually exciting and mutally contradictory theories. The composition of matter and the origins of the universe are in any case questions which still inspire such respect as to make the most complacent modernist seem small. They are also questions which divide the expert from the layman by a gulf which is formed not merely by ignorance, but also by a kind of revulsion: if the truth is so abstruse, alarming and remote from any ordinary kind of empirical verification as the experts' theories maintain, then the layman tends to feel that he would rather not think about it at all.

These feelings may still arise whe ɪ we contemplate the findings of astro-physics in the past fifteen years. Let us take a series of statements from Professor Steven Weinberg's recent book *The first three minutes*, which reconstructs the opening stages of the existence of our universe, using at one point the image of a cinematic film. The film starts not at the absolute beginning, but after a lapse of about one-hundredth of a second. At this moment 'The temperature of the universe is 100,000 million degrees Kelvin ($10^{11}$ °K). The universe is simpler and easier to describe than it ever will be again. It is filled with an undifferentiated soup of matter and radiation, each particle of which collides very rapidly with the other particles.' As to its size, 'Since the temperature of the universe falls in inverse proportion to its size, the circumference at the time of the first frame was less than at present by the ratio of the temperature then ($10^{11}$ °K) to the present temperature (3°K); this gives a first-frame circumference of about 4 light years.'

The thoughtful reader of these sentences may experience much the same conflict of feelings as a Milesian reader of Anaximander's treatise of the mid-sixth century BC on the origins of matter, a work in which the idea of the Infinite was put forward, probably for the first time, as the origin of all things, and which was the more arresting because the author expressed himself in the new medium of continuous prose. For Anaximander, the world (itself one of many worlds in the universe) was the product of conflicting pairs of elements, separated out from the Infinite, whose interaction was controlled by some kind of law or justice. Man's development was itself a form of evolution from these beginnings. The symmetry and elegance of Anaximander's abstractions, and their obvious social analogies, might have evoked the same degree of respect in the minds of contemporaries as does the precision of Professor Weinberg's physics and mathematics, and their objective basis, in ours. But the respect would be mixed with doubts: in the earlier case, Does he *really* know this? in the later, Did this *really* happen? and in either instance, By what means is the layman ever going to be able to establish whether the theory is even approximately right? This reaction is disarmingly anticipated by Weinberg himself: 'I cannot deny a feeling of unreality in writing about the first three minutes as if we really know what we are talking about.' In both cases, too, we suspect that there is some kind of lingering paradox: how did the Infinite come to be there anyway? What was it that exploded during the first one-hundredth of a second to produce the universe? And if the layman holds religious views of any kind, there will be the further worry: how can I possibly reconcile this account with my own, or perhaps with any, religious beliefs? Just how serious this last consideration was in Anaximander's day is debatable, but one can again suspect that in the sixth century BC it would probably have brought the thinker into acute trouble anywhere but in Greece. And even in Greece, another Ionian scientist, Aristarchos of Samos, found it still a threat three hundred years later: his contemporary and fellow-intellectual, Kleanthes the Stoic, felt that he should be prosecuted for impiety in 'disturbing the hearth of the universe', because of his revolutionary doctrine that the earth both rotated and revolved round the sun (Plutarch, *Moralia* 923 A).

It has never been too difficult, however, for later ages to appreciate the moral courage of the Ionian thinkers. Where our own generation is especially fortunate is in being able to see itself, once again, as their intellectual heir. We suddenly find ourselves placed, as they were, in a state of genuine uncertainty about these most fundamental of questions; and we live, as they evidently did, in a social and religious climate which does not discourage, at any rate to the point of active prevention, speculations and calculations aimed at answering the questions. Whether the analogy is strong enough to allow of any guesses as to their impact on their society, or of society's influence on them, is more doubtful. For what it is worth, it does not suggest that the former effect was immediately significant: it does not appear to make any difference to our behaviour whether we accept or reject the view that the universe is expanding and cooling, though at a deeper level there may be some ultimate effect. But the converse factor, the influence of the social system on the individual thinker, is widely thought to have been important then (as it doubtless is now). Some hold that the successful evolution of the early Greek state fostered the belief that mind alone could solve any other problem equally well; others, that the acceptance of a new form of social justice in the city encouraged the search for a similar operation of justice and order in nature. There may be truth in both contentions; but perhaps a more fundamental factor was that early Greek society, by permitting the individual to function as citizen or express himself as artist, was also (probably at first unwittingly) offering the chance for him to indulge in speculative thought; and at the same time, if less directly, the chance for his listeners and readers to study, question, interrupt and answer his expositions. The philosophical meeting was as revolutionary and durable an innovation as the political assembly. Other societies before had achieved the level of prosperity which permitted the growth of a leisured class from which the intellectual could emerge, but they had not combined this with a withdrawal of the constraints on his thought.

Before we leave the Ionian scientists, we should attempt some summary of the elements of their own view of science. They did not see it as a vehicle for social, material or any other sort of progress, except that of their own vocation. This of course limited their social impact, and may even help to explain some of the respects in which Archaic Greece failed to develop as fast as might have been expected. But at the same time, they pioneered not only fields of study, but *methods* of study, on which we still depend today. The mere rejection of supernatural causes for natural phenomena was perhaps the most important single step for the subsequent growth of science; by taking this step, they inevitably brought into focus problems whose very existence had, in some cases, hitherto been obscured by religious dogma, but which have occupied scientists ever since. By applying mathematics to natural phenomena, too, they set modern physics on its path, though they did not themselves care to follow it very far. Further, the whole notion of empirical research, although seldom conspicuous in modern accounts of Ionian thought, is nevertheless an essential background to it; this too is a foundation-stone of all subsequent science.

One field where we should expect to find this last method in operation is that of medicine. The progress of Archaic Greek *Plate 28* medicine is essentially charted for us in individual terms, as is so much of the thought of the times: it is the attainments of a few outstanding doctors which the sources mainly record, although modern experts have also detected passages of Archaic origin embedded in the later corpus of Hippokratic writings. Alkmaion of Kroton was one of the leaders of a school of medicine in that city (Cyrene had another distinguished school), which won proverbial fame over the whole Greek world in the later sixth century; he was a philosopher as well (probably a pupil of Pythagoras) and applied to medical practice the philosophical theory, going back to Anaximander, of the conflict of opposites, in what might seem to us a rather doctrinaire way. But then we learn that Alkmaion also operated on the eye, and that he was perhaps the first to locate the centre of thought in the human brain; these were hardly the activities of either a pure theoretician or a primitive. His fellow-citizen and perhaps slightly older contemporary, Demokedes, is best known from a long and exciting, but in part patently fictitious, story in Herodotus (iii, 129–37). The bare bones of the story, however, cannot have been simply invented; and the picture of a Greek doctor not only successfully treating King Dareios of Persia for a severe ankle-sprain, but specifically excelling his Egyptian rivals in so doing, is a credible one by the late Archaic period. Here again, the story contains a tell-tale element (also credible) as to the influence of the Greek social and political system on the career of Demokedes: on emigrating to Aigina and arriving there without any medical equipment, he nevertheless establishes a surgery there with such success that, a year later, his services are retained at a very handsome annual salary by the state of Aigina; there then ensues, in subsequent years, an auction for his services between other Greek states, as a result of which his salary rises from about 15 to about 30 times the wage of a skilled workman. Finally the fortunes of war bring him to Persia as a captive, with the result that we have seen; but it was his reputation in the Greek world which brought him to the Great King's notice, and this had been essentially created by two Greek features: the existence of public (as against royal) employment, and the scope given to individual excellence.

Our consideration of philosophy, astronomy, geography and medicine has brought us down to a late stage in the Archaic period. As a manifestation of what was possible in Greece when some of the constraints on individual freedom of thought and action were lifted, this achievement is certainly very remarkable. But it is by no means the earliest such manifestation. For that, we may fittingly turn to literature and the visual arts. We have given some consideration to the development of these, and their relation to each other, at an earlier stage, the second half of the eighth century (above, pp. 65–73). But quite soon after that, the whole course of development in both fields changed dramatically. It is difficult and possibly misguided to look for evidence of one medium influencing the other, except in isolated instances of common subject-matter; they are better regarded as independent manifestations of the same historical process (and once again, it is a process wholly confined to Greece). It is in literature that we can follow this process more clearly, if in social terms also more narrowly.

Already in Homer, there are fleeting signs that an Epic poet, entirely dependent on aristocratic houses for his employment and his immediate cultural response, could yet voice in passing, or put into the mouths of his characters, sentiments that were critical of the aristocratic ethos, or at least showed that there were other values which might command equal respect. At the turn of the century, Hesiod in his *Works and Days* makes a principle of such sentiments, and repeatedly cautions the aristocrat against abuse of his position. In positive terms, however, he has little to offer either of political alternatives or of ideals: hard work is his prescription, a laudable but hardly an inspiring one. The rise of the Greek state had not yet, it seems, generated an articulate literary expression of its accompanying ideology. But the gap was soon filled, and the thing which perhaps did most to bring this about was the emergence of a new poetic form, the short lyric. In a poem of short compass, much can be said; but the more personal the statement, the greater is likely to be the impact. Choral anthems and brief narratives in Epic style continued to be written, but the most talented writers saw that a whole new field of personal expression was opened to them, which the great length and timeless subject-matter of the Epic had not offered. They took their opportunity with startling promptness. The expression of anything like an ideology did not come at once; first, there had to be the discovery of an individual voice and of its ability to command attention. But, within perhaps a generation of the *Odyssey* and the *Works and Days*, we are confronted with the extraordinary figure of Archilochos of Paros.

Modern comment on Archilochos tends to fall into two distinct categories, according to whether it dates from before or after 1973. For it was in that year that potentially the greatest single step forward in our understanding of the Greeks of early Archaic times for at least a century, the most direct new communication from them to us, was made possible by the reading of a papyrus with a long fragment of a lyric poem of epode form – easily the longest surviving and restorable extract of Archilochos. On the strength of the smaller fragments that had been known previously, and of a number of references in later writers (for Archilochos was seen to be a great poet in antiquity), a reasonably consistent and recognizable picture had been built up: the first surviving personality of the western world emerged as that of a cynical, headstrong, sometimes coarse pragmatist. Critics have long since agreed that it is a fallacy to take all first-person statements of Archilochos and his successors literally, as being necessarily autobiographical. Nevertheless, it is likely that the man did experience more or less the kind of career with which we credit him: born probably in the lifetime of Hesiod, of aristocratic family but possibly illegitimate, politically a maverick who combined a mocking distrust of the propaganda of his own class with contempt for his inferiors, he fell from favour in his native island of Paros and spent at least a period of his life abroad and at sea, fighting; at one time he seems to have served as a mercenary, at another he was a leading figure in the foundation of the most famous Parian colony, Thasos. But he found time to write some of the fiercest Greek love-poetry that has survived and later biographers (perhaps falling victim to the 'autobiographical fallacy' mentioned above) linked his name with the daughters of a prominent Parian named Lykambes.

The new discovery belongs to this last context. The surviving part of the papyrus gives us thirty-five lines – apparently the middle and end – from the new poem, and then starts on another poem which was already known and attributed to Archilochos. This was the first strong hint that Archilochos might be the author; the next was the appearance of the familiar name of one of Lykambes' daughters in line 16. The metre and dialect do nothing to contradict the inference. Nevertheless, within under a year a group of respected scholars had come out against the attribution and, although they appear to remain in a minority, their view cannot simply be ignored. Even they, however, must admit the likelihood that the new poem was *accepted* as being by Archilochos in antiquity, not only because the manuscript is of the second century AD, but also because in the fifth century AD the lexicographer Hesychios recorded a four-word phrase from line 10, translated below as 'besides the main one', and gave its (by then probably long accepted) explanation as meaning 'apart from sexual intercourse'. No one would have troubled to interpret this phrase if they had realized that its context was that of a mere Hellenistic pastiche of Archilochos (which is what some at least of the sceptics suppose the poem to be). I will say no more than that the poem seems to me almost certainly genuine, and simply give what seems from some points of view the most satisfactory published translation of the poem, that of Professor John Van Sickle of Brooklyn College. Professor Van Sickle has preceded his translation by a series of plausible, though entirely conjectural, restorations of the possible content of the missing lines at the beginning of the poem, incorporating also one or two single known lines of Archilochos which could belong to this passage; while even the main section of the poem has lost letters or words from the beginnings and ends of lines, through the tearing of the edges of the papyrus, so that the text contains many smaller restorations here too. By his generous permission, I print the whole:

. . . but
    longing that makes a man's limbs go slack, my friend, still breaks my stride
. . .
    . . . once I saw
alone Lycambes' child, the younger one,
    gathering flowers in the close of Hera . . .
. . . spoke to her these words:
    '. . . keen desire . . . heart . . .
. . . you . . . here . . .
    . . . now . . . my very own.'
So much I said. She answered point for point:
    '. . .

. . .
totally keeping yourself, and I'd hold out to do the same;
but if you are pressed, if your heart drives hard,
    here in our household there is – and wants so much to marry now –
a lovely, tender girl: you won't I think,
5     find any fault in her looks. Make her, not me, your very own.'
So much she said. I answered point for point:
    'Daughter of Amphimedo, that woman excellent and wise
whom now the moldering earth keeps down below,
    many delights are derived from Aphrodite for young men
10   besides the main one. One of those will do;
    while as for this, in good time, whenever you have grapes grown ripe,
both you and I, god willing, will decide.
    I'm going to do as you say: you think I'm pressing very hard;
but here beneath the rim and shading gates
15   don't make a thing of it, dear, since I will keep my course to
grassy gardens – that for now. Neobule, no!
    Somebody else marry her! *Aiai*! She's more than overripe:
her girlhood flower has withered and dropped off,
    also the grace that was there. Her fill she never ever got;
20   the woman's crazed; she long since showed her prime.
    Out to the crows! Keep her off! May never he who rules the gods
decree that I, for keeping one like her,
    stand as a neighbourhood butt. Instead I much prefer you,
for you are neither faithless not two-faced.
25   She, though, is only too keen, makes many men her very own
I fear I'd get a misfit – premature –
    pressing on quickly with her: just like the hasty bitch, blind pups.'
So much I said, but then I took the girl
    into the flowers in bloom and laid her down, protecting her
30   with my soft cloak, her neck held in my arms.
    Though out of fear like a fawn she hindered, I encouraged her
and her breasts with my hands I gently grasped.
    She, then and there, herself showed young flesh – the onset of her prime –
and, all her lovely body fondling, I
35   also let go with my force, just touching, though, her tawny down.

One further comment is necessary: by accepting the explanation in Hesychios of the first half of line 10 (see above), we determine to some degree our interpretation of what happens in the last line. Some, apparently rejecting the Hesychian gloss, and at the same time succumbing once again to the 'autobiographical fallacy', have branded 'Archilochos' as an unregenerate seducer, even a psychopathic rapist. But on the other view, it seems likely that the narrator practises some form of last-minute restraint. Again, I will only state my view that the context favours the latter alternative. If the delicacy of this and other episodes in the poem then seems hard to reconcile with the crude Archilochos that we know from elsewhere, the ferocity of the passage on Neobule in lines 16 to 27 may once again revive our faith in the authenticity of the poem.

It seems a pity to dull the impact of these lines with so much exposition, but their message comes through none the less. This is a poem of sophistication, showing a relationship between the sexes which would pass as entirely normal today in, say, a Mediterranean country or any other society which lags somewhat behind full western emancipation. The apparent aristocratic background of the participants has little effect on the content: the poet seeks to interest us in their experience for its own sake, and we have to care about them as individuals in order to become involved. As if in one stride, Archilochos carries us from traditionalism to modernity. Yet it must be admitted that, as a genuine work of the seventh century BC, the poem is hardly typical of its kind (that indeed is the main importance of its discovery). What is unusual is the absence of any attempt to give the narrator's experience a permanent or general significance, or to pass on a message to society. Even Archilochos, the archetypal misfit, usually felt moved to involve the community as a whole in his complaints and insults, and to give it the benefit of his advice; he was capable, too, of looking beyond the confines of his native Paros and its colony to the wider world around. In the work of his younger contemporaries and successors, these qualities become much more conspicuous.

Some poets, notably the elegists Tyrtaios of Sparta and Kallinos of Ephesos, addressed the community with whole poems of exhortation, in which the new civic virtues of solidarity, moderation, frugality and, presently, justice were extolled at the expense of their opposites. Another important feature of the rise of seventh-century lyric is indeed the fact that its practitioners were often drawn from other walks of life, notably the political and the military: Terpander of Lesbos, a pioneer of the lyre, had been summoned to Sparta, traditionally as early as 676 BC, to play a statesman's role in settling political disputes there, and he was the first of a long line. Tyrtaios and Kallinos were particularly concerned with the citizen as a soldier; Tyrtaios might have been equally well fitted by the description which Archilochos gave of himself, as first a servant of the war-god and then a poet. But in other respects, the military contexts of these three men's poems look rather different. Archilochos portrays himself as a freelance warrior, sometimes a mercenary; although evidently familiar with the new-style equipment, he is interested in the individual fortunes of war and not in general morale or tactics. Kallinos too, though a little later (*c.* 640), seems still to express the values of the aristocratic champion, in a way that recalls the other evidence for Ionian backwardness in adopting phalanx warfare (see above, p. 108); but his object is both communal and propagandist. Tyrtaios, at the same period, has similar aims, but writes like a man determined to impress the precepts of massed infantry tactics on an army with different and less disciplined habits.

But whereas the great military reform of the seventh century, once fully achieved, could be taken for granted in the more static conditions that followed, the political situation in most Greek states remained unstable. The result was that the role of the poet as an instructor in the conduct of civilian life continued, and was even extended, in the later Archaic period. Tyrtaios contributed here as well, with typically earnest generalities in a conservative vein that was well designed to win acceptance at Sparta; later in the century, we find Alkman inculcating in the Spartans some other ideals of the new, state-centred morality: he praises simple food and urges collaboration of neighbour with neighbour (meaning of course citizen (Spartiate) neighbour). But one of the most eloquent spokesmen for civic virtues is also one of the most obscure: Phokylides of Miletos. A recent study suggests that he lived in the first half of the sixth century, a time when Miletos was passing through first tyranny and then two generations of political unrest. To Phokylides – or to a later writer who used his persona – we are indebted for the quintessential statement of what differentiated the Archaic Greek state from its older and more powerful Eastern neighbours:

> Phokylides says this too: a small, well-ordered city
> When it is built on a rock, is better than senseless Nineveh.
>
> (fr. 5)

The general sentiment had been anticipated by other poets: Archilochos had rejected both the wealth and the political power of Gyges, king of Lydia; while Alkaios of Lesbos had discerned that it was men, not fortifications, that made up the Greek city. What is new here is the insistent claim on the reader's attention of the individual authority: repetition of his name in this same formula is a feature of Phokylides' surviving fragments. New, too, is the attempt to identify the essential differences between Greek and other political systems; and, one might add, the unique near-contemporary reference to what had been the most formidable to date of all such alien systems, the Assyrian Empire based on Nineveh, which fell in 612 BC. Other lines credited to Phokylides express complementary attitudes, and give advice of the expected kind. Like Hesiod, he advocates arable farming (though no longer from first principles) and discourages ill-timed borrowing; like Archilochos, he distrusts fine appearances and self-styled 'breeding'. At one point, he even appears to anticipate Bertolt Brecht's dictum, 'Erst kommt das Fressen, dann kommt die Moral'; but when Phokylides says 'Seek first for a livelihood; when you have it, then look for virtue', it is probable that he is using the Greek word for virtue in its older sense of 'quality' or high social status. Neither a revolutionary ('I want to have a middle place in the city') nor a diehard reactionary like his younger contemporary Theognis of Megara, Phokylides is the authentic spokesman for the citizenry of an Archaic Greek state and for the values that it had adopted; his apparent lack of originality does not detract from this.

By the early sixth century, the poet-statesman is joined by a different and equally significant figure, the statesman-poet. That Solon should have used elegy as the medium, first for his political appeals and then, after holding office, for his justificatory propaganda, is both a token of his poetic gifts and a recognition of the great power which lyric poetry had won as a means of public communication. For that, Archilochos must take the greatest credit: by proving that such verse could be forceful, memorable and quotable, he fashioned an instrument for others with wider concerns than his. A further tribute was paid later in the sixth century by Xenophanes of Kolophon, the most radical of the great philosophers of Ionia; he abandoned his predecessors' use of the prose treatise, and instead put his theories – which were in their nature intended for a wider public – into verse-form. Where others had sought scientific alternatives to the received account of the universe, Xenophanes tackled head-on those aspects of the traditional religion which he found obsolete, and dared to propose his own form of monotheism. This was one of many assaults on established convention: nicknamed the 'Homer-trampler', he apparently found the values of the Epic poets unacceptable in the community of his day; he disliked the violent and divisive tendencies in the subject-matter of their lyrical successors; he ridiculed the aristocratic love of luxury and the popular adulation of athletes. Xenophanes was not only ahead of his times, but in many respects too advanced even for later Classical thought. One is not surprised to learn that he became a political exile, but at least he seems to have reached a wide audience.

This raises again a question which we encountered at the very beginning of this chapter: how far could an intellectual in Archaic Greece communicate beyond a closed circle, or at most a restricted élite? Each of the activities that we have been describing had its origins in some fairly exclusive social setting: where epic poets had often sung in the great hall of an aristocrat's household, the lyric poet typically performed at a private *symposium* or drinking-party. In one respect, as has been observed, this change actually increased the exclusiveness of the occasion, since women (or at any rate respectable women) would no longer be in the audience. Philosophers presented their theories to small groups of educated colleagues. A man like Xenophanes, who combined the last two roles, was evidently at home in either milieu. The basic requirement of leisure for these activities in any case made them exclusive socially. This might suggest that new ideas, new art-forms and new methods of thought were unlikely to spread very widely among the population. Yet the evidence is very much against this conclusion. On the contrary – to anticipate a little and give almost random examples – we shall find that the citizen population as a whole was receptive to new political ideas, that literacy spread to a degree apparently unprecedented in earlier cultures, that religious festivals involved the participation of all classes, that the tastes of craftsmen and their customers were often the same at different social levels.

It is easy to point out some of the 'egalitarian' factors which brought about this state of affairs: for instance, lyric poets might be lionized in the aristocratic symposium, but they also composed choral odes which were both commissioned and performed publicly, and were heard by everyone; the widespread tradition of citizen assemblies meant that political oratory was judged by large audiences; the writing-system was an easily accessible one. Music would be heard as widely as poetry *Plate 2*⟨⟩ (indeed, at this time it existed *only* as an accompaniment to poetry), and in Greece it must have acted as a unifying force. The musical instruments of Archaic Greece were not extensive either in number or in range; characteristically, they had been adopted from the neighbouring cultures of the East at the beginning of the Archaic period, with just a few modifications being devised later. It is hardly surprising that there is little evidence for a distinction between 'highbrow' and 'popular' in Greek music. Perhaps most important of all, the structure of Archaic thought was in general such that it could be widely comprehended. I mean by this that there had not yet taken place that growth of *theory*, as such, which later ages have taken so much for granted. There was as yet no real political theory, only individual political measures; military theory was for long kept to the minimum, if not excluded, by the Archaic forms of warfare; the social sciences were not yet founded and, as we have noted, economic theory did not come into being even in the Classical age; philosophical theory was only in its infancy. The rarity of prose writing may have acted as a deterrent factor. There may be some quickening of development in the last decades of the Archaic period – perhaps in military and naval theory for example (see pp. 151–3), but until then the doctrines of intellectuals were couched in more accessible form than they have ever been since. But there is also a particular proof of the diffusion of culture through Archaic society, and it is to be found in works of art.

If there is one product of the visual arts in Archaic Greece which stands duty for the whole period, it is the type of standing nude male figure which we conventionally call the *kouros*. Not only is it the commonest single category of Archaic statue, but for experts it forms a kind of framework to which other works of art must be related: it provides both a chronological index of the progress of the sculptor's art and, to some extent, a guide to regional style, enabling us to discriminate between artistically 'advanced' and 'backward' schools or to distinguish, for example, 'graceful' Attic from 'sinewy' Peloponnesian or 'fleshy' Ionian characteristics. It is also often used as an illustration of the inborn Greek love of order, symmetry and discipline, taking over the role assigned in the preceding era to Geometric vases; and it is cited as an early example of the lasting pre-occupation of Greek art with mankind as a subject, and with physical beauty as both an ideal in itself, and a symbol of other admired qualities (good birth, good exercise, even sexual desirability). All of these claims have some justification, but some are more debatable than is often realized; and all, it could be argued, miss the most important points.

In the first place, the kouros-type as a criterion of the artistic attainments of Archaic Greece is almost entirely misleading. From most specialist treatments and from virtually all general books, one would infer that the cream of sculptural talent used the kouros as a prestigious medium in which to display their highest skill and their newest anatomical discoveries. This view is based on the undoubted frequency of occurrence of the type, which in turn arises from its equally undoubted versatility of function in society: a kouros could serve as a grave-monument or as a dedication to a deity, in both cases without any necessity for the person concerned to be of appropriate age and appearance. On occasion, it could even serve as the actual cult-statue of a male deity in his sanctuary. It thus had an extremely broad social significance; but this does not mean that it had an equally wide *artistic* importance. A good case could be made for saying that, on the contrary, after the early stages the better sculptors came to regard it as a tiresomely inhibiting and convention-bound medium, which they were compelled to adopt for the majority of their commissions, but from which they would escape with relief when opportunity arose. The advantages of the kouros-type would be most apparent to the mediocre sculptor: its pose might have been designed (indeed, probably *was* originally designed) to require the minimum modification of a tall, prism-shaped block of about 6 feet by 1 foot by $1\frac{1}{2}$ feet (or of other dimensions in similar proportion) – equivalent to two small building-blocks superimposed on end. The task of getting the proportions right, always a difficult one for beginners in representing the human figure, could be greatly eased by the practice of drawing in the frontal, profile and back views on the appropriate faces of the block, before the carving was begun; and this process in turn became easier if even an approximate scheme of accepted ratios existed for the various measurements (as seems very likely in the early stages of Greek sculpture), for then a grid of guide-lines could be drawn in, as the first step, and the positions of the limbs easily plotted. We have already considered some evidence (p. 143) which has a bearing on this process: the existence of 'pre-carved' kouros statues either *in situ* at a quarry, or nearby. Our conclusion then was that either the quarryman had been closely briefed by the sculptor, or the quarryman *was* the sculptor. The former alternative becomes more credible, and is perhaps *only* credible, if there existed a system of proportions of the kind mentioned above. But the latter is also easy to accept, if we reflect for a moment on the background of the first sculpture in Greece.

A civilization which is undertaking or reviving the practice of a new art must of necessity recruit its practitioners from another art (or from another country – for which supposition there is no evidence whatever in Greece at this time, although Egyptian *influence* is highly likely). The quarrying and carving of hard stone was, in seventh-century Greece, the preserve of the building trade, which would therefore be the obvious place to look for established expertise. The idea of the sculptor's trade as an independent occupation would take time to develop; its growth into an *art* would take longer still. The evidence mentioned just now – the residual influence of the four-sided block, the probable scheme of proportions, the pre-carved figures – mostly relates to the early stages of Archaic sculpture, between c. 650 and 575 BC. It seems very likely that during this period statues were still often produced by men whose professional training had been as masons or quarrymen (both professions, incidentally, which appear to have achieved quite high standards in Archaic Greece). As such, their aim would probably be to produce very competent, beautifully-finished products which would also conform to the social requirements for human figure-sculpture – such as those of standard pose and proportions for an upright male statue. They might have 'artistic' aims as well, but not necessarily those which we would consider appropriate to the art of sculpture: a well-executed decoration in pattern form, for instance, would come naturally to men who were already applying patterned mouldings to architectural members. Much less plausible would be the aim, which has nevertheless been imputed to kouros-sculptors by their most influential student, the late Gisela Richter, of a conscious progress towards a naturalistic rendering of the body. Since this aim had never been fully realized before, least of all by sculptors in Greece, it is highly unlikely that an Archaic sculptor would have even *recognized* it as an aim. There is little ground for believing that Archaic sculptors often worked from the living model, and less for thinking that medical dissection was practised. More likely, as at other periods, artists will have looked primarily at other works of art. What society asked from them was recognizable 'schemata' (to use E. H. Gombrich's term) for the human figure, in three dimensions and with a certain minimum size; that is, typical renderings, effective as representations of the human body but not consciously trying to simulate its appearance. Even the very pose of the kouros, we may note, is an unnatural one, both feet being flat on the ground even though the position of the legs is for walking.

But during these same years, there began to appear men who, by some unexplained inspiration, were not content with this achievement. They wanted to give their products both originality and individuality. The originality was to prove, within the field of sculpture, total and unqualified: they had ideas which, unknown to them, were to lead sculpture into doing what it had never done before, anywhere in the world. The individuality was not usually that of the subject, in the sense of producing the recognizable appearance of some individual, real or imaginary; it was that of themselves as creators. One sign of this is their wish to have their statues recognized as having been produced by no one else; to this end, they began the frequent practice of inscribing bases with their own name, either as well as or instead of that of the dedicator (as had been the older custom). We cannot prove that they were full-time sculptors even now; to a certain extent they had been forestalled by practitioners of other arts (notably vase-painting), and there may have been at least some indirect influence from there. But to adapt these new aims to the sculptor's art was none the less a huge advance.

Where can we see their handiwork? There are some much-admired statues from as early as about 600 BC. A fragmentary kouros from the Dipylon cemetery in Athens is perhaps the first Greek statue carved with real sensitivity as well as skill: the sculptor was aiming for something 'extra'; if it was naturalism, then he can hardly be said to have significantly excelled his contemporaries but, even if that provided some of the impulse, the ultimate effect has more often been described as 'architectural' (an appropriate term perhaps in more ways than one). To the same period belong the twin kouroi from Delphi, executed and signed by an Argive sculptor to celebrate a famous and poignant *Plate 30* episode in his city's history, the exploit of Kleobis and Biton (see above, p. 63). Some critics have seen in his work a conscious attempt to express the essential quality of the brothers, their physical strength, and the great exertion required by their feat. Even if they are right, the distinctive aim is still of a generic, not a specific kind, and it was not apparently often repeated in the medium of the kouros. What we instead find is that, when male statues of truly outstanding quality appear, a high proportion of them are not kouroi at all: this is one argument for the view advanced earlier (p. 179) as to the artistic status of the kouros type.

One of the earliest works which actually seizes our attention *Plate 31* by its quality is the Calf-bearer from the Athenian Akropolis, a work of about 570–560: the complexity of this, a true group-sculpture, is of a kind that required deep thought on the sculptor's part. A man carrying an animal was not an uncommon subject in early art, but nowhere had the two been integrated as fully as by this sculptor. The result shows many stylistic features of his time – the group is still a brilliant piece of design rather than a study of nature – but to these he added several of his own: above all, a feeling for the roundness of human and animal limbs. This last is a naturalistic feature, but that does not mean that naturalism is being systematically or even consciously pursued. If there were any kouroi of this period of a quality approaching this, then we simply do not have them. The same could be said of two other brilliant works of about the middle of *Plate 32* the century, the 'Sabouroff' head in Berlin and the 'Rampin' horseman (the head, found long ago, is in Paris), both probably Athenian too. There are also outstanding grave-reliefs of this *Plate 33* period from Athens, one of a discus-thrower (probably by the sculptor who carved the horseman) and a magnificent study of a boxer; again, we look in vain for similar quality of carving among the kouroi. (I am confining this discussion to male statues, in the hope of keeping the comparisons fair; if female figures were included, the same arguments would not apply because the main concentration is on drapery as much as on the human figure.)

Above all, there began to appear, from this time on, sculptures of vigorous and even violent action. The context which permitted this was not, of course, that of the kouros, nor even that of the isolated statue or group of any kind; it was that of architectural sculpture, and in particular of temple pediments. The claim that relief-sculpture is simply a different medium, with different ideals and different practitioners, has some general force; but it wears thin when it is applied to figures in sculptured pediments which, from about the mid-century, begin to be carved almost entirely in the round and on a scale approaching life-size. To compare these studies of striding, lunging, crouching and collapsing figures with their contemporary kouroi is to realize what a limiting medium the kouros had become; and yet it still had three generations' life in front of it. It is the pedimental figures which should be held up as examples of the attainment of Archaic sculptors; for very practical reasons, they are not given the same degree of finish as a statue which could be studied at eye level and at close quarters, but their adventurousness in pose and subject was the biggest contribution of the age to later sculpture. Where the Archaic pedimental sculptors sowed, Classical, Hellenistic and ultimately Renaissance artists reaped; the full fruit of the discoveries was denied to their immediate contemporaries by the force of the conventions that bound free-standing sculpture.

What was it that made possible, indeed perhaps necessitated, this artistic enterprise? The answer is clear: narrative and, specifically, mythical narrative. The fact that the narrative art had by this time reached such heights in Greece – first in the medium of epic poetry, then more tentatively in some of the two-dimensional arts, and then with increasing confidence in lyric and choral ode, vase-painting and work in shallow relief – made it inevitable that, when placing a series of figures side by side in the triangular frame of a pediment, sculptors would try to relate them to each other by involvement in a story. So that their portrayal would be clearly intelligible to a spectator looking up from ground-level, actions and gestures had to be forthright and *Plate 34*   expressive. If the contest of Herakles against a monster was to be shown, it was not enough for Herakles to take up a statuesque pose facing his enemy; he must actually fight it. Thus it is that we find this very subject represented, virtually in the round, in a pediment on the Athenian Akropolis by the mid-*Plate 23*   century; a generation later, a Battle of the Gods and Giants adorned the new temple which the tyrants constructed, and here the participants on both sides are shown in postures of contortion as well as exertion. By the end of the century, pedimental groups at Eretria and Aigina were showing such ambitious sub-*Plate 35*   jects as Theseus abducting the Amazon queen Antiope, archers crouching to shoot, or Greeks and Trojans fighting and dying.

By this fusion of the twin arts of narrative and sculpture in the round, the Greeks were simply carrying to a more spectacular level the process which had begun with the first tentative compositions of the Dipylon Master and his associates in the vase-painting of the mid-eighth century. The role played by the element of narrative does something to validate E. H. Gombrich's claim that it was this 'free evocation of mythological events' which enabled the Greeks to steer the visual arts into this unprecedented course. The theory is not without difficulties, but it does fit in impressively with some of the evidence: the age-long devotion of the Greeks to myth as the subject-matter for the visual arts, for example, might perhaps to some degree result from the richness and power of their mythology, but it is much more convincingly explained by the view that myth provided not merely a subject-field for the arts but an actual driving force behind their development. As we have seen, this same theory accounts persuasively for the fact that in sculpture – an art which we today instinctively associate with free-standing, self-contained works – the most enterprising early developments should have taken place in what would seem an ancillary field, the architectural sculpture grouped in the gable-ends of temples. By comparison, the kouros type appears as the embodiment of artistic conservatism. It is, I would argue, a medium which tells us more about social convention than it does about sculptural progress. Some of the inhibitions which society imposed lasted throughout the 150 years of the life of the kouros type: the uncomfortable pose, the narrow permissible range of age and physique, the almost total absence (in the funerary statues) of any attributes which would express the manner of life or of death. But other vogues were less durable and one of them, the notorious 'Archaic smile' which appeared during the sixth century and vanished at its end, has aroused much inconclusive discussion. It is not only found on single statues, but appears in group-sculptures, on the faces of figures engaged in life-and-death combat. One thing that seems clear is that it is better explained by social than by artistic causes. Indeed, as a convention it should not be unintelligible to an age which shows similar tastes in photography – even when (to pursue the analogy) the photograph illustrates a newspaper story in which the violent death of the subject is reported.

The same society which exacted such conservatism from its artists in one medium is hardly likely to have been the motive force behind the developments in another, closely-related field. Therefore this free play of the inspiration of myth was, we infer, something which operated on the artists directly, or else through a different kind of social influence. The latter possibility is created by the fact that the kouros must have been essentially the medium of a priviliged clientèle, rich enough to pay for many months of a sculptor's time; whereas architectural sculpture was typically executed for the community and paid for by the state, belonging as it usually did to the temple, which itself had the same connotations. So it is conceivable that the upper-class ethos denied to the sculptor of private dedications that freedom which the community as a whole encouraged in architectural sculptors. But this is perhaps too formal a rationalization; the simple fact is that Greek myth was a force so potent, so accessible and in a sense, as we shall see, so egalitarian that it was at the disposal of any group, including the artisan class from which sculptors came, who wished to make use of it.

All this makes the development of Archaic sculpture as much an intellectual as an artistic advance; and I believe that this is a fair description. The innovatory sculptors of the sixth century were making a contribution to Western thought which stands comparison with that of their contemporaries the philosophers. Their advances required a similar exercise of individualism and a similar kind of intellectual, perhaps even moral courage. Their achievement was also typical of their age in another way. Technologically, the two great steps forward were the introduction of life-sized stone statues in the mid-seventh century, and the discovery of a means of hollow-casting life-sized bronzes. This second step is placed by our literary sources just a hundred years later, in the mid-sixth century; the surviving physical evidence, which begins a generation after that, suggests that they are not far out in their dating. But both techniques had been mastered centuries earlier in Egypt; and the chronology of Greco-Egyptian relations, despite some difficulties in the case of the earlier development, is just compatible with the view that both ideas were borrowed from Egyptian sculptors. That is exactly what one might expect from other instances of the period (see above, pp. 148–54), and it is strongly supported by the general resemblance in the poses of standing and seated figures, and by one or two more specific details of anatomy and proportions. Typical, too, is the sequel: sculpture proved to be a means of giving physical shape to several ideas that were in the forefront of the Greek mind, and so it had to develop. Within two generations of the first contact, sculptors were beginning to abandon the notions which they had uncritically borrowed (such as the carving of colossi) and to attempt things which the Egyptians had never practised (such as the first tentative use of narrative pedimental compositions). From then on, the speed of development was such that, arguably, it outran technology; the introduction of life-sized bronzes was delayed perhaps later than one would have expected, and it certainly came late enough to lead, this time, to an *immediate* breakaway from Egyptian practices. Bronze statues had no sooner appeared than they were adopting freer poses than their marble contemporaries, with arms extending free of the body; and although bronze was not normally acceptable for architectural sculpture, its influence made itself felt there too, one of the results being the revolutionary freedom of pose in the Eretria and Aigina pediments (p.184).

Sculpture once created was, like choral odes, political speeches and alphabetical writing, widely accessible. Even the funerary kouroi of an aristocratic family stood in a cemetery where anyone could look at them. The myths which were narrated in temple sculptures were not the recondite material of higher education or priestly mystique, they were myths which everyone knew. The language of the visual arts could be comprehended without literacy (only a minority of narrative works were inscribed), and in this way art could function as a medium of popular culture. For proof that it did so, however, we have to turn away from sculpture and look at painted pottery. The two arts are linked by the fact that both were produced by men who were essentially regarded in their own time (as distinct from later antiquity) as artisans – men with exceptional skill who could expect to be paid accordingly, but who would be admitted only exceptionally and on sufferance to the cultural élite of their city. The important difference is in the context and the cost of the sculptor's work as against the vase-painter's. One natural result of this difference is that, whereas a modest collection of literary comment (most of it considerably later) on Greek sculpture survives from antiquity, the art of the vase-painter rose, flourished, declined and vanished with barely a single notice in any literary source to acknowledge its existence. There may be other contributory reasons for this too, such as the chronological: we today generally consider that the greatest age of Greek vase-painting was the last century, and particularly the last half-century, of the Archaic period. The great age of sculpture has, rightly or wrongly, been considered since antiquity to have begun just at the time when vase-painting was going into decline, and we find that very few of the ancient literary passages on sculpture refer back to the Archaic period. Yet there were still fine vases painted in the heyday of Classical sculpture and literature; but they were neither mentioned at the time nor, it seems, treasured long enough for later antiquity to admire them. So it is a fair inference that the status of the two arts was different. Greek vases, however finely decorated, were with rare exceptions functional objects, as their shapes make clear. They were produced in large quantities, dozens of them at a time in each firing of the kiln, and were not often commissioned pieces; their price was within the range of all but the poorest customers and, equally important, the people who produced and decorated them were probably from no more elevated a social stratum than that of most of their customers.

This last statement stands in need of a little closer examination. What we know about Greek potters is not much, and mostly derives from the internal evidence of their works. A potter's workshop was a small business, with an owner and a few employees, including the painters. The only vase-painter fleetingly portrayed in Classical comedy (Aristophanes, *Ekklesiazousai* 995–6) is clearly not a rich man, although in the Archaic period the occasional potter did become rich enough to make a sculptural dedication. The paintings themselves convey evidence on two main questions: that of geographical origins and that of literacy. The potters' and painters' names, signed on a minority of the Athenian vases, contain a surprising number (though relatively speaking again a minority) of foreign names – foreign, that is, to Greece and not just to Athens. Many of them look less like personal names than foreign ethnics – 'the Lydian', 'the Mysian', 'the Scyth', 'the Kolchian', 'the little Syrian', 'the Brygan' (a tribe in Thrace) – such as might be used by an Athenian populace which could not master some unpronounceable proper name. The significance of these names, if they mean what they appear to mean and are not simply nicknames, is that those who bore them can never have been Athenian citizens. Their status must have been either that of metics (resident aliens with certain rights that did not include political ones) or else that of slaves; even the former, though it would not exclude them from becoming rich, would not make for easy access to the world of private education, the symposium, the philosophical or the political debate. These same inscriptions, together with the much more numerous ones explaining or commenting on the content of the pictures, are in fact the most copious general source of evidence, of any kind, about literacy in the Archaic period. As applied to the vase-painters themselves they are a little ambiguous, since we cannot always be sure that it is the same man who is painting the figures and writing the captions. What they suggest is that the painters lived in a world of partial literacy, with at times a hazy knowledge of spelling; and that is entirely compatible with the other inferences made above. The first painted alphabetical inscription is before 700 BC, but even in the sixth and fifth centuries they are hardly frequent.

So we come to the content of the paintings themselves. Leaving aside the problematical era of the later Geometric paintings (see above, pp. 65–78), and confining ourselves to the human figure-scenes, we find certain general features to be present throughout the seventh, sixth and early fifth centuries. Firstly, for a long time myth predominates very heavily in the subject-matter of these scenes and even when, in the late sixth century, genre scenes begin to be commoner they do not yet displace mythology as a focus of interest. Secondly, the mythological pictures show certain marked biases: heroes appear with greater frequency than divinities, and the exploits of the heroes are somewhat selectively portrayed with an eye to a simple and intelligible picture: that is presumably why we have among the deeds of Herakles, for example, over five hundred representations of the Nemean Lion and not a single one of the Augean Stables. Such an approach leads to repetitiveness, especially when coupled with the age-long tendency of artists to observe each other's work and choice of subjects.

To these general characteristics we can add another, less commonly discussed outside specialist circles: the vase-painters' approach to the iconography of a given subject. Even when he is directly inspired by a literary source, an artist in any other medium has to make a conceptual change or adjustment of some

kind, and none more than the painter. It is obvious that he cannot 'paint a story' just as he has heard or read it; what is less
obvious is what he must do instead. The 'simple' solution of
picking a single, climactic moment in the story and representing
that is in fact neither so simple nor necessarily appropriate. The
notion of taking a story – that is a set of parallel sequences of
events on a personal scale – and portraying those stages of the
sequences which happen to be *exactly* simultaneous in time, is
one that has become familiar to our minds mainly since the
invention of still photography; and it is in fact a rare photograph
which encapsulates, in itself, the elements of a whole sequence
of events. This solution is thus seldom adopted in narrative
vase-painting. In a different way, the next most natural alternative for us was equally unlikely to be appropriate for them,
namely the presentation of a series of pictures in which one or
more characters appear repeatedly, on the analogy of the car-
toon strip or the cinematograph, to show the successive
episodes of a story. Historically, the Greeks appear to have
adopted this method only in the Hellenistic period, and to have
left its full exploration to the Romans; but a more serious objection is anyway that the surface of a vase is generally too small an
area to allow of such treatment; and the few apparent breaches
of this limitation are in fact examples of something slightly different, a series of pictures on one vase representing a *series* of
exploits by the same hero, each separate tale having one picture.

What Greek narrative painters, together with most other early
artists, adopted instead was a method which seems descriptively
more complex than either of the above, although psychologically
it is doubtless more primitive. This is the method best called
'synoptic', in which the artist presents as contemporaneous a
*Plate 36*   number of events which are in fact successive, either by taking a
climactic episode and expanding it forwards and backwards in
time, or by mentally arranging the episodes in their proper order
and then simply telescoping them together (expert opinion differs as to which of these two variants predominated). The
method came so naturally to the artist that he probably used it
without thinking; and so naturally to his public (ourselves

included) that we often do not notice it unless it is pointed out. For instance, every picture of the living Gorgon Medusa, accompanied by the winged horse Pegasos, is an example of the 'synoptic' method since the story relates that Pegasos was born by emerging from the Gorgon's headless trunk after her decapitation. Less obscurely, any scene of the blinding of Polyphemos *Plate 37* in which the victim holds a cup is a further example since, as Homer relates, the deed could only be done when Polyphemos had fallen asleep, and his sleep was in turn the effect of the drunkenness which the cup in turn is there to symbolize. There is, in short, more of a history of analytical thought, however primitive, behind the simple forms of a Greek vase-painting than might appear.

But as well as being produced by a different form of thought-process from that of a literary version of a myth, the vase-paintings sometimes show independence at a more detailed level: that is, they sometimes tell what is recognizably the same myth in different terms. It is tempting, when this happens, to say that they have simply got the story wrong. If a vase-painter is clearly representing a well-known literary episode, such as the chariot-race in book xxiii of the *Iliad*, and shows the 'wrong' hero winning the race, then indeed we may perhaps be entitled to suspect a mistake. But often the position is more ambivalent than this. We looked at this question briefly in the context of the Late Geometric paintings (p. 72) and the tentative conclusion there was that the surviving literary accounts of the Greek myths may have been neither complete nor incontestable. There are later pictures on Greek vases which show clear and coherent legendary scenes that are otherwise virtually unknown to us: Ajax and Achilles playing dice is an unusually familiar example; as well as appearing on one of the most famous of Greek vases, it was frequently represented over a period of fifty years or so, in sculpture as well as on pottery. There are many other pictures which tell a well-known story in an unfamiliar form, yet are not necessarily to be explained as misunderstandings of the familiar literary version. After all, even within the literary tradition there was room for gradual modification of the details of a story through time (as we see, for instance, by comparing a Homeric and a fifth-century tragedian's version of the same myth); room, too, for two or more absolutely contradictory versions to have existed, even contemporaneously.

The importance of the vase-paintings for this question is, firstly, that they go back to a date earlier than most of, in some cases earlier than all, our literary accounts of a given myth; and secondly, that they bring to light 'buried' stories, or versions of stories, which were not merely the result of an individual artist's whim. Sometimes an early vase gives a version of a story which is only confirmed by some very obscure, or very much later, literary source. A clear example is the story of Tydeus and Ismene (cf. p. 72). As representatives of opposite sides in one of the great wars of the Heroic Age, the expedition of the Seven against Thebes, these two might have been thought unlikely to become acquainted, still less intimate; even if they had, the 'accepted' version of the sequel, as given in Sophokles' *Antigone* (*c.* 440 BC), is one in which Ismene, Antigone's sister, plays an important secondary role in the action at a time when Tydeus, along with most of the Seven, has already been killed in battle. Yet on a Corinthian vase of about 550 BC we see Tydeus threatening Ismene with imminent death as she lies in bed, while a naked man named Periklymenos makes his escape. It is only in an introduction to the text of the *Antigone*, written nearly a thousand years later, that a commentator named Sallustius tells us why. Tydeus, he explains, killed Ismene at Athena's command for committing adultery with a man named Theoklymenos (rather than Periklymenos). What is most significant is that this commentator refers the story back to the Archaic poet Mimnermos of Kolophon; he thus shows that a version of this myth was current in Archaic times that was not merely different from, but directly contradicted by, the more familiar version. He also gives, unsolicited, a vindication of the vase-painter, whose work he cannot possibly have known, and whom we might otherwise have thought a mere victim of confusion. If anyone, it is Sophokles who emerges as the likeliest 'heretic' in the transmission of the legend.

29 Attic red figure amphora with kithara-player, *c*. 525 BC

30 Archaic kouroi, Kleobis and Biton

31 The Calf-bearer (Moschophoros)   32 'Rampin' horseman from Athenian Akropolis

33 Grave-stele of discus-thrower from Athens, *c*. 550 BC

34 Herakles and Triton from
limestone pediment, Athens,
Akropolis

35 Theseus and Antiope from
pediment of Temple of Apollo,
Eretria

36 Attic black figure cup with scene of Circe and Odysseus' sailors, *c.* 550 BC

37 Protoattic amphora with blinding of Polyphemos
(*above*) and Gorgons (*below*), *c.* 670 BC

38 Attic red figure amphora with Theseus and Korone, *c.* 510 BC

39 Attic red figure cup with Greek fighting Persian, *c.* 480 BC

40 View of Temple of Aphaia at Aigina, *c.* 500 BC

41 Kore dedicated by Euthydikos

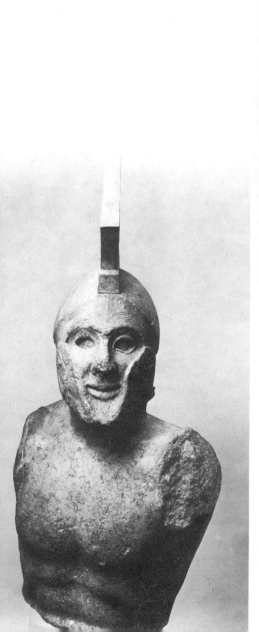

42 Torso of warrior ('Leonidas')
from Sparta

43 Figure number III in East pediment from Aigina

At one level, this can be taken as just another example of the way in which Greek vase-painting often does duty as a primary source. Just as, through his genre scenes, the vase-painter quite often informs us of real-life practices which are not known to us from literature, so too he acts as guardian, through his myth-scenes, for stories of whose currency we should otherwise be ignorant. But there may be more to it than that. The vase-painter has, I would argue, a kind of social significance, as a link between the social and intellectual élite and the common man. In the Classical period, such a role is primarily filled (at least from our point of view) by the comic poet, who might have a fairly high social status, but presented genre settings and down-to-earth characters. In Archaic times, comedy did not yet exist in the full dramatic sense. The vase-painter is the reverse of the comedian in that, having relatively *low* social status, he decorated his products in such a way that they would appeal to aristocrats, among others. More particularly, the genre scenes on late Archaic vases show a very marked social exclusiveness in their subject-matter: few Athenians had the leisure or wealth to frequent the gymnasium, the wrestling-school or the symposium; to engage musicians and reciters; to keep mistresses or solicit beautiful boys with gifts; to own horses and serve in the cavalry (or even, come to that, in the heavy infantry). Yet these are the commonest of genre subjects, and painted vases were owned and used by a far wider clientèle than that represented in the scenes. Likewise, the 'love-names' on vases, praising the beauty of boys (and occasionally girls, see below) in contemporary Athens, are usually applied to people of aristocratic birth, whom the painters are unlikely to have known personally. Many societies since then (our own not least) have sought to divert their masses with the spectacle of the upper class at play, and it seems that late Archaic Athens was another such.

But the subject-matter of myth and legend was one of the interests that were common to all; and mythical narration was an activity that could not be kept exclusive. The trite repetition of established 'favourites' among the mythological repertoire is usually seen as a popular feature; and I believe that the occurrence of the numerous 'aberrant' versions of myths should also be seen as a kind of vernacular or 'alternative' culture for the many who lacked a literary outlet, and in some cases were even without literary access. There is an attractive instance of this on a vase of just before 500 BC painted by Euthymides. A famous

*Plate 38* exploit of Theseus had been his abduction (at a very early age, long before the Trojan episode) of Helen. On this vase, however, Theseus is carrying off a girl with the name, unknown to mythology, of Koronĕ, while it is another woman, evidently trying to restrain him, who is labelled as 'Helen'. There is an obvious temptation, which most authorities have not resisted, to say that Euthymides became confused over his captions, that the abduction-victim should have been 'Helen' and the other girl (perhaps an obscure maidservant in the story) 'Koronĕ'. But when we learn that Koronĕ was the name of a pretty girl in Athens, fervently praised for her looks on another vase of approximately the same date, then a different and more pleasing explanation comes to mind. The attractions of a reigning beauty are being presented as superior even to those of Helen, and she is temporarily given a legendary context in which to prove the point: even Theseus cannot resist her.

Such examples, rare as they are, can illustrate for us a genuinely popular handling of myth, and thus lift the curtain for a moment on the thoughts and actions of ordinary people in Archaic Greece. At this time, we may be sure, there was no great contrast between town and country life: urban citizens owned land in the open country, rural citizens came to the town to take part in certain festivals, and to attend assemblies. For both alike, much of life consisted of a round of work (mainly agricultural) and sleep; recreational activity would be dominated by the festivals, some local, some involving the whole state. By the fifth century, these had become sufficiently numerous in Athens to cover something like sixty days in a year (not an excessive number for a civilization which knew no week-ends or sabbaths). The performance of rituals ensured that the religious inspiration of these occasions was remembered; but this did not prevent religion being used, as so often in the Greek world, as an excuse for many other things. The festival would involve a visit to a sanctuary of some kind, where new and advanced works of sculpture might be on view; a choir might perform a hymn, either traditional or specially written for the occasion, accompanied by musicians whose art was as widely appreciated as was the poet's. Not that all the contributions would be of such an obviously appropriate kind: there were festival contexts for which a poem like Archilochos' story of seduction (above, pp. 170–3) would be in the expected genre – thus perhaps strengthening our doubts about its autobiographical element. At a festival, people hoped to eat meals of a quality that they did not taste in the rest of the year; lavish consumption of wine was often not merely permitted but expected. The presence of aristocrats and other well-to-do people who might have attended inter-state festivals in places like Delos and Olympia would have acted as some sort of guarantee of artistic standards; yet, at local festivals in particular, almost all classes of the community, including women, participated. For these and the other reasons that we have considered, it seems likely that the values of Archaic Greece – artistic, intellectual and (so far as they went) spiritual – were broadly based and universally shared.

In such circumstances, one would expect that political ideas, too, would be actively shared by a wide range of the population. That they must have been in late sixth-century Athens at least is guaranteed by the way in which the decisive steps were taken towards one of the last great achievements of Archaic Greece – democracy. In 508 BC, with the tyrants gone for good and the apparatus of aristocratic politics undergoing hasty repairs after decades of disuse, the politician Kleisthenes took a fateful step. He realized, apparently, that the rule of Peisistratos and his sons had changed Athens too deeply for a reversion to the old system to be acceptable. An even stronger incentive may have been that, under this briefly-revived 'old system', his own party was getting the worst of the struggle. He was a member of the family of the Alkmaionidai which, despite an earlier phase of compromise with the tyranny in the 520s when Kleisthenes himself had held high office, could claim to have been latterly the focus of

resistance to the tyrants. By some combination of all these considerations, he conceived the idea of 'taking the people into
partnership', as Herodotus puts it (v 66, 2), and thus securing
his own position. But he could only do this by offering a programme which commanded wide support, and here he showed a
level of statesmanship and administrative insight which is still
impressive from our own distance of time. His programme
embraced an extension of the citizenship to a number of new
people – metics, foreigners, even slaves according to Aristotle
(*Politics* 1275 b 37); this was a traditional and often effective
measure, whose popularity was in this case all the greater for
the fact that his opponents had just been violently reversing it
by a purge of the citizen-rolls. It has been plausibly suggested
that Kleisthenes was here re-instating one of the popular policies
of the tyranny, possibly even reinstating the very 'new citizens'
whom the tyrants had enrolled and his opponents purged.

By far his greatest undertaking, however, was a proposed
reform of the whole government and organization of Attica. The
traditional four tribes of an Ionic polis were to be replaced, for all
political purposes, by ten new ones, each of which would meet
to elect one general and fifty members of a newly-established
Council of 500, which in turn was to have direct control of a
wide range of state affairs. Some old institutions – the archons
(annual magistrates) and the long-established aristocratic council
of the Areiopagos, composed of former holders of the archon-
ship – were allowed to survive, but gradually declined in power
and prestige: by 487 it was found acceptable to decide the
appointment of archons by lot, while in 462 the Areiopagos was
deprived of its last political powers. Most complex of all was
Kleisthenes' proposed system for his tribal divisions: each tribe
was composed of three *trittyes* ('ridings'), of which there were
therefore thirty; but the three had to be drawn, one each from
three geographical divisions of Attica – the City, the Coast and
the Inland – which Kleisthenes proposed to form. Each tribe
would therefore be a microcosm of the Attic state, with no room
for undue bias derived from either locality or kinship. At the
lowest level, an equally important change was made with the

reorganization of the *demes*; these already existed as centres of population, but under Kleisthenes their number was to become probably 139 in all Attica, and they were now designated as sub-divisions of each trittys (although in a very populous area, where there was an established deme which could not easily be divided, there might be only one deme to a trittys). A recent

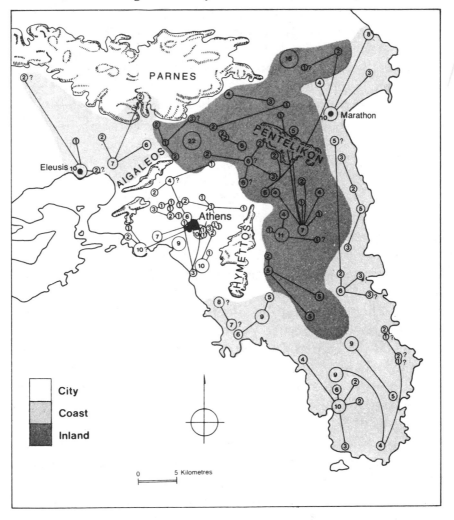

Fig. 14 The geographical effect of Kleisthenes' reforms (after J. S. Traill, *The political organization of Attica* (*Hesperia*, supplement 14, 1975)). The circles are the *demes*, the networks are the *trittyes*, the numerals show the number of counsellors elected

discovery suggests that a similar system of artificial tribes, each with members recruited from three different geographical districts, existed at Corinth by the mid-fifth century, and probably goes back to a time earlier than Kleisthenes' reforms at Athens. If this is right, it underlines two salient features of Kleisthenes' thinking: first, a willingness to adopt ideas from external sources which makes him more of an eclectic reformer than a visionary or radical; and secondly, an absence of anything that was *necessarily* democratic about his administrative provisions, as is shown by the fact that Corinth was a thorough going oligarchy at the time in question.

There is, accordingly, much to be said for the modern view that Kleisthenes, for all his administrative ability, was a skilled manipulator of the traditional forms of Archaic politics who unwittingly stumbled on a democratic solution. On this view, he misjudged the majority of his fellow Athenians, who proceeded to harness his measures to their own purpose with a speed which can only be explained by the existence of a strong, ready-formed movement towards democracy. The political actions of the next four years after 508 are dazzling in their self-confidence and heady with success. The first and hardest test came within months: the Spartans, whose army had been the actual instrument that brought about the fall of the Athenian tyranny in 510, had been hoping to secure a powerful ally under the leadership of Isagoras, Kleisthenes' chief opponent, who favoured government by oligarchy. Now they were dismayed at the radical turn which Athens' affairs had taken. When Isagoras called for help – democracy was indeed seeking 'brilliant Athens and us' – King Kleomenes of Sparta was quick to answer, and a Spartan force was soon installed on the Athenian Akropolis. But the plan failed: by a great spontaneous convulsion, the people of Athens repudiated Isagoras and the Spartans, and the resistance was led by the Council. This showed the mettle both of the electors and of the men they had chosen to represent them.

Kleomenes and his Spartans were allowed to leave under truce; but they could not easily accept such a reverse and in 506 they were back in the field with a more dangerous plan: a three-cornered invasion of Attica by the Boiotians from the north, the Chalkidians from the north-east, and the Spartans and their allies from the south-west. This time, Isagoras was actually to be installed as tyrant, showing that Sparta found democracy even more menacing than tyranny. But the new democracy stood its ground: the allies of the Spartans refused to take part in such a blatantly interventionist move and withdrew, provoking a split in the Spartan leadership; the Athenian army, in a brilliant double victory, meanwhile routed the Boiotians and the Chalkidians severally. Even this was not the end: the Boiotians incited Aigina to launch a naval war against Athens, and in about 504 there was one more abortive plan by the Spartans, which this time aimed at no less than the restoration as tyrant of Peisistratos' son Hippias, whom they themselves had expelled in 510 and who was now living under Persian protection. It was to no avail: the solidarity of the Athenians with their state and its new constitution was unshakable. Yet all these decisive achievements were carried through anonymously, as it were, and without the names of individual leaders coming down to us. Kleisthenes was not in continuous control any longer: he had been exiled by Isagoras during the first attempted counter-revolution and could take no part in the crucial events of that year; he soon came back, but presently faded from the picture. One item of his policy, that of submitting to the Great King of Persia in return for Persian help against Sparta, was unacceptable to the Athenians, and they repudiated it utterly when the attempt to restore Hippias was made in 504. The democracy was in a mood to take on all comers if necessary.

These events of the last decade of the sixth century are a brilliant example of the power of political ideas in the field of action, as well as a vindication of the principle of the independent city-state. They stand comparison with any of the similar and better-known episodes in later Western history, such as those in England after 1642, in France after 1789 or in Russia after 1917; and the fact that they were carried through without a Cromwell, a Napoleon or a Lenin is perhaps the most significant thing about them. The individual Greek had begun by expressing himself in poetry, in thought and in art; now the individual Athenian was claiming, as of right, the responsibility of political participation in a democracy, and backing his claim with extra-ordinary success. Other Greeks, some in a directly political way, others less consciously, were soon to follow along the path that had been opened to them.

# 6

# *The End of Archaism*

The houses of our City
Are real enough but they lie
Haphazardly scattered over the earth . . .

                                    . . . Where the
Power lies remains to be seen,
The Force, though, is clearly with Them: perhaps only
      By falling can She become
Her own vision, but we have sworn under four eyes
      To keep Her up . . .

      W. H. Auden,
      'On installing an American Kitchen in Lower Austria'

The claims made for Archaic Greece in the preceding chapters
may seem inflated. If so much had been done, then what worlds
were there left for the Classical Greeks to conquer? And why
should we continue to regard the later fifth century BC as the
climax of Greek civilization? These are reasonable questions, and
it might seem that we could answer them by a kind of hypothetical test. The Archaic period is conventionally divided from the
Classical by a military episode, the Persian Wars and the con- *Plate 3*
temporaneous wars of the Sicilian Greeks against Carthage;
although it is an episode for which scholars have tried to discern
correlatives of a more cultural kind, making it into a landmark
for the arts and for political developments too. I hope to show
that some of these attempts have been misguided; but even if I
am wrong, it must always be borne in mind that such demarca-
tions of history as 'Archaic' and 'Classical', 'Medieval' and
'Renaissance', although reasonably accepted for the convenience
of later ages, are entirely artificial categories which would have

been only dimly perceptible, if that, to the people who lived through the transition.

Accepting, then, the landmark of Xerxes' invasion of 480–479 BC as the terminus for the Archaic period, let us put the question first in the hypothetical form: suppose that the predictable (and indeed the widely-predicted) had happened, and the armies and fleets of the Greek states had gone down before the overwhelming numerical superiority of the forces of Persia. What then would be our estimate of the contribution of the Greeks to Western civilization? The question, however, contains a hidden assumption: that the later development of Greek culture, with the country permanently incorporated in the Persian Empire, would have been stunted beyond recognition. That is not perhaps an extravagant assumption; the best evidence that we can cite in its support is the experience of the Ionian Greeks in the two final generations of the Archaic period, during which many of them were in fact subjects of the Persian Empire. The experience was not a happy one: both culturally and economically, Ionia seems to have suffered a marked regression; politically, too, the Persians had at first pursued an interventionist policy, installing pro-Persian tyrants in most of the cities that they controlled. The mass-exodus of leading cultural figures and the elimination of the former political leadership did nothing to help. If this is the pattern that would have been imposed on mainland Greece, then we must assume an equally discouraging outcome. Yet even then the evidence is not entirely unambiguous: for it is also true that in the fifth century, with their independence of foreign powers restored, the Ionians did not enjoy anything like a restoration of their former glories; the economic picture is particularly cheerless. If this was because, in exchange for Persian rule, they found themselves subject to the increasingly exacting demands of membership of the Athenian confederacy, then this constitutes another 'hidden variable' for which allowance must be made.

In fact, the tissue of superimposed hypotheses soon becomes unmanageable, and it is better to re-phrase our question in a different and less hypothetical way. What was it that the Greeks sought to preserve by fighting the Persians? What was it that drove, firstly the Ionian Greeks to make their unsuccessful attempt to shake off Persian rule in 499–494; then the Athenians and Eretrians, having supported that revolt, to stand their ground against the inevitable Persian retribution in 490, with results as triumphant for the one as they were disastrous for the other; and finally, the thirty-one Greek states to send their contingents into action against Xerxes' forces in 480–479? By any rational calculation, the odds against success on each occasion were long; they had not appreciably shortened even at the moment when the opposing armies faced each other for the final encounter on the field of Plataia in 479. The alternative course of entering into some kind of peace-negotiations was open throughout, and was specifically offered to the Athenians, on very favourable terms, as late as 479 when the Persian general Mardonios saw the chance of exploiting a conflict of interest between Athens, in her exposed position north of the Isthmos, and the bulk of her allies who lived in the Peloponnese. Many Greek states – not just the northern ethnē of Macedonia and Thessaly, but powerful poleis like Thebes, Argos and, for a time, Aigina, took what seemed the reasonable course and submitted to Persian rule. Likewise, in Sicily, the powerful city of Selinous was committed to the side of the Carthaginian invaders.

The behaviour of the remaining states can only be explained by some intuitive belief, backed by one or two favourable portents like the good showing of the Chian navy in the Ionian Revolt and the signal success of the Athenian infantry at Marathon, that the reasonable would not happen, and that the risk of war was worth taking. Other factors doubtless contributed to their calculations, such as a well-founded faith in the superiority of Greek arms and armour when the fighting came to close quarters (this is a recurrent theme in Herodotus' accounts of the battles – see v 49, 5; vii 211, 2; ix 62, 4 and 63, 3). Then there were the geographical features in central and southern Greece, which favour a defender who not only knows the country, but also prefers fighting on battlefields of restricted extent by land, and in enclosed waters at sea; this last factor largely

explains why the decision of the northern Greeks, with their different physical environment, tended to be against resistance. But
still the question remains: the risk of war was worth taking, but
for the sake of what?

The answer of an individual Greek would almost certainly
have included the word 'freedom'. When submitted to closer
analysis, his use of the word could probably be broken down
into two main headings, one affecting the community as a whole
and the other referring to the individual; and he might have
added that neither could properly be applied to the soldier who
faced him in the Persian army. A community, first of all, is a
group of people who share some kind of common life and who
give and receive some kind of reciprocal services and benefits; its
organization need by no means be democratic, as long as the
roles performed by its different classes of membership are
widely accepted. The soldier in a Greek army could point to an
obvious fact here: whatever it was that he was fighting for, his
fellow citizens were all in the fight beside him. Some of the
richest landowners might still have their horses waiting out of
sight, but when the battle joined they were in their place in the
infantry line; so too was the army commander (in two of the
three main land-battles of the Persian Wars, Marathon and
Thermopylai, the Greek commander was killed fighting bravely
in the front line). The poorer classes might be unable to afford
the arms which could give them a place in the phalanx, but they
were still there in some strength as auxiliaries, to face the risk of
Persian missile-fire and the possible consequences of defeat;
while in a sea-battle between fleets of oared ships, their contribution as rowers was the primary one. The soldier in the Persian army could not make similar claims; he might be a member
of any one of the subject peoples (including Ionian Greeks) who
had been conscripted into service in the Persian forces, or he
might be Persian-born; in either case, he was probably
thousands of miles from home, under the command of representatives of an inaccessibly remote monarch, many of them cavalry
officers who could contribute to victory, but were likely to desert
him in defeat. Nor did the consequences of victory offer him

much positive advantage, beyond being preferable to those of defeat. He had played no part whatsoever in the choice of the representatives who had brought about the war, or who led him in the battle. Many such considerations could have run through the minds of the ordinary Greek (and Persian) soldiers as they prepared to fight; and in the Western conflict similar factors applied, for the Carthaginian army was again a confederacy of subject peoples, even though at Carthage itself the same extremes of authoritarianism did not prevail.

As for the freedom of the individual, this will have meant different things to men of different contingents and statuses. We may start at the darkest end of the spectrum: the thousands of Helots who marched out on campaign with their Spartan masters did so not from any free choice, but probably on pain of death. Yet even they could hope for a grant of their personal freedom if they distinguished themselves in the fighting; failing that, victory offered them the security of keeping as their masters men who were at least fellow-Greeks and whose ways were long familiar to them. These ways could run in very sinister directions: on occasion, brave or otherwise distinguished Helots were victimized as being a menace to the security of the system (e.g. Thucydides iv 80, 4). But the hard fact is that the Helots as a whole were trusted to fight rather than desert, and did so; which implies that they expected no improvement in their lot from a Persian victory, a belief which may or may not have been justified. The Helots, however, represent an extreme and a minority case of the Greek side; the Greek armies and navies were otherwise largely composed of free citizens, men with a civilian occupation which they had abandoned in preparation for war. The majority of these could expect, if they survived, to go back to the same work and the same life-style after the fighting was over, whoever won; so it was hardly this that they were fighting for. If they had an economic motive at all, it could be connected with a distinguishing feature of the Greek system which had been pointed out fifty years earlier, according to Herodotus (i 153, 1), by no less a figure than King Cyrus of Persia, when he said 'I have never yet been afraid of a people who have a special place set aside in their city where they can come together and tell each other lies under oath'. The permanent market (to which he was referring) was certainly by now a regular feature of a Greek town and this anecdote, even if apocryphal, suggests that that was not the case in the Persian Empire.

But the opportunity for individual enterprise in trading was only one instance of a whole set of values which had grown up in the shelter of the Archaic Greek state: the right to attend the assembly and, if not to participate in the taking of decisions, at least to hear them justified; the right to appeal to a recognized code of laws; the right to speak one's mind about politics, morality, the arts and, up to an appreciable point, even religion – these were some of the things which a Greek of 480 BC had already come to expect, and which he could have felt to be at stake in the war against Persia. They were, however, somewhat abstract ideals and not always easy to articulate. In so far as a more explicit sentiment appears in the expressions of Greek feelings at this time of crisis, it is to do with self-respect: the revulsion at the degree of servility expected of the subjects of the Great King, and the fanatical extremism which, under the stress of warfare, showed itself in both the Persian and the Carthaginian military systems. This again reflects the implicit expectations of the Greek, that even though all men were not yet to be regarded as equal, yet there was an irreducible minimum of esteem (and self-esteem) for the free individual in society. If taxed with the condition of the Athenian slave or the Spartan Helot, he might well have replied that it was in order to escape this same condition for himself that he was fighting.

Every historian of Greece suffers the temptation of extending false generalizations, based on the unique case of Athens, to Greek culture as a whole; and this is especially true in the late Archaic period when the Athenian experiment in democracy was so isolated. Nevertheless Athens did play an outstanding part in the resistance to Persia and it is justifiable to point out the way in which her institutions contributed to her achievement. The freshly established board of ten generals, one elected by each of Kleisthenes' new tribes, was put to the supreme test within less than a generation, when the landing of a Persian force, first on Euboia and then on Athenian soil at Marathon, demanded a series of swift strategic and tactical decisions. Warfare by democracy is not everybody's prescription for success, yet that is essentially the process that Herodotus describes (vi 103–110) in the tense days before battle was joined, with the vote of the majority of the Assembly going in favour of Miltiades' proposal to send out the army to Marathon, and that of the majority of the generals eventually supporting the best tactical proposal, that for a frontal attack. Even more crucial was the vote of the Assembly a few years later, against applying the new-found revenues of the Laurion silver-mines to a free hand-out to all citizens, and in favour of the building of a fleet as proposed by Themistokles, who had begun this policy ten years earlier by fortifying the great natural harbour of the Piraeus. In 480, this fleet was to contribute more than any other single force to the deliverance of Greece; in Classical Athens, the political advancement of the poorer classes who manned its galleys was a direct result of this decision and an equally direct influence on Athenian policy.

But how far can these years, militarily so crucial, be judged to form a precise cultural landmark, such as is conventionally seen in the division of Archaic and Classical? It is my contention that most of the main contributions of the Greeks to later civilization were the result of processes already well under way in Archaic times, if in some cases only from near its end. The orthodox view, by contrast, takes its stand essentially on literature and art, and claims that in these fields a great new era came into being after, and at least partly as a result of, the Greek victory in the Persian Wars. In the words of J. B. Bury, 'Men seemed to rise at once to the sense of the high historical importance of their experience'. The two great literary genres used to illustrate this view are drama and prose (especially historical prose); while in art, the favoured examples are the rise of free painting and the achievements of so-called fifth-century sculpture (meaning, nearly always,-sculpture between 480 and 400). Now as long as the criterion is that of the *survival* of literary works in their own right, and of works of art together with later copies and literary descriptions of them, then the case is clear and beyond question: of surviving Greek drama and prose literature, something over 99 per cent must date to after 480 BC, while in the case of art there is a glaring contrast between the scrappy and unreliable testimonies about Archaic art and the relatively copious flow of detailed information, and of later copies, from the early Classical period onwards. These survivals are, however, essentially the product of opinions formed in later centuries (in some cases, very much later) and it is not self-evident that, had it the choice, our own age would necessarily have shared all those opinions. Furthermore, we do have some factual knowledge which tells against regarding the Persian Wars as an absolute and epoch-making division.

For a start, many of the writers and artists who became famous in the years immediately after 480 had, naturally, begun their careers well before that date. To name the most conspicuous, Aischylos and Pindar had both reached early middle age by the time of Xerxes' invasion, had formed their styles and had won some fame, in the same way as the outlines of Athenian policy in the fifth century were shaped by statesmen like Themistokles whose greatest achievements were by then behind them. Tragedy, in particular, was an established medium in Athens, where a *cause célèbre* broke out over the production, probably in 492, of a play about the fall of Miletos in the Ionian revolt, by Phrynichos (another artist active both before and after the Persian Wars). The revolution in Greek wall- and panel-painting, which is associated with the names of Polygnotos of Thasos and Mikon of Athens, looks like a clear case of a post-war development, in as much as their most famous works were to be seen in buildings only erected at that time, and indeed on occasion made use of the Persian Wars themselves as subject-matter. Closer examination, however, has revealed some interesting features: the influence of this revolution has been detected in Athenian red-figure vases, some of which are thought to date from rather before 480; at least one innovatory painter, Kimon of Kleonai, was believed to have lived in the late Archaic period. Famous late Archaic buildings, such as the Treasury of the Athenians at Delphi and the new Temple of *Plate 40* Aphaia on Aigina, require the eye of an expert to distinguish them from architecture of the full Classical period. Above all, there is the evidence of sculpture to support the notion that, independently of the Persian Wars, and well before, for mainland Greece, their issue had been decided, the great series of innovations which brought into being what we call the 'Early Classical' or 'Severe' style, was already well under way.

In the case of sculptural development, enough evidence survives either in monumental form or in descriptions to make the conclusions fairly secure. Once again, we can point to the names of great artists, like the Aiginetan sculptors, Onatas and Glaukias, whom we know to have been active and successful before 480, but whose reputation was at its peak in the 470s and 460s, suggesting that the revolution in style was not an entirely post-war phenomenon. No original works survive which can be definitely attributed to them, however. What we have instead is a series of works, original but anonymous, which adequately illustrate the nature and timing of the change that took place in sculpture. It has been fully studied in several books, of which one of the most recent, Brunilde Sismondo Ridgway's *The Severe Style in Greek Sculpture*, gives an acceptable summary of the features of the new style. By comparison with most Archaic sculpture, the aptly-named 'Severe' style presents a new simplicity: surface elaboration is rejected in favour of a greater feel for volume and three-dimensionality; the ornate and mannered drapery-folds are drastically pared down; the 'Archaic smile', for inactive figures, is finally banished in favour of a serious expression, while figures involved in physical activity are given expressions of appropriate emotion; the use of bronze for the most prestigious works is greatly increased. Perhaps most significant, the poses of free-standing statues begin to show the freedom which had hitherto been confined to architectural sculpture. Instead of the hundred-year-old pose of the kouros, male figures could now be shown in violent action: an athlete sprinting or throwing

the discus, a soldier in battle, a satyr stepping quickly backwards. Statues, in short, have begun to have a subject instead of
merely conforming to one of a narrow range of types.

If we examine these features one by one, we shall find nearly
all of them present in the sculpture of the years between 500 and
480, and one or two perhaps even earlier than that. There is first
the stratigraphic evidence from the Athenian Akropolis. When
the Persians occupied Athens in the weeks before the battle of
Salamis, they destroyed or damaged many of the buildings and
sculptures that they found; the Athenians, returning after their
victory, evidently decided to dispose of a group of irreparably
damaged dedications on the Akropolis, most of them of the type
of standing female statue known as the korē, by burying them in
a trench near the site of the later Erechtheion, and there they lay
undisturbed until discovered by the excavators of the 1880s. Any
statue found in this particular deposit will almost certainly have
been carved before 480, particularly if it shows signs of burning;
but we have to be more careful with other groups of Archaic
sculpture found elsewhere on the Akropolis; they may not have
been buried in identical circumstances, especially since they are
sometimes associated with other works which, on the accepted
stylistic chronology, would be dated *after* the Persian Wars.
However, there is one critically important work of which at least
one piece seems to have been buried in the main deposit: it is
Plate 41  the korē Akropolis 686, dedicated by a man named Euthydikos,
which should therefore be counted as a victim of the destruction
of 480. It is critical because it shows several of the features of the
'Severe' style: the drapery has been simplified, in the cause of
emphasizing the underlying bodily forms; the expression is so
remote from the old Archaic smile as to give the statue its nick-
name of 'La Boudeuse' (the sulky girl). With this objective
dating-evidence before us, we may even think again about the
accepted post-war dating of certain other works, which look
stylistically even later, but were buried at other spots on the
Akropolis.

Other works of sculpture, in different ways, support an early
dating for 'Severe' style characteristics: anguished expressions

are found on the face of a dying figure, both on a relief from a temple in far-away Selinous in western Sicily, which is normally dated to about 500, and in the mysterious 'second east pediment' of the Temple of Aphaia on Aigina, which is thought to have been installed as a replacement for the original east pediment and cannot therefore be dated by the temple to which it belongs. Nevertheless, the orthodox stylistic date for this later pediment is between 500 and 480; it includes other figures represented in very ambitious poses, in particular two warriors who *Plate 43* are in the act of falling over backwards and are shown off balance; but here again there are vase-paintings, universally dated before 480, which show closely similar poses. Next, a freestanding statue of a warrior in a vigorous, thrusting pose was found *Plate 42* in the 1920s at Sparta, near the site of the tomb of Leonidas, and was thought by its discoverers to be a memorial to that Spartan king who died so heroically at Thermopylai in 480. Later students have seen stylistic features which look too early for that date, and have therefore doubted the identification; but its pose remains typical of what we call 'Early Classical'. More famous in antiquity was another work, remarkable once again for its pose (to judge from Roman copies, for the original is lost this time), but much more so for its subject, which was politically almost explosive: the group of the Tyrannicides, Harmodios and Aristogeiton, shown in the act of striking down Hipparchos (the brother of Hippias), as they had done in 514 BC. Here, surely, is the very embodiment of the 'Severe' style, in terms of pose and execution, but even more in terms of subject; furthermore, we know that the group was originally erected two years after the final Persian defeat, in 477, so that it would seem to tell *against* my argument about the chronology of sculptural development. But then we learn that it was merely a replacement for an original group, carved by the Archaic sculptor Antenor some time soon after the establishment of the democracy in 507. We know nothing of the pose of Antenor's group – perhaps it was simply a pair of kouroi side by side, like Kleobis and Biton – but the point is that the *intellectual* step of representing in sculpture a highly topical political subject had been taken well before the end of the Archaic period. Even the Persians paid their tribute to this revolutionary artistic advance, by carrying off Antenor's group to their capital (from where it was returned to Athens centuries later), rather than destroying it like the other sculptures. As to the popularity of bronze in the new style, this was certainly exemplified by the work of Aiginetan sculptors like Kallon, Onatas and Glaukias, and their influence can in turn be detected in the 'second east pediment' of Aphaia, mentioned just now; even Antenor's Tyrannicides were bronze (Arrian, *Anabasis* iii 16, 7). And so on.

It seems to me that the notion of a great war as an inescapable influence, actually *causing* artistic change, may in this case at least be misconceived. There is a more recent parallel which comes to mind. Let us imagine that a historian, thousands of years hence, has documentary evidence proving that the First World War broke out in 1914, but has (like us) only vaguer archaeological dating for the great innovations of the early twentieth century in painting and music. If he were to conclude that these changes were directly caused by the great disruption of the established order in Europe, he would be making the same kind of deduction which has led some authorities to think that the 'Early Classical revolution' in art was caused by the Greek triumph in the Persian Wars. But consider how wrong he would be. Of the great early twentieth-century movements in painting, many of the most distinctive and innovatory began well before 1914: the 'Fauvisme' of Matisse and his school is detectable from about 1904, and Cubism from 1907; Kandinsky painted his first abstract work in 1910 and, with Marc, set up the 'Blaue Reiter' group in 1911; German Expressionism becomes prominent from 1912 on. Or take music: Schoenberg's First String Quartet was first performed in 1907, and the break away from acceptable tonality had begun; Stravinsky's *Firebird* was heard in 1910 and his *Le sacre du printemps* in 1913; Webern's *Five Orchestral Pieces* were composed in 1911. In no accepted sense of the word can these developments have been 'caused' by the cataclysm of 1914; if there was a connection of any kind, it would be more reasonable to say that a feeling, detectable among European artists, of dissatisfaction with conventions which had been accepted for centuries past also showed itself subconsciously in some collective urge towards conflict in a political and ultimately in a military sense.

That some similar process worked itself out in the last generation of the Archaic period is likely enough, though impossible to prove. The invasion of Xerxes was, after all, simply a further act in a drama which had been inaugurated in the 540s when the Persians reached Ionia, and which had been approaching a climax since the outbreak of the Ionian Revolt in 499. Many Greeks, artists among them, will have felt that a supreme crisis was shortly to be upon them, and their thoughts may have turned more strongly in the direction of change. But I have not laboured this point at such length merely in order to establish a detail of relative chronology. If we modify the original hypothesis, made at the beginning of this chapter, from one of a final Greek defeat in the Persian Wars to one in which the final confrontation had not occurred at all – once again, a far from inconceivable eventuality historically – then the inference will become clear. It is that, irrespective of the great military events of 480 and 479, the society of Archaic Greece (and especially of Archaic Athens) was embarked on a course which would certainly have generated major political and cultural developments, and possibly ones essentially similar to those which, in the event, did take place. I am not for one moment disputing the fact that the onset of the Persians, once we remember that it was a process covering two generations, was the catalyst which brought Archaic Greece to its highest pitch of achievement. But the decision of the thirty-one states to march and sail against a people whose empire already stretched from the Indus to Cyrenaica, and whose soldiers had been seen far up the Nile and north of the Danube, was a decision as important in its antecedents as in its sequel. It was the culmination of a long process of ferment among the Greeks, resulting in the conclusion that it was worth almost anything to be able to carry on following their own ways and serving their own values.

We cannot know that such thoughts went through the minds

of the participants. But I hope that at least the foregoing chapters have made clear what some of these ways and values might have been. Looking back over the generations which had contributed to them, I still find that the most remarkable developments are the initial ones, and that the 'structural revolution' of the later eighth century was the greatest turning-point in Greece's earlier history. It was a greater step to conceive of the small independent state than to let it develop along its own course. The idea of citizenship, of the free members of such a state having certain inalienable rights, led naturally to the extension of those rights. Yet the independence of the state was also a guarantee of the many variations in the speed of developments, allowing one state to learn from the example and the experience of others. Together, these ideas were almost a prescription for political innovation, so long as the precarious balance of power within Greece, and the equally precarious immunity from external interference, were maintained. It was Greece's good fortune that, for over two centuries, these conditions were permitted to exist; by the end, it was clear to most Greeks that the gains that they had made were worth fighting for.

In the same way, the introduction of the military innovations of the first half of the seventh century (see above, pp. 99–107) is in many ways a more remarkable event for its time than is their employment, two hundred years later and after only minor modifications, to defend Greece successfully against the Persians. This outcome itself runs so very much counter to man's experience of warfare in other periods of history, when the long-entrenched system of warfare has almost inevitably fallen victim to the new and untried opponent with no such preconceptions, that it argues an exceptional degree of precociousness in the original introduction. So, too, does the promptitude with which these innovations were imitated by other peoples all over the Mediterranean area in the seventh and sixth centuries; we have already noted (p. 111) the fact that this was almost the first episode since the Bronze Age in which the doings of the Greeks became a matter for serious concern in neighbouring lands. Doubtless it was in part this experience which gave rise to the entirely unfeigned self-confidence with which the Spartans, at any rate, contemplated the rising power of Persia. Their message to King Cyrus when he threatened the cities of Ionia (it drew the rejoinder mentioned earlier, on p. 205) exemplified this attitude: 'The Spartans would not permit him to molest any city of Greece.'

Likewise, the fact that the individual gained the liberty to express himself at all – in poetry, in the arts, in oral speech or in prose – is in retrospect almost as notable as the use to which this freedom was later put. Archaic Greece, by no means in all ways a permissive society, seems to have generated from an early stage a wide freedom of spontaneous comment in some areas. Because of the tension between this freedom and that love of order which was equally clearly present in early Greek society, we find an alternate ebb and flow in the degree of self-expression permitted. But in some instances at least, the high tide of this freedom can be observed in the first half of the seventh century BC, the era which produced the poem of Archilochos which we considered earlier (pp. 170–3), together with a brief outbreak of imaginative creativity in the visual arts – including vase-painting, a medium where such ideas seem to have been firmly repressed both earlier and later. If one looks at the products of the 'Protoattic' school of this period, in particular, one sees the mysterious and unexpected at every turn. The painter of the Polyphemos amphora from Eleusis (c. 675 BC), not *Plate 37* content with an unprecedented use of internal shading in the figure of Odysseus in his main scene, has also drawn his Gorgons in the picture below, on the body of the vase, with cauldrons for heads, thus anticipating by over 26 centuries Picasso's much-admired use of the same kind of idea, when he gave the head of his bronze 'Baboon and young' the shape of a child's toy motor-car. A little later, the painter of the Orestes krater in Berlin is not the only artist of his day who introduced into the margins of his mythological scenes strange, sometimes hairy, dwarf-like figures, which certainly contribute to the aura of tension, but whose exact significance – since they vanish without trace under the régime of sobriety and order that follows –

remains unexplained. This brief, exuberant interlude is in equally strong contrast with the style of the preceding Geometric period, when the contrary principle had prevailed almost to excess, and with the later development of painting in the sixth and fifth centuries, where in a more sophisticated form it dominates once again.

In the literary field, the outbreak of spontaneity is not such an abrupt and ephemeral thing. It has been observed, for example, that the erotic scene in the Archilochos poem owes something to the Homeric episode of Hera and Zeus in book 14 of the *Iliad*; although to compare the two is to see the measure of Archilochos' liberation as well. Here, too, the latitude once gained was extended to later writers in certain genres, such as Classical comedy. Similarly, it seems clear that the elaborate tissue of double standards which the Greeks wove around the question of male homosexuality also came into existence during the Archaic period; as a recent authority observes, 'overt homosexuality was already widespread by the early part of the sixth century BC'. This is an issue on which Homer is notably restrained; some would attribute this to a convention of the epic craft rather than to the general tenor of Greek opinion in the eighth century; but, even if this is true, one can still claim that the inhibitions on *literary* expression in this matter were lifted. These cases are alike in that the initial concession of freedom was the really significant step in all of them.

I hope these claims on behalf of the Archaic Greeks will not appear to have been pushed to excessive lengths. But I do believe that the famous revolution in Greek culture which occurred towards the close of the Archaic period is matched in importance by that which occurred at its beginning. When seen in the short term, both were fairly gradual processes, occupying more than one generation. Modern scholarship, by compressing the later revolution into what I believe is an artificially short span of time, has made it appear much the more dramatic. But that is an argument which cuts two ways, since, if it was the climax of the Persian Wars which transformed Archaic Greece, all at once, into Classical Greece, then all those remarkable events which clearly

antedate 480 BC remain unadulterated 'Archaism': the establishment of Athenian democracy and the achievements of its first
five years, the original decision of several Greek states to chal-
lenge Persia, the foundation of tragic drama, the building of
Athens' fleet, the undermining of the canons of Archaic statu-
ary, and so on. It is wiser, I think, to recognize that we are dealing with processes, rather than events, at both periods.

It is relevant to the comparison that the later revolution is
immeasurably the better-documented of the two, in both ancient
and modern sources. Indeed, the very fact that our knowledge
of the earlier one is to some extent derived from archaeology
may have made some of the more traditionalist historians fight
shy of it, and even perhaps doubt its reality. Yet, ironically, it is
by working backwards from our earliest *historical* documentation
that we reach the point, in the later eighth century BC, where we
are faced with two stark alternatives: either the pattern of
Archaic civilization was established at this period, or it goes back
beyond it; and, if the latter, then there is really no convincing
reason for stopping our backwards search through history until
we arrive at the Mycenaean era. The civilization of Classical
Greece will then have grown organically out of the Mycenaean
civilization. This latter view has had some distinguished supporters and is not entirely indefensible even today; but in totally
rejecting it, as I have in this book, I have preferred to appeal to
the arguments, rather than invoke the support of the great
majority of modern authorities with whom, here at least, I am in
agreement. I have portrayed the Archaic period as a long era of
restrained experiment, bounded at either end by shorter periods
of more hurried, at times almost feverish innovation. This reconstruction may prove mistaken, but here again I do not think that
it runs violently counter to general opinion.

The achievement of the generations after 750 BC, although we
can establish something of its magnitude by empirical means,
remains historically an obscure one, whereas there has been by
comparison a floodlight trained on the era of the Persian Wars
and what appears to be their direct consequence, the Classical
achievement. As with history, so in literature and the arts there

had been successive waves of reverberation from the events of
the Persian Wars and successive resurrections of later fifth-
century Greece, from the *Persai* of Aischylos in 472 BC to the
nineteenth century of our era, before the modern rediscovery of
Archaic art had even occurred, and before the modern rehabilita-
tion of the early poets had progressed very far. Now at last, in
the later twentieth century, the wheel has turned full circle.
Archaic art suddenly finds favour where the 'complacent', 'life-
less', 'too-perfect' or 'boring' Classicism palls; the earlier periods
of ancient history are heavily in favour with younger resear-
chers. It is a fashion, to whose influence doubtless the present
writer is also subject. But behind the fashion lies a serious and
justifiable interest in the more spontaneous and unaffected
epochs of art, and the more innovatory and experimental cultures of history. To find the real roots of innovation is perhaps
the underlying quest which unites these modern approaches;
the aim is a very elusive one, and I doubt whether these pages
have brought its attainment much closer. But the achievements
of this period deserve wider attention – and here I include expert
attention. The range of expertise, however, needs to be wider
than that of the disciplines traditionally concerned with the
period. There was a time when the achievements of Classical
Greece were judged to be little, if at all, short of miraculous;
what I have claimed as the achievement of Archaic Greece is that
it made many of them predictable.

# Bibliography

On the period as a whole, the most continuously valuable ancient sources are Herodotus, *The Histories* and Aristotle, *The Politics* (Penguin Classics translations by A. de Selincourt, 1954 and T. A. Sinclair, 1962 respectively).

The following recent studies in English concentrate on the Archaic period, or aspects of it (the abbreviations used for some of them in these notes are given on the left hand side):

| | |
|---|---|
| (LSAG) | L. H. Jeffery, *The local scripts of Archaic Greece* (1964) |
| | J. Boardman, *The Greeks overseas* (1964, 2nd ed. 1973) |
| (Forrest) | W. G. Forrest, *The emergence of Greek democracy* (1966) |
| | A. R. Burn, *The Warring States of Greece* (1968) |
| | M. I. Finley, *Early Greece: the Bronze and Archaic ages* (1970) |
| | G. A. Christopoulos and J. C. Bastias, *History of the Hellenic world* ii, *The Archaic period* (translation, Athens, 1975) |
| | R. J. Hopper, *The early Greeks* (1976) |
| | J. Charbonneaux, R. Martin and F. Villard, *Archaic Greek art* (1971) |
| (AGCS) | L. H. Jeffery, *Archaic Greece: the city states, c.700–500 BC* (1976) |
| | A. W. Johnston, *The emergence of Greece* (1976) |
| (ESH) | M. M. Austin and P. Vidal-Naquet, *Economic and social history of ancient Greece* (1977), with a long review of the earlier French edition by J. K. Davies in *The Phoenix* 29 (1975), 93–102 |
| (Starr) | C. G. Starr, *The economic and social growth of early Greece* (1977) |

These regional studies concentrate on the Archaic period:

> G. L. Huxley, *Early Sparta* (1962)
> G. L. Huxley, *The early Ionians* (1966)
> T. Kelly, *A history of Argos to 500 BC* (Minneapolis, 1976)

Other abbreviations used are:

(Humphreys)          S. C. Humphreys, *Anthropology and the Greeks* (1978)

(*JHS*)              *Journal of Hellenic Studies*

CHAPTER 1

Recent works that cover this early period in some detail include J. N. Coldstream, *Geometric Greece* (1977) and, less fully, my *The dark age of Greece* (1971). There is also a very useful, though undocumented, article in English by J. Sarkady, 'Outlines of the development of Greek society in the period between the 12th and 8th centuries BC' in *Acta Antiqua Academiae Scientiarum Hungaricae* 23 (1975), 107–125.

*Pp. 19–24*: see in general E. A. Wrigley, *Population and history* (1969); on early Greek demography and other questions, my *Archaeology and the rise of the Greek state* with references (notes 6, 12) for the statistics in figs. 1 and 2; see also *The dark age of Greece*, 360–67. For Perati, Sp. Iakovidis, *Perati: to Nekrotapheion* ii (Athens, 1970), 28–9, 391–410, 422, 467–8 and for Lefkandi, V. R. Desborough, *The Greek dark ages* (1972), 188–99.

*P. 25*: the reference is to D. Roussel, *Tribu et cité* (Paris, 1976) and F. Bourriot, *Recherches sur la nature du genos* (Lille, 1976). There are three useful articles dealing with the early state in Homer and elsewhere, by W. Hoffmann in *Festschrift für Bruno Snell* (Munich, 1956), 153–65; C. G. Thomas in *La Parola del Passato* 21 (1966), 1–14; and F. Gschnitzer in *Chiron* 1 (1971, 1–17. The observations on Phoenician cities on page 32 owe much to discussion with Martin Bernal.

*Pp. 28–47*: the classic account of Greek state-forms is by V. Ehrenberg, *The Greek state* (2nd edition, 1969); see also *ESH*, chapter iii.

*Pp. 36–7*: on the medieval agricultural revolution, see Lynn T. White, *Medieval technology and social change* (1962), chapter ii; for Athens, *ESH* 97, passage no. 66.

*Pp. 38–40*: on hero-cults, see J. N. Coldstream, 'Hero-cults in the age of

Homer', in *JHS* 96 (1976), 8–17, with a different explanation for their distribution. Fig. 7 is based on this map.

*P. 40*: two of the fuller recent reports on Pithekoussai are by G. Buchner in *Archaeological Reports* (supplement to *JHS*) 17 (1970–1), 63–7 and by D. Ridgway in *Greeks, Celts and Romans* (ed. C. F. C. Hawkes) (1973), 5–38.

*Pp. 43–4*: see E. Kirsten, *Die griechische Polis als historisch-geographisches Problem des Mittelmeerraumes* (Bonn, 1956), 100–101 with figs. 12–13.

CHAPTER 2

*P. 53*: I list not only the publications referred to here, but also the most important earlier publications of metal dedications from sanctuaries, for general reference: A. Furtwängler, *Olympia: die Ergebnisse* iv (Berlin, 1890); C. H. Waldstein, *The Argive Heraeum* ii (Boston and New York, 1905); P. Perdrizet and others, *Fouilles de Delphes* v (1908——); Chr. Blinkenberg, *Lindos* ii (Berlin, 1931); H. G. G. Payne, *Perachora* i (1940). In recent years, these have been supplemented by full and up-to-date studies of the same and other sites: C. Rolley in the latest instalments of *Fouilles de Delphes* v (fascicles 2 (1969) and 3 (1978)), and (for Delos) in *Études déliennes* (*Bulletin de Correspondance Héllénique*, suppl. 1 (1973), 491–524; J. Ducat, *Les kouroi du Ptoion* (Paris, 1971); for Olympia terracottas, W-D. Heilmeyer, *Frühe Olympische Tonfiguren* (*Olympische Forschungen* 7, Berlin, 1972); on Philia (and Pherai) in Thessaly, K. Kilian, *Fibeln in Thessalien* (*Prähistorische Bronzefunden* xiv, 2, Munich, 1975); on Samos, various authors, *Samos* i—— (Berlin, 1961——).

*P. 53*: for the grave-finds, see my *The dark age of Greece*, chapter 5.

*P. 54*: Colin Renfrew, *The Emergence of Civilization* (1972), especially chapter 21.

*Pp. 55–62*: recent discussions of sanctuary excavations, to be added to those listed above under *p. 53*; on Corinthian exports of pottery to sanctuaries, J. N. Coldstream, *Greek Geometric pottery* (1968), chapter 14; on early temples at various sites and their interpretation, H. Drerup, *Griechische Baukunst in geometrischer Zeit* (*Archaeologia Homerica*, chapter O, Göttingen, 1969), to which must now be added, for Eretria, communications in *Bulletin de Correspondance Héllénique* 96 (1972), 752–65 and 98 (1974), 687–9; for Corinth, H. S. Robinson in *Hesperia* 45 (1976), 203–39; for Isthmia, O. Broneer, *Isthmia* i: *The Temple of Poseidon* (Princeton, 1971).

*P. 62*: the two inscriptions referred to appear in Jeffery, *LSAG* 339, 334, no. 53; and 72, 77, no. 21. The view of Delphi expressed here follows W. G. Forrest, 'Colonization and the rise of Delphi', *Historia* 6 (1957), 160–75.

*Pp. 65–7*: the process is charted in detail by Coldstream in *Greek Geometric pottery*, chapter 2. On Thucydides, R. M. Cook, *Annual of the British School at Athens*, 50 (1955), 267–9.

*Pp. 67–75*: the more controversial matters of interpretation have been discussed at great length by a series of writers, of whom I single out two for their forceful and lucid expression of views contrary to mine: K. Fittschen, *Untersuchungen zum Beginn der Sagendarstellungen bei den Griechen* (Berlin, 1969) and J. Carter, 'The beginning of narrative art in the Greek Geometric period', in *Annual of the British School at Athens* 67 (1972), 25–58; in the same periodical, 50 (1955), 38–50 appeared T. B. L. Webster's article 'Homer and Attic Geometric vases'; J. M. Hemelrijk's remark is quoted from a review in *Gnomon* 42 (1970), 169. Funerary scenes are fully discussed and illustrated by G. Ahlberg, *Prothesis and ekphora in Greek Geometric art* (Göteborg, 1971). For shields (*p. 75*) cf. P. Cassola Guida, *Le armi difensive dei Mecenei nelle figurazioni* (Rome, 1973), 38–44. fig. 3.

*P. 76*: for the Salamis burials, see V. Karageorghis, *Salamis in Cyprus: Homeric, Hellenistic and Roman* (1969); for those at Eretria, C. Berard, *Eretria iii: L'Héroön à la porte de l'ouest* (Berne, 1970).

*P. 77*: see the edition of *Fragmenta Hesiodea* by R. Merkelbach and M. L. West (1967). Discussions of the Siamese-twin pictures appear in Fittschen, Carter and Ahlberg (see above under *pp. 67–75*).

*Pp. 78–84*: the classic study of the early alphabet is Jeffery, *LSAG*. The reference on *p. 82* is to H. T. Wade-Gery, *The poet of the Iliad* (1952).


CHAPTER 3

*P. 86*: the fullest, though hardly the most reliable, ancient account of the First Messenian War is in Pausanias, *Description of Greece* iv, 4–13.

*Pp. 87–92*: fuller accounts of the early state are given by Austin and Vidal-Naquet in *ESH*, chapters 3 and 4, and by Jeffery in *AGCS*, especially chapter 3.

*Pp. 93–4*: on Solon's reforms, see *ESH* 59–60 and 69–72 with passages nos. 36–38; Starr, 181–6.

*Pp. 96–7 and 111–16)*: on tyranny, see A. Andrewes, *The Greek tyrants* (1956), with further details of specific early tyrants in Jeffery, *AGCS*: Chios inscription, *LSAG* 336–7, no. 41.

*Pp. 98–9*: on early cavalry, see P. A. L. Greenhalgh, *Early Greek Warfare* (1973), chapter 3.

*Pp. 101–7*: there has been a considerable recent literature on the military reform. Since the appearance of my *Early Greek armour and weapons* (1964), additions and modifications have been proposed by J. K. Anderson, *Military theory and practice in the age of Xenophon* (Berkely and Los Angeles, 1970), chapter 2; and by Greenhalgh, *Early Greek warfare*, chapter 4. See also a series of articles in *JHS*: my 'The hoplite reform and history' in vol. 85 (1965), 110–22; J. Salmon, 'Political hoplites?', 97 (1977), 84–101; and, especially relevant to Sparta (*pp. 109–10*), P. A. Cartledge, 'Hoplites and heroes', 97 (1977), 11–27. It will be seen that I have tried in some places to accommodate the criticisms of Greenhalgh, Salmon and Cartledge, in others to consolidate on such common ground as exists between the four of us. On the two graves at Argos, see P. Courbin in *Bulletin de Correspondance Héllénique* 81 (1957), 322–86 and E. Protonotariou-Deilaki in *Arkhaiologikon Deltion* 26 (1971), *Chroniká*, 81–2, fig. 13.

*P. 105*: the details of the relevant Olympia publications are:
   E. Kunze, *Archäische Schildbänder (Olympische Forschungen* 2, Berlin, 1950)
   F. Willemsen, *Dreifüsskessel von Olympia (OF* 3, 1957)
      (I have not yet seen M. Maass, *Dreifüsse in Olympia (OF* 10, 1978))
   H. V. Herrmann, *Die Kessel der orientalisierenden Zeit i (OF* 6, 1966)
   On armour, see E. Kunze and others, *I – VIII Bericht über die Ausgrabungen in Olympia* (Berlin, 1936–67), supplemented by shorter reports in *Arkhaiologikon Deltion* 17 (1961–2), *Chroniká*, 107–24 and *Bulletin de Correspondance Héllénique* 84 (1960), 714–20 and 88 (1964), 751–5.

*Pp. 113–15*: on Athenian cults, see H. W. Parke, *Festivals of the Athenians* (1977) (for the suggestion about Peisistratos' palace, J. Boardman, *Greek sculpture: the Archaic period* (1978), 153–4).

*P. 118*: the quotation is from A. M. Andreades, *A history of Greek public finance* i (translation, Harvard, 1933), 231.

*Pp. 118–20*: on the lawgivers, see Jeffery, *AGCS* 42–4 and *passim*; Forrest, 143–5.

*P. 121*: the quotation is from p. 113 of Roussel's book, where he is

224 *Bibliography*

criticizing the view represented by Forrest, chapter 2 and A. Andrewes, *The Greeks* (1967), chapter 5.

CHAPTER 4

*Pp. 123–6*: very helpful accounts of these problems are to be found in *ESH*, chapter 1 with passages nos. 1–6, and in Starr, *passim*.

*Pp. 127–8*: the most valuable attempt at the quantification of Greek pottery-production remains R. M. Cook's article, 'Die Bedeutung der bemalten Keramik', in *Jahrbuch des deutschen archäologischen Instituts* 74 (1959), 114–23.

*P. 129*: for Megara Hyblaia, see G. Vallet and F. Villard, *Mégara Hyblaea* ii: *La céramique archaïque* (Paris, 1964); for Phokaian colonies, J. P. Morel, 'L'expansion phocéenne en Occident', in *Bulletin de Correspondance Héllénique* 99 (1975), 853–96; for Istria, P. Dupont's study 'Une approche en laboratoire des problèmes de la céramique de Grèce de l'Est', first delivered at a colloquium in Naples in July 1976 and to be expanded for inclusion in *Histria*, vol. v (Bucharest); a fourth illustration, more complex but giving some parallel results, is provided by M. Farnsworth, I. Perlman and F. Asaro, 'Corinth and Corfu: a neutron activation study of their pottery', in *American Journal of Archaeology* 81 (1977), 455–68.

*P. 130*: Olympia dedications, Jeffery, *LSAG* 219–20, no. 12; W. Dittenberger and K. Purgold, *Olympia* v (Berlin, 1896), no. 258; E. Kunze, *VII Bericht über die Ausgrabungen in Olympia* (Berlin, 1961), 207–10.

*P. 133*: on Spartans at Samos, see Jeffery, *AGCS* 216–7.

*Pp. 134–6*: this account of early coinage owes most to C. M. Kraay's fundamental article, 'Hoards, small change and the origin of coinage', in *JHS* 84 (1964), 76–91 (see also his *Archaic and Classical Greek coins* (1976)); and to P. Grierson, *The origins of money* (1977). For the early Lydian coins, see A. R. Bellinger in *Essays in Greek coinage presented to Stanley Robinson* (1968), 10–15.

*Pp. 137–9*: for ship-representations, cf. Humphreys, 166–9, with references to recent studies published by B. Bravo; on Sostratos, see M. Torelli and A. W. Johnston, in *La parola del passato* 26 (1971), 44–67 and 27 (1972), 416–23 respectively; for Kolaios, cf. Humphreys, 168, and Starr, 52, 210 n. 69.

*Pp. 138–40*: iron ore transport: Pithekoussai, G. Buchner, 'Recent work at Pithekoussai', *Archaeological Reports* (suppl. to *JHS*) 17 (1970–1), 63–7; Motya, B.S.J. Isserlin and others, 'Motya, a Phoenician-Punic site near Marsala, Sicily', in *Annual of the Leeds University Oriental Society* 4 (1962–3), 84–131; Bassai, N.Ph. Yalouris in *To Ergon tis Arkhaiologikis Etaireias* 1959, 106–9.

*P. 140*: far-travelled finds, J. Boardman, *The Greeks overseas* 205–6, 213–14, 260; sanctuary-dedications, see publications listed above under *p. 53*, and Coldstream, *Geometric Greece*, 334–8, on tripod-cauldrons.

Pp. 140–3: on marble provenances, see the exchange in the *Annual of the British School at Athens*, vol. 63 (1968), 45–66 (A. C. Renfrew and J. Springer Peacey); 65 (1970), 1–2 (B. Ashmole); 68 (1973), 349–53 (R. E. Wycherley). On travelling sculptors and unfinished works at quarries, G. M. A. Richter, *Kouroi* (3rd edition, 1970), 6, 11.

*Pp. 144–6*: on Solon, see above, under *pp. 93–4*; for the statues, see Richter, *Kouroi* (above) and *Korai* (1968).

*Pp. 147–80*: on the diolkos, see now R. M. Cook's note, 'Archaic Greek trade: three conjectures' in *JHS* 99 (1979), 152–5.

*Pp. 148–9*: on Greek technological thinking, compare J-P. Vernant, 'Remarques sur les formes et les limites de la pensée technique chez les Grecs', *Revue d'Histoire des Sciences et de leurs Applications* 10 (1957), 205–25.

*P. 148*: for Ugarit, F. Thureau-Dangin, 'Vocabulaires de Ras Shamra', in *Syria* 12 (1931), 228–30, no. 5.

*Pp. 149–51*: J. J. Coulton, 'Lifting in early Greek architecture', *JHS* 94 (1974), 1–19.

*Pp. 151–4*: on military changes, see chapters 3 and 4 of my *Arms and armour of the Greeks* (1967); on the origins of the trireme, the most recent stage of the controversy is represented by an exchange between A. B. Lloyd and L. Basch in *JHS* 95 (1975), 45–61 and 97 (1977), 1–10; on Samian engineering feats, R. Tölle-Kastenbein, *Herodot und Samos* (Bochum, 1976), part ii.

*Pp. 154–8*: for these sites, see respectively: Athens, H. A. Thompson and R. E. Wycherley, *The Agora of Athens* (*The Athenian Agora*, vol. xiv, Princeton, 1972); Corinth, C. A. Roebuck, 'Some aspects of urbanization at Corinth', *Hesperia* 41 (1972), 96–127; Smyrna, J. M. Cook and others, 'Old Smyrna', *Annual of the British School at Athens* 53–4 (1958–9), 1–181; Megara Hyblaia, G. Vallet, F. Villard and P. Auberson, *Mégara Hyblaea* i: *Le quartier de l'Agora archaïque* (Paris, 1976);

Selinous, E. Gabrici, 'Studi archeologici Selinuntini', *Monumenti Antichi* 43 (1956), 205–408.

CHAPTER 5

*Pp. 161–8*: painfully attenuated though it is, this account owes much to G. E. R. Lloyd's *Early Greek science: Thales to Aristotle* (1970) and, here and in the treatment of other intellectuals (*pp. 176–8*) to Humphreys, chapter 9, to J-P. Vernant, *Les origines de la pensée grecque* (Paris, 1962), and to W. Donlan's article in *Historia* 22 (1973), 145–54.

*Pp. 170–3*: on the new epode of Archilochos, I refer to the publications by John Van Sickle in *Classical Journal* 71 (1975), 1–15 and *Arethusa* 9, 2 (1976), 129–150. The first edition of the text was by R. Merkelbach and M. L. West in *Zeitschrift für Papyrologie und Epigraphik* 14 (1974), 97–113.

*Pp. 170–5*: there are stimulating discussions of Archilochos and Tyrtaios in Forrest, 78–88 and 125–35.

*Pp. 175–6*: on Phokylides, see M. L. West in *JHS* 98 (1978), 164–7.

*Pp. 178–82*: on kouroi, the references are to Richter, *Kouroi* and E. H. Gombrich, *Art and Illusion* (1960), chapter 4.

*Pp. 181–4*: the works described here are conveniently collected and perceptively discussed in M. Robertson, *A history of Greek art* (1975), 93–9, 109, 159–67 with plates 24–5, 27, 30 and 50; and by J. Boardman, *Greek sculpture: the Archaic period* (1978), 72–5, figs. 112–4, 117.

*Pp. 188–9*: on the status of vase-painters, see J. Boardman, *Athenian black-figure vases* (1974), 11–13, with references to earlier work on page 235; T. B. L. Webster, *Potter and patron in Classical Athens* (1972).

*Pp. 189–94*: the pioneer study of Greek myth-iconography was Carl Robert's *Archäologische Hermeneutik* (Berlin, 1919); on the recent writings of N. Himmelmann-Wildschütz, see especially J. M. Hemelrijk's review (in English) in *Gnomon* 42 (1970), 166–71; the latest general treatment is Jane E. Henle, *Greek myths: a vase-painter's notebook* (Bloomington and London, 1973). On subjects, see especially J. Boardman, *Athenian red-figure vases: the Archaic period* (1975), chapters 7 and 8.

*P. 194*: the vases naming Koronē (there are several) are discussed by D. von Bothmer, *Amazons in Greek art* (1957), 96–7, whose lead I have followed.

*Pp. 194–5*: on Athenian festivals, see Parke, *Festivals of the Athenians*, with calendar on pp. 26–7.

*Pp. 195–9*: for the interpretation of Kleisthenes' reforms, I follow Forrest, chapter 8; the sequence of events is described and documented by Jeffery in *AGCS* 99–105 with notes 8 and 9; the resultant arrangements are presented in impressive detail by J. S. Traill, *The political organisation of Attica* (*Hesperia*, supplement 14, Princeton, 1975).Corinth: *AGCS* 153. 160 n. 6.

CHAPTER 6

*P. 202*: on Ionia in the 6th and 5th centuries, see Jeffery, *AGCS*, chapter 13 and J. M. Cook, *The Greeks in Ionia and the East* (1962), chapter 10.

*P. 205*: on the Helots, compare *ESH* pp. 86–90 with passages nos. 50, 58–61.

*Pp. 209–12*: the sculptures mentioned are discussed, illustrated and documented in B. S. Ridgway, *The severe style in Greek sculpture* (Princeton, 1970), chapters 2 and 3, although her chronological conclusions are the opposite of mine; on the Tyrannicides, see her chapter 6: also Robertson, *A history of Greek art* 165–7, 173–4, 184–6 with plates 50, 52, 54.

*P. 215*: on Protoattic vases, Robertson *A history of Greek art* 27–8, 50–1 and J. D. Beazley, *The development of Attic black-figure* (1951), chapter 1; Picasso's 'Baboon and young' is illustrated in Gombrich, *Art and illusion* 89, figure 70. On homosexuality, see K. J. Dover, *Greek homosexuality* (1978); the quotation is from page 1; cf. 194–6 on the development from Homer on.

# Index

# Index